African Security

SERIES IN HUMAN SECURITY

Series editors: Geoffrey Dabelko, Brandon Kendhammer, and Nukhet Sandal

---

The Series in Human Security is published in association with Ohio University's War and Peace Studies and African Studies programs at the Center for International Studies and the Environmental Studies Program at the Voinovich School of Leadership and Public Affairs.

Technologies of Suspicion and the Ethics of Obligation in Political Asylum, edited by Bridget M. Haas and Amy Shuman

Exiting the Fragility Trap: Rethinking Our Approach to the World's Most Fragile States, by David Carment and Yiagadeesen Samy

Women's Perspectives on Human Security: Violence, Environment, and Sustainability, edited by Richard A. Matthew, Patricia A. Weitsman, Gunhild Hoogensen Gjørv, Nora Davis, and Tera Dornfeld

African Security: Local Issues and Global Connections, edited by Abu Bakarr Bah

African Security

Local Issues and Global Connections

Edited by

ABU BAKARR BAH

OHIO UNIVERSITY PRESS I ATHENS

Ohio University Press, Athens, Ohio 45701
ohioswallow.com
© 2024 by Ohio University Press
All rights reserved

To obtain permission to quote, reprint, or otherwise reproduce or distribute material from Ohio University Press publications, please contact our rights and permissions department at (740) 593-1154 or (740) 593-4536 (fax).

Printed in the United States of America
Ohio University Press books are printed on acid-free paper ∞ ™

Library of Congress Cataloging-in-Publication Data
Names: Bah, Abu Bakarr, 1969– editor, author.
Title: African security : local issues and global connections / edited by Abu Bakarr Bah.
Other titles: African security (Ohio University. Press) | Series in human security.
Description: Athens : Ohio University Press, 2024. | Series: Series in human security | Includes bibliographical references and index.
Identifiers: LCCN 2023043682 (print) | LCCN 2023043683 (ebook) | ISBN 9780821425503 (paperback) | ISBN 9780821425497 (hardback) | ISBN 9780821425510 (pdf)
Subjects: LCSH: Security, International—Africa. | National security—Africa. | Terrorism—Africa—Prevention. | Rule of law—Africa. | Africa—Politics and government—1960–
Classification: LCC JZ5584.A35 A375 2024 (print) | LCC JZ5584.A35 (ebook) | DDC 327.172096—dc23/eng/20230918
LC record available at https://lccn.loc.gov/2023043682
LC ebook record available at https://lccn.loc.gov/2023043683

Contents

Introduction
Local Issues and Global Connections in African Security
ABU BAKARR BAH   1

Chapter 1   African Realities and Knowledge Production
*Conceptions of Civil Wars, International Interventions,
and State Building*
ABU BAKARR BAH AND NIKOLAS EMMANUEL   30

Chapter 2   Proscription Regimes and the Internationalization of
National Security Threats
Countering Terrorism in Nigeria
FOLAHANMI AINA   55

Chapter 3   Countering Violent Extremism through Community Policing
in Likoni, Mombasa, Kenya
JOHN MWANGI GITHIGARO   87

Chapter 4   Militarized Response to Domestic, Regional, and International
Security Issues in Nigeria and Uganda
MICHAEL NWANKPA   112

Chapter 5   The Conundrums of International Military Interventions in Africa
The Cases of Côte d'Ivoire and Mali
ALFRED BABO   142

Chapter 6   African Agency in Securitization
Assimilating International Capacities
TENLEY K. ERICKSON   181

VI

Chapter 7 The African Union on the Periphery of Peacebuilding
The Role of External Powers and Regional Bodies in Libya
NORMAN SEMPIJJA, AKRAM ZAOUI, AND NOAMANE CHERKAOUI   215

Contributors   239

Index   241

Introduction

Local Issues and Global Connections in African Security

ABU BAKARR BAH

African security continues to face challenges emanating from both domestic and global problems. In 2023, the United Nations (UN) had six peacekeeping operations in Africa, and many other countries are facing significant conflicts. Between 1960 and 2020, the UN has had twenty-five peacekeeping operations in Africa.[1] Indeed, Africa has been experiencing instability and political violence since the start of independence in the 1960s. Earlier conflicts in Africa were connected to the struggle for decolonization, the Cold War, and agitations for ethnic/regional autonomy and democracy.[2] Some of the most notorious cases were those of South Africa, Angola, Mozambique, Zimbabwe, Zaire, Nigeria, and Rwanda. In all of these countries, political violence stemmed from colonial policies that created oppression and ethnic domination, and in some cases from the very reluctance by White settlers to end colonial rule. Many of these conflicts were woven into the Cold War as Western powers and communist states inserted themselves into the conflicts as arms suppliers and exploiters of natural resources.[3] While many of these conflicts faded with the end of the Cold War and the global push for democracy during the 1990s, some of the wars persisted and new ones emerged. Notably, the war in Zaire never seemed to have ended as political and regional conflicts morph from one war to another in what has become the war from Congo to Zaire and back to the Democratic Republic of Congo (the DRC).[4] Even more problematic, new wars have emerged, notably warlord-driven civil wars and terrorism warfare. Currently, two major forms of new wars continue to plague Africa: (1) warlord-driven civil wars over the rule of law and democracy and (2) the Global War on Terror wars. In some cases, such as those of Somalia, Mali, and Libya, these two forms of war have mixed, leading to catastrophic state failure, if not state collapse. In addition, protracted violent communal conflicts cause major social disorder and dislocation, though not archetypal civil wars. Northwestern Nigeria has been heavily affected by these kinds of communal conflicts.

The democratization process during the 1990s led to some notable cases of transition to multiparty democracy in countries such as Ghana, Nigeria, Kenya, Senegal, Namibia, and Zambia.[5] However, that democratization process also produced major civil wars in countries such as Liberia, Sierra Leone, Côte d'Ivoire, the DRC, and Burundi.[6] Even countries that did not descend into civil wars—such as Guinea, Togo, Kenya, and Nigeria—were plagued by major political violence. Many of the wars became what has been dubbed new wars as warlords mixed banditry with insurgencies in the name of democracy.[7] Sierra Leone, Liberia, and the DRC are clear cases where warlords exploited minerals to support war enterprises that claimed to fight for democracy while violating basic rule of law, committing war crimes and even violating the rules of democracy.[8] These kinds of new wars have prompted regional and international military interventions under the Responsibility to Protect (R2P) doctrine undertaken by the UN often in collaboration with the African Union and/or its Regional Economic Communities.[9] In some cases, major Western powers, notably Britain, France, and the United States, have been deeply involved in this form of military humanitarianism, as well as neighboring African states engaged in proxy wars. Some of the cases include the peacekeeping missions in Sierra Leone, Liberia, Côte d'Ivoire, the DRC, Mali, Somalia, and South Sudan. In many of these cases, international military intervention became massive security- and state-building ventures geared toward a culminating multiparty election and postwar reconstruction agenda to transform the countries into liberal democracies.[10] Overall, the results have been mixed as most countries have quickly slid back into political conflicts and authoritarianism, even as they claim to uphold democracy. In both Sierra Leone and Côte d'Ivoire, for example, the postwar democracies have steadily been plagued by political violence and violations of core tenets of multiparty democracy by the governments in power. In Libya, NATO's dubious intervention under R2P has produced one of the most catastrophic conflicts in the region.

As Africa seemed to have settled the new wars, especially in countries where there were major international military and humanitarian interventions, such as in Sierra Leone, Liberia, and Côte d'Ivoire, the Global War on Terror triggered a new breed of new wars in Africa in the form of terrorism warfare.[11] Starting with Somalia, groups related to and inspired by al-Qaeda and ISIS have emerged across the Sahel and in countries such as Nigeria, Mozambique, Burkina Faso, the DRC, and Libya. These terrorism warfare forms of conflicts have dovetailed with environmental and poor governance issues to destabilize countries that were fairly stable, and in some cases even democratic, such as Mali. Wars connected to the Global War on Terror often lead to more covert external military interventions in the form of counterterrorism programs and in worst cases more overt Global War on Terror missions such as the French missions in Mali and the Sahel, notably Operation Barkhane and Operation Serval. The Global War on Terror has been exerted on countries plagued by terrorism warfare largely as a way to protect Western national security interests. In the process, many African countries are becoming frontiers in the war between Western powers and jihadists who exploit state fragility and local grievances connected to environmental problems and political oppression in Africa to fight Western domination. More terrorists are infiltrating African countries as terrorism spreads and becomes permanent mobile wars that seem to be endless (as we have learned from Afghanistan and the Middle East).

A deep reading of African and international politics would show an interesting mix of domestic and external drivers of violent conflicts, leading to entanglement in Western-dominated agendas in Africa. A basic question for understanding security in African countries, and the continent as a whole, is: What are the domestic and external drivers of African conflicts? Indeed, studies of Africa fully capture the myriad conflict drivers, both domestic and external. However, the intersection of domestic and external factors is often not probed in ways that explain the nature of contemporary conflicts and the (in)adequacy of neoliberal solutions often rooted in global liberal governance.[12] This edited collection examines the fusion of domestic and external drivers of African conflicts and how that mixture of conflict drivers shapes the nature of African conflicts. The core argument that runs throughout this book is that African conflicts are shaped by the cross-pressures of local grievances and external interests that transform African conflicts into glocalized security situations. As such, the ultimate aim of this book is to trigger new ways of thinking of solutions to African security—solutions that understand the eclectic and glocalized nature of African conflicts and are capable of addressing both the domestic and the external dimensions of African conflicts. An important departure point for this glocalized security approach is a recognition of the domestic and external conflict drivers as articulated in the extant literature.

DOMESTIC AND EXTERNAL CONFLICT DRIVERS

In terms of domestic drivers of conflicts, the common culprits are patrimonialism, ethnicity, and natural resources. As Robert Jackson and Carl Rosberg noted long ago, patrimonial rule is endemic in African politics to the point that it is a system by itself.[13] Patrimonial rule takes many forms that manifest in the political, economic, and social realms.[14] Politically, patrimonial rule is associated with one-person rule and dictatorship, which stifle the rule of law, inhibit democracy, and unleash political oppression. Patrimonial rule by civilian and military dictators has proved to be problematic. Ultimately, this form of political oppression breeds political violence. Some of the most notorious cases include those of Liberia, Sierra Leone, the DRC, Sudan, and Libya, where autocratic rule led to armed insurgencies to remove the autocrats from power.

Patrimonial rule also breeds corruption tied to social networks and nepotism in the distribution of state resources and offices. Such forms of corruption undermine economic development as resources are increasingly diverted from public good into personal wealth, thereby generating a sense of social injustice, especially among groups excluded from power. In some of the worst cases, this form of corruption leads to state decay and the collapse of state institutions and basic services, compounding the adverse effects of the abuse of power. In Sierra Leone, for example, corruption led to state failure, which led to civil war.[15] In Sudan, before the secession of the South, corruption and social injustice inflamed southern demands for equity and the civil war. Sudan continues to be plagued by massive social injustice in the distribution of resources, which has bred new wars, especially in Darfur.[16] South Sudan, too, has been plagued by massive corruption and social injustice, which has led to civil war.[17] In all these countries, corruption and nepotism have been tied to the personal rule of a dictator. Conflicts arising out of this sense of injustice create major ethnic and regional animosities that make them very difficult to resolve as marginalized groups increasingly see secession as the only real way of ending their marginalization. This has been the case in countries such as Ethiopia, Sudan, Nigeria, and Cameroon.

In many ways, the problems of patrimonial rules feed into ethnic and regional grievances, propelling ethnicity into a conflict driver by itself. Ethnic conflicts have plagued countries such as Rwanda, Ethiopia, Kenya, Nigeria, Côte d'Ivoire, and Guinea. Ethnicity dovetails with political and economic grievances and manifests itself in political violence, especially concerning elections and military coups, as members of various ethnic groups compete for political power.[18] A key problem in ethnicity is the winner-takes-all nature of African multiparty democracies that seems to guarantee ethnic marginalization. This is very problematic, as the state is the most important economic entity given its control of natural resources and the major forms of foreign aid. As such, political power feeds into economic marginalization. Despite some efforts to mitigate the effects of ethnicity on politics by requiring certain margins and distributions of vote to win the presidency and some form of decentralization (e.g., Kenya and Nigeria), politics in African countries is still plagued by ethnic voting and political blocs.[19] Overall, ethnicity remains a conflict driver from both the social justice and the political perspectives.[20]

Access to natural resources is another key driver of violent conflicts in Africa. Conflicts over national resources typically take two forms: (1) civil wars over control and access to revenues from natural resources such as oil and diamonds and (2) communal conflicts over access to land and water resources. Civil wars over mineral resources have erupted in countries such as Sudan, South Sudan, Nigeria, the DRC, and Angola. These wars tend to be prolonged and intense as revenues from mineral resources are used by governments and rebel groups to fund the war. In Sierra Leone and Liberia, for example, diamonds and timber became critical in prolonging the wars as rebel groups were able to gain significant revenues with which to purchase weapons.[21] In Nigeria, minorities in the Niger Delta have waged war to ensure access to the huge revenues from oil extracted from their lands. More recently, environmental factors are fueling more intense conflicts among communities, especially herders and farmers.[22] In Nigeria, for example, there are numerous violent conflicts between Fulani herders seeking grazing lands and farming communities resisting encroachment on their ancestral lands. Similar conflicts over natural resources have been reported in countries such as Kenya, Sudan, Chad, the Central African Republic, and Ethiopia. A growing trend, especially in the Sahel, is the fusion of natural resource–based conflicts with terrorism warfare wherein local communities seeking to defend themselves have been labeled as terrorists, especially the pastoralist communities. In some cases, terrorist groups exploit communal conflicts by offering protection as the states are unable to provide security.[23]

The literature on Africa also points to external factors contributing to conflict. Indeed, the external drivers of African conflicts are directly rooted in colonialism and geopolitical rivalries among major and emerging powers that see Africa as a place to garner natural resources, spread ideologies, or simply exert power within the context of international politics. Indirect external factors are also connected to the global economy and environmental issues. External factors such as war logistics, economic interests, geopolitics, neoliberalism, national security doctrines, and environmental changes affect African conflicts. Most of these factors feed into the neocolonial and global liberal governance frames of Africa's encounters with the rest of the world, especially Western powers.

The clearest form of external conflict driver is the supply of weapons, which ties into the issues of war logistics, economic interests, and geopolitics. African wars are typically fought with weapons imported from outside Africa.[24] During the Cold War, the sale and supply of weapons to African governments and rebel movements were part of deliberate efforts by the Soviet Union and Western powers to gain access to minerals and deny other powers a geopolitical space in Africa.[25] Some of the most affected countries have been Zaire (the DRC), Angola, Sudan, Ethiopia, and Nigeria. The sale of weapons often goes with concessions to exploit minerals. In that sense external powers fuel African conflicts by providing logistics to wage war, irrespective of whether the war is reasonably justified or whether the destruction caused is disproportionate to the causes of war. The fusion of economic interests in minerals with strategic geopolitical positioning entrenches the interests of external powers and their involvement in African conflicts, as is most evident in the extensive French military bases and agreements with francophone countries.[26] More recently, China is also emerging as a significant military player in Africa as it subtly supports oppressive regimes in order to create the security needed to pursue its economic interests, such as in Sudan and Djibouti. The problems of weapons supply and geopolitical positioning have been worsened by the Global War on Terror.

The Global War on Terror has led to expansive notions of national security by Western powers and more intense geopolitical competition among major and emerging powers. The Global War on Terror has been elevated into an ideology of security that pits communities and jihadists against Western powers and the governments with which they collaborate.[27] Even though the Global War on Terror in Africa has been cast as a benevolent effort to protect African states against international terrorist networks, in reality the Global War on Terror mostly enforces a statist approach to security that de-legitimizes even genuine grievances over state corruption, marginalization, and broader human security issues.[28] Ironically, the Global War on Terror itself has become a conflict driver in many parts of Africa because of the way it attracts jihadists and alienates local communities through excessive and dubious counterterrorism operations. The clearest case is that of Mali, where NATO intervention in Libya drove militants and huge amounts of weapons into Mali that further destabilized the country. Moreover, French counterterrorism in Mali inadvertently caused more problems for local communities and undermined Malian governments, plunging Mali into deeper insecurity and repeated military coups. Similar problems are playing out in Niger, Nigeria, Burkina Faso, Chad, Somalia, and Kenya, where counterterrorism has become a form of iatrogenic violence.[29] The application of the Global War on Terror in these countries is transforming groups that were once mere political or religious radicals into major terrorist groups.[30] Arguably, groups such as Boko Haram in Nigeria and Al-Shabaab in Somalia became terrorist mostly in reaction to the militarization of the Global

War on Terror, which invites more external military intervention, sinking African countries deeper into terrorism warfare.

Another form of external conflict driver is intervention by African countries in neighboring countries plagued by war, usually by way of strong support for one party to the conflict. This form of quasi–external conflict driver is typical in regional conflicts pitting African countries against one another in proxy wars. These proxy wars have been most common in central and eastern Africa, especially in the DRC and South Sudan, where various African countries have become active participants in the wars in ways that are not necessary within the scope of peacekeeping missions.[31] This form of African interventions intensifies the conflicts, often creating stalemates that make it very difficult to resolve the conflict either through military victory or peaceful negotiation. In the DRC, for example, countries such as Rwanda, Uganda, Kenya, Angola, Namibia, Burundi, and Zimbabwe have all been involved in the fight supporting different sides to the conflict. In South Sudan, countries such as Uganda and Sudan have been deeply involved in the war by supporting the government or the rebels.[32] Unlike the interventions under UN or African Union mandates, interventions by African countries seem to be clandestine and rarely tied to any international peacekeeping mission. In the process, African countries claim a stake in the outcome of the conflict under some expanded idea of national interest. However, such interventions by African political elite are often connected to cross-border ethnic and political ties and the desire to exploit natural resources.

Beyond the more explicit external drivers of conflict, some indirect external conflict drivers exist. These are factors that contribute to the social and economic de-stabilization of vulnerable African countries, which manifests as political violence. Key among these are neoliberal policies that are imposed on African countries as conditionalities for aid and access to loans from Western financial institutions, notably from the International Monetary Fund. Such neoliberal conditionalities come in the form of structural adjustment programs that require deep cuts in government spending on essential services. Structural adjustment programs have adverse effects on the poor that often lead to violent protests and demands for regime change. Demands for regime change breed major violence, especially when authoritarian regimes are bent on holding onto power. During the 1990s, for example, this was the case in countries such as Côte d'Ivoire and Zaire, which ended in deep civil wars as autocrats resisted calls for multiparty democracy ignited by protests against economic austerity measures.[33] More recently, global crises such as the COVID-19 pandemic and the war in Ukraine have led to huge increases in prices for basic goods and services, notably food and transportation. In Sierra Leone, for example, severe economic problems led to a major instance of political violence in August 2022 in which dozens of people were killed.[34] In October 2022, around fifty people were killed in Chad as protesters demanded change of government in the context of a dramatic increase in food prices.[35] The severe effects of external economic and political issues on Africa also dovetail with global environmental issues that are adversely affecting the livelihoods of farming and pastoral communities, leading to more conflicts over land and water resources. Communal conflicts induced by environmental changes are notorious in the Middle Belt region of Nigeria, the Sahel, and eastern Africa, where communities have formed militias to protect themselves from other communities.[36]

GLOCALIZED SECURITY: LOCAL ISSUES AND GLOBAL CONNECTIONS IN AFRICAN SECURITY

Clearly, conflicts in African countries have both domestic and external drivers. Also, these conflict drivers are intertwined in ways that produce new conflict dynamics that defy orthodox modes of approaching African security and peacebuilding. Indeed, frames such as state actors, non–state actors, rebels, ethnic militia, jihadists, terrorists, and bandits do not do full justice to the complex fusion of domestic and external conflict drivers. This reality requires novel ways of conceptualizing African security and peacebuilding. African security issues have been theorized mostly through the lenses of neocolonialism, liberal peace, Responsibility to Protect (R2P), and collective security. However, very few works see African conflicts through the fusion of external and domestic factors. Perhaps a more useful way to think of African conflicts is through the lens of glocalization. In many ways, African security has become a glocalized phenomenon. While the notion of glocalized security does not replace extant theories in explaining African conflicts, it does provide a new lens that captures the fusion of domestic and external drivers of African conflicts and the glocalized nature of African security.

Indeed, the earliest theoretical works on African security are those on neocolonialism. African scholars, such as Ali Mazrui, understood African political reality in relation to its neocolonial position in the international system. As Mazrui aptly framed it, "The question that has arisen lately, however, is whether real decolonization is not the wining of formal independence, not the changing of guard on independence day, the raising of new flags, or the singing of new national anthems, but the collapse of the colonial state itself, the cruel and bloody disintegration of colonial structures. Liberation and decolonization can no longer be equated."[37] Mazrui touched on the constant themes of the institutional vestiges of colonialism and the global structures of power and domination that undermine African security. As Basil Davidson notes, African states would end up in constant instability largely as a result of the burdens of colonial structures on the states, especially how they play into ethnicity.[38] The violence of colonialism and the postcolonial state, which breeds not only trauma but also constant war, is well captured in Frantz Fanon's classic book *The Wretched of the Earth*.[39] The diabolical structure of the colonial state soon started to manifest in political violence and military coups.[40] Colonialism dovetailed with the Cold War to produce another frame for explaining African war.[41] The Cold War has been used to explain many of the wars, especially during the 1970s and 1980s in countries such as Ethiopia and Angola.[42] In many ways, the Cold War simply became a variant of neocolonialism in Africa.[43] Neocolonialism has morphed not only into Cold War theories but into a much broader idea of the political economy of war, especially in relation to the connection between natural resources and civil wars in Africa with countries such as Nigeria, the DRC, and Angola standing out as notorious cases.[44]

Another theory that addresses African security is liberal peace. In some ways, liberal peace loops back to the literature on patrimonial rule in Africa. Liberal peace sees dictatorship and illiberal governance as the root causes of African conflicts. As such, the solution to African insecurity lies in the implementation of multiparty democracy and inculcation of the rule of law.[45] Liberal peace in Africa has been fused into peacekeeping and peacebuilding works, especially through the United Nations missions that see multiparty elections as a critical marker of peace and security, irrespective of the problems of conflict relapse and the challenges of postwar reconstruction.[46] Indeed, liberal peace captures core domestic conflict drivers, but it tends to underestimate the effects of the external conflict drivers. At the same time, it does not pay full attention to the agency and capacities of local actors in solving the problems. As such, liberal peace seems to be idealistic in its solutions to African conflicts. Peacebuilding, as first developed by Boutros Boutros-Ghali and further expanded by the UN, goes a bit deeper than classic neoliberalism. In a way, it provides for a more holistic human development approach to peace.[47]

Since the Rwandan genocide, African conflicts have often been framed around the notions of new wars and R2P. While the notion of new wars, as popularized by Mary Kaldor, refers to brutal wars waged by violent non–state actors deliberately targeting civilians, R2P connects with international military interventions in new wars under the banner of humanitarianism and the responsibility of the international community to protect civilians whose governments cannot protect them from mass violence.[48] The notion of new wars rests on discourses of the state, especially issues of state decay and state failure.[49] The R2P discourse taps into neoliberal peace but goes further in recognizing the broader causes of civil wars and the moral responsibilities of major powers in those wars. Moreover, R2P extends into issues of postwar reconstruction that go beyond narrow liberal peace. In some cases, R2P is tantamount to international state building, especially as R2P is deployed in countries where the state has failed.[50]

State failure too connects to collective security theory. Collective security rests on the understanding that other countries have an interest in the security situation of other countries, as they too can be adversely affected. As such, countries can come together to defend their collective security interests or support an allied country in protecting its national security interests.[51] Under this model, countries may come to support other countries as part of a shared security agreement. Collective security works at the global and regional levels. One strand of the collective security theory is the idea of regional security complex along with security evolution.[52] Collective security explains why and how countries intervene in African conflicts, beyond the R2P doctrine and UN peacekeeping. While under R2P intervention is seen as largely a benevolent moral action, under collective security intervention is tied to national security interests and security obligations that countries have to fulfill in order to ensure their own security. A notable articulation of collective security is countering violent extremism in the form of the Global War on Terror. Since the 9/11 terrorist attacks on the United States, the war on terrorism has expanded from Afghanistan and the Middle East to African countries where terrorism warfare has emerged, especially in the Sahel and the Horn of Africa. Within Africa, too, neighboring countries and regional organizations have intervened under a regional security complex frame, especially in response to the conflict in the DRC.

Collectively, the various theories capture the multiple dimensions of (in)security in Africa. However, they tend of be skewed either toward the domestic or the external drivers of conflicts, or they simply focus on the nature of insecurity rather the causes of conflict.[53] For example, while neocolonialism sees external factors as the drivers of African conflicts, liberal peace sees domestic factors as the causes of African conflicts. In the case of collective security, what is more important is the nature of insecurity threat rather than the causes of conflict, as we see from the Global War on Terror. Perhaps a more holistic understanding of conflict drivers, and the nature of conflicts, can provide a better picture of the nature of African conflicts and point to more-pragmatic solutions. In this book, African security issues are framed through the lens of glocalized security. Glocalized security draws upon sociological critiques of globalization to examine the fusion of domestic and external drivers of African conflicts. As such, the notion of glocalized security is used to weave the domestic and external dimensions of (in)security, akin to the way the notions of globalization and glocalization have been deployed to understand the intricacies and dialectics of global homogenization and local resistances.[54]

The notion of glocalization comes out as a critique of the homogenization of Western values and practices under globalization. A key figure in the development of the notion of glocalization is Roland Robertson, who alluded to it in his article "Globality and Modernity," published in 1992 at *Theory, Culture & Society*, and further developed the concept in his studies of globalization, culture, and migration.[55] Other scholars, such as Ulrich Beck, have also critiqued the homogenizing nature of globalization through a cultural relativism standpoint that accentuates the importance of the local, notably the non-Western, through the notion of contextual universalism.[56] These kinds of critiques of globalization

Introduction

essentially point to the notion of glocalization. In this work, *glocalization* refers to the fusion of domestic and external factors in ways that produce new political, economic, and social dynamics and realities. In this sense, glocalization rests not on an additive approach to causality but on a deeper sociological understanding of intersectionality and the dialectical relations between the local and global.[57] Though the concept of glocalization has been used in studies of social movements, culture, and globalization generally, it is hardly used in relation to security issues.[58] Interestingly, Samuel Marfo et al. tried "to make a case for a 'glocalized peace and security architecture,' a comprehensive peace and security design which is both domestically or inward-looking relevant and internationally or outside-looking practicable." As they argue, a glocalized peace and security architecture "attempts to suggest an approach which can foster a peaceful co-existence among states without necessarily endangering domestic politics in a seemingly chaotic global environment."[59] Overall, the notion of glocalization has been missing in the African security discourse. We use the notion of glocalized security to refer to the fusion of domestic and external conflict drivers and the transformation of conflicts into theaters of war where local grievances and external interests are exerted. In such conflicts, the local and the global are weaved together through complex and dialectical securitization and peacebuilding agendas of African states and external powers.

As we shall see in this work, glocalized security goes far deeper than extant security theories in capturing the depth, scope, and nuances of African conflicts and the competing forms of solutions. As compared with neoliberalism, glocalized security captures the external frames and global forces that shape African conflicts. Yet glocalized security does not fall into the pitfalls of the neocolonialism discourse, which tends to leave out the agency of African actors and the problematic nature of governance institutions in African countries. Glocalized security also goes beyond collective security and R2P in unearthing the geopolitical and ideological interests that drive external securitization in Africa and the local factors in the conflicts. In many ways, glocalized security brings into security studies a deep sociological lens that is useful not only for African conflicts but also for other conflicts connected to global liberal governance.[60] A glocalized security provides a unique holistic approach in which the intersecting and dialectical elements of conflicts are clearly defined, and their collective transformative effects are made evident.

African security issues are plagued by a plethora of intersecting and dialectical forces within and outside the countries themselves. This book shows the glocalized nature of African security by simultaneously addressing the domestic and external drivers of African conflicts and pointing to the transformed nature of African security. Glocalized security is most evident in the Global War on Terror–related cases, notably in Libya, Mali, Nigeria, and Kenya as shown in this book. In all of these cases, violent conflicts are rooted in domestic issues of governance and ethnic marginalization, but those conflicts have been significantly transformed by the emergence of terrorist groups that exploit domestic grievances to further violent extremism. A poignant illustration of this glocal element is the radicalization into violent extremism that has been going on in countries such as Nigeria, Kenya, and Mali. In northwestern Nigeria, conflicts between farmers and herders over natural resources have degenerated into insurgencies that easily fuse with jihadist insurgencies in Nigeria and neighboring countries. Even in the DRC, where there are myriad domestic conflict drivers and deep regional factors, external conflict drivers have been infused into the conflict through the exploitation of mineral resources and the emergence of groups linked to terrorist networks such as the Allied Democratic Forces. Even more, counterterrorism programs and external military interventions in Libya and Mali have actually *exacerbated* terrorism by producing iatrogenic violence. Glocalized security is not just a way to bridge the domestic and external conflict drivers but a way to understand the very nature of African conflicts. African conflicts are wars that occur on African soil, but the factors that fuel them, the people who direct them, and the means through which they are fought extend far beyond Africa. All these elements rest deeply in the forces of global liberal governance.[61]

SCOPE AND THEMES: RULE OF LAW, GLOBAL WAR ON TERROR, AND AGENCY

In examining the glocalized nature of African security through the fusion of domestic and external drivers of conflicts, this book focuses on three issues in African security, namely (1) governance and the rule of law, (2) the Global War on Terror, and (3) African agency in its security matters. These themes emerge from the various chapters in ways that connect to the domestic and external drivers of African conflicts and the glocalized nature of African security problems. The themes not only dovetail with extant theories on African security but also tie in neatly with a glocalized security lens.

The issue of governance and the rule of law is intrinsic to all the chapters, notably Babo's chapter on Mali and Côte d'Ivoire, Fola's chapter on Nigeria, Nkwanpa's chapter on Uganda and Nigeria, and Bah and Emmanuel's chapter on the conceptions of African civil wars. Extant studies of issues of governance and rule of law are firmly anchored on the liberal peace theory, which sees patrimonial rule as the primary cause of African conflicts. The chapters in this book also show that, but they go much further by demonstrating how these domestic issues connect with external conflict drivers. This is most evident in Babo's chapter on Côte d'Ivoire and Mali in which he discusses the problems of governance, failed democracies, and state decay under the weight of externally driven democratization and securitization. In both countries, democracy could not work because of domestic and external problems. Anina's chapter on proscription of terrorist groups in Nigeria shows how groups fighting for economic and social justice can be easily designated as terrorist groups, thereby delegitimizing their grievances and justifying state violence. However, the proscription approach to security fails to address core problems of governance and the rule of law. Moreover, Anina shows how proscription becomes part of the Global War on Terror as countries accept other countries' designations of groups as terrorists. Nwankpa also shows how the militarization of the War on Terror diverts from making efforts to address genuine grievances over political oppression and economic injustice. In a way, the Global War on Terror provides a problematic military fix to deep-rooted domestic problems of the rule of law and governance. In the end, the military fix becomes iatrogenic violence.

The chapter by Bah and Emmanuel on the conceptions of African civil wars also captures this problem of governance and the rule of law as it is presented in the external bodies of knowledge about Africa, especially in international relations studies. For Bah and Emmanuel, African security needs to take into account African knowledge and perspectives that go beyond liberal peace as they draw richly on the colonial history of Africa. In this chapter, external knowledge about African conflicts is juxtaposed with an African knowledge of African security, especially as it has been developed in international relations studies. Erickson's chapter on assimilating international norms and capacities shows the neoliberal frame of peace as embodied in European normative and security institutions, and how those norms are supposed to be replicated in Africa. In the chapter on Libya by Sempijja, Cherkaoui, and Zaoui, the Libyan peace process is viewed in terms of the possibilities of creating a stable multiparty democracy, which has been elusive as more external powers exert themselves into the Libyan war for strategic interests. Githigaro provides a ground-level look at how human rights violations occur against Somali people in Kenya through the Global War on Terror. As he points out, Somali people face systemic marginalization, which is often ignored as they are associated with Al-Shabaab terrorism in Kenya. As this case shows, liberalism seems to be suppressed under the weight of the Global War on Terror.

The second theme is on the Global War on Terror, which shows up in nearly all the cases. The Global War on Terror has already been noted as an external conflict driver. Moreover, it fits into the notion of collective security. The chapters show that the Global War on Terror is a glocalized security issue in Africa. Babo's chapter shows how Mali's domestic issues are fused with terrorism warfare, generating improper French intervention in Mali. French intervention became focused on French national security interests at the expense of Mali's stability. So too in Libya; as Sempijja et al. show, NATO intervention pushed a domestic uprising into terrorism warfare that has drawn in even more external powers such as Russia and Turkey. In the process, the African Union became marginalized from the peace process despite the wider regional implications of the Libyan war. In Nigeria and Uganda, too, the Global War on Terror is central to how those countries approach security. As Nwankpa shows, the Global War on Terror approach has led to excessive militarization of the conflicts.

In two of the chapters, the Global War on Terror takes a deeply local form. In Nigeria, local criminal networks referred to as bandits are proscribed as terrorist groups. As Anina points out, the Global War on Terror has been far-reaching in its application to the point that even truly local community forms of violence have been brought under the Global War on Terror frame. Through proscription, Nigeria is failing to

Introduction

focus more on domestic conflict drivers and increasingly turning to external tools and solutions in dealing with violent conflicts. In Kenya, too, Githigaro shows how the designation of "Global War on Terror" has been applied to Somali communities through community policing. Unfortunately, the Global War on Terror has generated too much distrust of the Kenyan state among Somalis, rendering the community-policing effort ineffective.

The final theme is about African agency in African security matters. African agency in its security matters has been challenging for individual African countries and for the continent as a whole.[62] Indeed, the extant theories on African security tend to swing between those that see African countries as totally responsible for the causes of their conflicts, notably the liberal peace theory, and those that see African countries as largely victims of external forces, most notably the neocolonial and R2P theories. By addressing the fusion of domestic and external conflict drivers, this book provokes the issue of African agency. Overall, the chapters show a mixed bag. In some cases, African countries have tried to show agency, but too often African agency is limited. Erickson's chapter on assimilating international norms and capacities shows a fair level of African capacity to adopt Western collective security norms as we see in the DRC and through peacekeeping missions led by the African Union (AU) and/or its Regional Economic Communities. However, this agency rests on African countries' adopting Western norms of security, and by implication liberal peace. African agency seems strong when African countries initiate and undertake security action, but too often that requires Western funding and training. In the chapter by Bah and Emmanuel on conceptions of African civil wars, the issue of African agency is accentuated through the discourse of knowledge about African security. The chapter shows how African knowledge is largely marginalized in international relations studies, even though the African experiences have been critical to international security. Even more, African agency becomes very limited when African security policies draw too heavily on bodies of knowledge that leave out African experiences and/or African scholars.

Overall, there is a significant deficit of African agency as security matters in Africa are dictated by external powers. This is most evident in Libya, where the AU has been marginalized from the peace process.

As Sempijja et al. point out, the marginalization of the AU is a result of an AU credibility deficit and lack of capacity as well as the entrenched interests of NATO and EU, and more recently by Russia and Turkey. Mali and Côte d'Ivoire show the limits of African agency. As Babo notes, French interventions in Mali and Côte d'Ivoire were fiercely resisted, especially in Mali, where France was asked to leave the country. However, the French simply relocated across the border to Niger, leaving them right in the neighborhood without any change in policy. In Côte d'Ivoire, despite the strong protest, France was able to determine the final outcome of the power struggle between northerners and southerners by militarily intervening.

In Nigeria, Kenya, and Uganda, African agency seems to be contingent on whether those countries get the support they want from external powers. When the countries receive military and other forms of aid, they participate in the Global War on Terror as requested. However, they can modify their participation to extract more support. As Anina shows, in Nigeria, proscription of terrorist groups was done by the Nigerian state. But too often, the Nigerian state takes Western intelligence and requests into account. Also, proscription of terrorist groups, especially Boko Haram, was a way of communicating Nigeria's commitment to the Global War on Terror. In Uganda, as Nwankpa shows, the government became a strong Western ally in the wars in the Great Lakes and the Horn of Africa at the expense of promoting meaningful democracy in Uganda. In Kenya, too, as Mwangi shows, community policing was used as a counterterrorism tool. Normally, community policing is for purely local matters. However, the Kenyan government became a key ally in the Global War on Terror and adopted various counterterrorism tools in a way that suggests limited agency.

This book is about the fusion of domestic and external issues in African conflicts and how that fusion generates a complex glocalized security landscape. Overall, the chapters explore the causes and nature of insecurity through case studies of Mali, Côte d'Ivoire, Nigeria, Uganda, Libya, and the DRC. The critical question for African scholars and policymakers is how to resolve African conflicts. Merely calling for neoliberal reforms or restating the structural damage of colonialism and calling for moral responsibility on the part of Western powers seem to be jaded idealistic "solutions." More-pragmatic solutions to African security issues would require an eclectic approach and understanding of the glocalized nature of African (in)security. African countries must be able to direct attention to core domestic drivers of conflict while finding ways to mitigate the external forces. Ultimately, African countries must develop creative institutional designs that can minimize ethnic marginalization and enhance regional and pan-African mechanisms. A key challenge for pan-African institutions is the weaknesses of member states. As such, African countries must enhance their own individual capacities by creating mechanisms for inclusive governance at the national level. African countries must also be active members of the international system. Indeed, African countries can bring formidable moral capital to the discourse on global issues of the environment, economics, and social injustice. However, African countries need to build more trust in order to gain moral leverage in the international system.

NOTES

1. United Nations Peacekeeping, "Where We Operate," United Nations, accessed November 7, 2023, https://peacekeeping.un.org/en/where-we-operate.
2. Jeffrey Herbst, "War and the State in Africa," *International Security* 14.4 (1990): 117–139; Taisier Mohamed Ali and Robert O. Matthews (eds.), *Civil Wars in Africa: Roots and Resolution* (Montreal: McGill-Queen's University Press, 1999); William Minter, *Apartheid's Contras: An Inquiry into the Roots of War in Angola and Mozambique* (Johannesburg: Witwatersrand University Press, 1994).
3. Peter Schwab, "Cold War on the Horn of Africa," *African Affairs* 77.306 (1978): 6–20; Adebayo Oyebade and Abiodun Alao (eds.), *Africa after the Cold War: The Changing Perspectives on Security* (Trenton, NJ: Africa World Press, 1998).
4. Gérard Prunier, *Africa's World War: Congo, the Rwandan Genocide, and the Making of a Continental Catastrophe* (New York: Oxford University Press, 2008); Séverine Autesserre, *The Trouble with the Congo* (New York: Cambridge University Press, 2010).
5. Abu Bakarr Bah, "Changing World Order and the Future of Democracy in Sub-Saharan Africa," *Proteus: A Journal of Ideas* 21.1 (Spring 2004): 3–12; Michael Bratton and Nicholas Van de Walle, *Democratic Experiments in Africa: Regime Transitions in Comparative Perspective* (New York: Cambridge University Press, 1997).
6. Adekeye Adebajo, *Building Peace in West Africa: Liberia, Sierra Leone, and Guinea-Bissau* (Boulder, CO: Lynne Rienner Publishers, 2002).
7. Mary Kaldor, *New and Old Wars: Organised Violence in a Global Era* (New York: John Wiley & Sons, 2013); Abu Bakarr Bah, "The Contours of New Humanitarianism: War and Peacebuilding in Sierra Leone," *Africa Today* 60.1 (2013): 3–26.

8. Stephen Ellis, *The Mask of Anarchy: The Destruction of Liberia and the Religious Dimension of an African Civil War* (New York: New York University Press, 2006).

9. Adebajo, *Building Peace in West Africa*; Abu Bakarr Bah (ed.), *International Security and Peacebuilding: Africa, the Middle East, and Europe* (Bloomington: Indiana University Press, 2017).

10. Abu Bakarr Bah, "People-Centered Liberalism: An Alternative Approach to International State-Building in Sierra Leone and Liberia," *Critical Sociology* 43.7–8 (2017): 989–1007.

11. John Davis (ed.), *Terrorism in Africa: The Evolving Front in the War on Terror* (Lanham, MD: Lexington Books, 2012); Michael Nwankpa, "Understanding the Local-Global Dichotomy and Drivers of the Boko Haram Insurgency," *African Conflict and Peacebuilding Review* 10.2 (2020): 43–64.

12. Mark Duffield, *Global Governance and the New Wars: The Merging of Development and Security* (London: Zed Books, 2014).

13. Robert H. Jackson and Carl Gustav Rosberg, *Personal Rule in Black Africa: Prince, Autocrat, Prophet, Tyrant* (Berkeley: University of California Press, 1982).

14. Patrick Chabal and Jean-Pascal Daloz, *Africa Works: The Political Instrumentalization of Disorder* (London: James Currey, 1998); Jean-François Bayart, *The State in Africa: The Politics of the Belly* (Cambridge, MA: Polity, 2009); Abu Bakarr Bah and Margaret Nasambu Barasa, "Indigenous Knowledge and the Social Construction of Patriarchy: The Case of the Bukusu of Kenya," *Critical Sociology* 49.2 (2023): 217–232; Abu Bakarr Bah and Ibrahim Bangura, "Landholding and the Creation of Lumpen Tenants in Freetown: Youth Economic Survival and Patrimonialism in Postwar Sierra Leone," *Critical Sociology* 49.7–8 (2023): 1289–305.

15. William Reno, "Corruption and State Politics in Sierra Leone," *Corruption and State Politics in Sierra Leone* (New York: Cambridge University Press, 1995); Abu Bakarr Bah, "State Decay and Civil War: A Discourse on Power in Sierra Leone," *Critical Sociology* 37.2 (2011): 199–216.

16. Chiara Tea Antoniazzi, "Land, Natural Resources, and Environmental Protection in the Juba Peace Agreement," *African Conflict and Peacebuilding Review* 12.2 (2022): 133–150; Jacopo Branchesi and Francesco de Rosa, "Economic Prospects and Challenges for Sudan after the Juba Peace Agreement: The Role of Development Endeavors in Promoting Peacebuilding and Community Stabilization in Darfur," *African Conflict and Peacebuilding Review* 12.2 (2022): 216–240.

17. Kimo A. Adiebo, "Resource, Economic, and Financial Management in South Sudan: Taking Stock of Chapter IV of the R-ARCSS," *African Conflict and Peacebuilding Review* 11.2 (2021): 39–63.

18. Abu Bakarr Bah, *Breakdown and Reconstitution: Democracy, the Nation-State, and Ethnicity in Nigeria* (Lanham, MD: Lexington Books, 2005); Abu Bakarr Bah, "Ethnic Conflicts and Management Strategies in Bulgaria, Sierra Leone and Nigeria," Programme on Ethnic and Federal Studies Monograph New Series, no. 3 (Ibadan, Nigeria: John Archers Publishers, 2003).

Introduction

19. Abu Bakarr Bah (ed.), *Post-conflict Institutional Design: Peacebuilding and Democracy in Africa* (London: Zed Books, 2020); Bah, *Breakdown and Reconstitution*.
20. Bah, "Democracy and Civil War"; Bah, *Breakdown and Reconstitution*; Gabrielle Lynch, "Negotiating Ethnicity: Identity Politics in Contemporary Kenya," *Review of African Political Economy* 33.107 (2006): 49–65.
21. Michael D. Beevers, "Governing Natural Resources for Peace: Lessons from Liberia and Sierra Leone," *Global Governance* 21.2 (2015): 227–246; Bah, *Post-conflict Institutional Design*.
22. Abosede Omowumi Babatunde, "Environmental Insecurity and Poverty in the Niger Delta: A Case of Ilaje," *African Conflict and Peacebuilding Review* 7.2 (2017): 36–59; Caroline Varin, "No Opportunity Lost: The ISWAP Insurgency in the Changing Climate of Lake Chad Region," *African Conflict and Peacebuilding Review* 10.2, (2020): 141–157; Matthew D. Turner et al., "Livelihood Transitions and the Changing Nature of Farmer-Herder Conflict in Sahelian West Africa," *The Journal of Development Studies* 47.2 (2011): 183–206.
23. Caroline Varin, "No Opportunity Lost: The ISWAP Insurgency in the Changing Climate of Lake Chad Region," *African Conflict and Peacebuilding Review* 10.2 (2020): 141–157.
24. Abdel-Fatau Musah, "Privatization of Security, Arms Proliferation and the Process of State Collapse in Africa," *Development and Change* 33.5 (2002): 911–933; Kimberley Thachuk and Karen Saunders, "Under the Radar: Airborne Arms Trafficking Operations in Africa," *European Journal on Criminal Policy and Research* 20.3 (2014): 361–378.
25. M Webber, "Soviet Policy in Sub-Saharan Africa: The Final Phase," *The Journal of Modern African Studies* 30.1 (1992): 1–30.
26. Marco Wyss, "The Gendarme Stays in Africa: France's Military Role in Côte d'Ivoire," *African Conflict and Peacebuilding Review* 3.1 (2013): 81–111; Bruno Charbonneau, "Dreams of Empire: France, Europe, and the New Interventionism in Africa," *Modern & Contemporary France* 16.3 (2008): 279–295.
27. Bah, *International Security and Peacebuilding*; Manfred B. Steger, *The Rise of the Global Imaginary: Political Ideologies from the French Revolution to the Global War on Terror* (New York: Oxford University Press, 2008).
28. Emeka Thaddues Njoku, "Merchants of Terror: Neo-patrimonialism, Counterterrorism Economy, and Expansion of Terrorism in Nigeria," *African Conflict and Peacebuilding Review* 10.2 (2020): 83–107.
29. Laurence McFalls, "Benevolent Dictatorship: Sovereign Authority and Humanitarian War," in *Contemporary State of Emergency: The Politics of Military and Humanitarian Intervention*, ed. Didier Fassin and Mariella Pandolfi (Brooklyn: Zone Books, 2010).
30. Nwankpa, "Understanding the Local-Global Dichotomy"; Usman Ladan, "Transnational Terrorism Revisited: Is Boko Haram an al-Qaeda Affiliate?," *African Conflict and Peacebuilding Review* 12.1 (2022): 105–126.
31. Gérard Prunier, "Rebel Movements and Proxy Warfare: Uganda, Sudan and the Congo (1986–99)," *African Affairs* 103.412 (2004): 359–383.

32. Melha Rout Biel, "IGAD and Regional Actors in the South Sudan Crisis: A Tale of Interests and Influence," *African Conflict and Peacebuilding Review* 11.2 (2021): 85–103.

33. Bratton and Van de Walle, *Democratic Experiments in Africa*; Obed O. Mailafia, *Europe and Economic Reform in Africa: Structural Adjustment and Economic Diplomacy* (New York: Routledge, 2005); Bah, "People-Centered Liberalism."

34. Umaru Fofana and Cooper Inveen, "Freetown in Shock after Dozens Killed in Sierra Leone Protests," Reuters, August 11, 2022, https://www.reuters.com/world/africa/six-police-officers-killed-sierra-leone-protests-police-head-2022-08-11.

35. Mahamat Ramadane, "About 50 People Killed in Chad Protests, Government Says," Reuters, October 20, 2022, https://www.reuters.com/world/africa/chad-police-fire-tear-gas-pro-democracy-protests-2022-10-20.

36. E. T. Akov, "The Resource-Conflict Debate Revisited: Untangling the Case of Farmer–Herdsman Clashes in the North Central Region of Nigeria," *African Security Review* 26.3 (2017): 288–307; T. A. Benjaminsen and B. Ba, "Farmer-Herder Conflicts, Pastoral Marginalisation and Corruption: A Case Study from the Inland Niger Delta of Mali," *Geographical Journal* 175.1 (2009): 71–81; G. J. Abbink et al., "Lands of the Future: Transforming Pastoral Lands and Livelihoods in Eastern Africa," *Max Planck Institute for Social Anthropology Working Papers* 154 (2014).

37. Ali A. Mazrui, "The Blood of Experience: The Failed State and Political Collapse in Africa," *World Policy Journal* 12.1 (1995): 28–34.

38. Basil Davidson, *The Black Man's Burden: Africa and the Curse of the Nation-State* (New York: Times Press, 1993).

39. Frantz Fanon, *The Wretched of the Earth* (New York: Grove Press, 1963).

40. Aristide R. Zolberg, "The Structure of Political Conflict in the New States of Tropical Africa," *American Political Science Review* 62.1 (1968): 70–87; Zolberg, "Patterns of National Integration," *The Journal of Modern African Studies* 5.4 (1967): 449–467; Bah, "Democracy and Civil War"; Bah, *Breakdown and Reconstitution*; Bah, *Post-conflict Institutional Design*.

41. Vladimir Gennadevich Shubin, *The Hot "Cold War": The USSR in Southern Africa* (London: Pluto Press, 2008).

42. Schwab, "Cold War on the Horn of Africa"; Olajide Aluko, "African Response to External Intervention in Africa since Angola," *African Affairs* 80.319 (1981): 159–179.

43. Douglas Little, "Cold War and Colonialism in Africa: The United States, France, and the Madagascar Revolt of 1947," *Pacific Historical Review* 59.4 (1990): 527–552; James L. Roark, "American Black Leaders: The Response to Colonialism and the Cold War, 1943–1953," *African Historical Studies* 4.2 (1971): 253–270.

44. Eghosa E. Osaghae, "The Ogoni Uprising: Oil Politics, Minority Agitation and the Future of the Nigerian State," *African Affairs* 94.376 (1995): 325–344; Philippe Le Billon, "Angola's Political Economy of War: The Role of Oil and Diamonds, 1975–2000," *African Affairs* 100.398 (2001): 55–80; Koen Vlassenroot

and Hans Romkema, "The Emergence of a New Order? Resources and War in Eastern Congo," *Journal of Humanitarian Assistance* 28 (2002): 24–39; Prunier, *Africa's World War*.

45. Ian Taylor, "What Fit for the Liberal Peace in Africa?," *Global Society* 21.4 (2007): 553–566; Roland Paris, *At War's End: Building Peace after Civil Conflict* (New York: Cambridge University Press, 2004).

46. Bah, "People-Centered Liberalism"; Bah, "Democracy and Civil War."

47. Boutros Boutros-Ghali, "An Agenda for Peace: Preventive Diplomacy, Peacemaking and Peacekeeping," *International Relations* 11.3 (1992): 201–218; United Nations General Assembly and Security Council, "Report of the Panel on United Nations Peace Operations" (A/55/305 S/2000/809), August 21, 2000 (Brahimi Report); Bah, "The Contours of New Humanitarianism."

48. Kofi Annan, "Two Concepts of Sovereignty," *The Economist* 352.8137 (1999): 49–50; Commission on Human Security, *Human Security Now* (New York: United Nations, 2003); Kaldor, *New and Old Wars*; Bah, "The Contours of New Humanitarianism."

49. Abu Bakarr Bah, "State Decay: A Conceptual Frame for Failing and Failed States in West Africa," *International Journal of Politics, Culture, and Society* 25.1–3 (2012): 71–89.

50. Abu Bakarr Bah and Nikolas Emmanuel, "Positive Peace and the Methodology of Costing Peacebuilding Needs: The Case of Burundi," *Administrative Theory & Praxis* 43.3 (2020): 299–318; Bah, "People-Centered Liberalism." See also: Abu Bakarr Bah and Nikolas Emmanuel, *International Statebuilding in West Africa: Civil Wars and New Humanitarianism in Sierra Leone, Liberia, and Côte d'Ivoire* (Bloomington: Indiana University Press, forthcoming, 2024).

51. Hans Kelsen, "Collective Security and Collective Self-Defense under the Charter of the United Nations," *The American Journal of International Law* 42.4 (1948): 783–796; A. Charles Kupchan and Clifford A. Kupchan, "The Promise of Collective Security," *International Security* 20.1 (1995): 52–61.

52. Barry Buzan and Ole Wæver, *Regions and Powers: The Structure of International Security* (New York: Cambridge University Press, 2003); Shiping Tang, *The Social Evolution of International Politics*, online ed. (Oxford: Oxford University Press, 2013), https://doi.org/10.1093/acprof:oso/9780199658336.001.0001.

53. Kenneth Waltz, "Reflections on Theory of International Politics: A Response to My Critics," in *Neorealism and Its Critics*, ed. Robert D. Putnam (New York: Columbia University Press, 1986); Robert D. Putnam, "Diplomacy and Domestic Politics: The Logic of Two-Level Games," *International Organization* 42.3 (1988): 427–460.

54. Thomas L. Friedman, *The World Is Flat: A Brief History of the Twenty-first Century*, updated and expanded ed. (New York: Farrar, Straus and Giroux, 2006); Ulrich Beck, *What Is Globalization?* (Cambridge, MA: Polity, 2000); Ulrich Beck, Natan Sznaider, and Rainer Winter (eds.), *Global America? The Cultural Consequences of Globalization* (Liverpool: Liverpool University Press, 2003); Roland Robertson, "Glocalization: Time-Space and Homogeneity-Heterogeneity," *Global Modernities* 2.1 (1995): 25–44.

55. Roland Robertson, "Globality and Modernity," *Theory, Culture & Society* 9.2 (1992): 153–161; Roland Robertson, "Globalisation or Glocalisation?," *Journal of International Iommunication* 1.1 (1994): 33–52; Robertson, "Glocalization"; Richard Giulianotti and Roland Robertson, "The Globalization of Football: A Study in the Glocalization of the 'Serious Life,'" *The British Journal of Sociology* 55.4 (2004): 545–568; Richard Giulianotti and Roland Robertson, "Glocalization, Globalization and Migration: The Case of Scottish Football Supporters in North America," *International Sociology* 21.2 (2006): 171–198; Roland Robertson and Kathleen E. White, "What Is Globalization," *The Blackwell Companion to Globalization* (2007): 54–66.
56. Ulrich, *What Is Globalization?*; Beck, *Global America?*
57. C. Wright Mills, "The Promise," *The Sociological Imagination* (1959): 3–24. http://people.uncw.edu/levyd/soc105/Mills,%20the%20Promise.PDF; Patricia Hill Collins, *Black Feminist Thought: Knowledge, Consciousness, and the Politics of Empowerment* (New York: Routledge, 2002).
58. Bettina Köhler and Markus Wissen, "Glocalizing Protest: Urban Conflicts and the Global Social Movements," *International Journal of Urban and Regional Research* 27.4 (2003): 942–951; Dannie Kjeldgaard and Søren Askegaard, "The Glocalization of Youth Culture: The Global Youth Segment as Structures of Common Difference," *Journal of Consumer Research* 33.2 (2006): 231–247; Giulianotti and Robertson, "The Globalization of Football"; Beck, *What Is Globalization?*
59. Samuel Marfo, Halidu Musah, and Dominic DeGraft Arthur, "Beyond Classical Peace Paradigm: A Theoretical Argument for a Glocalized Peace and Security," *African Journal of Political Science and International Relations* 10.4 (2016): 48.
60. Duffield, *Global Governance and the New Wars.*
61. Duffield; Bah, *International Security and Peacebuilding.*
62. Abu Bakarr Bah, "African Agency in New Humanitarianism and Responsible Governance," in *International Security and Peacebuilding: Africa, the Middle East, and Europe,* ed. Abu Bakarr Bah (Bloomington: Indiana University Press, 2017), 148–169.

BIBLIOGRAPHY

Abbink, G. J., et al. "Lands of the Future: Transforming Pastoral Lands and Livelihoods in Eastern Africa." *Max Planck Institute for Social Anthropology Working Papers* 154 (2014).

Adebajo, Adekeye. *Building Peace in West Africa: Liberia, Sierra Leone, and Guinea-Bissau.* Boulder, CO: Lynne Rienner Publishers, 2002.

Adiebo, Kimo A. "Resource, Economic, and Financial Management in South Sudan: Taking Stock of Chapter IV of the R-ARCSS." *African Conflict and Peacebuilding Review* 11. 2 (2021): 39–63.

Akov, E. T. "The Resource-Conflict Debate Revisited: Untangling the Case of Farmer–Herdsman Clashes in the North Central Region of Nigeria." *African Security Review* 26.3 (2017): 288–307.

Ali, Taisier M., and Robert O. Matthews, eds. *Civil Wars in Africa: Roots and Resolution*. Montreal: McGill-Queen's University Press, 1999.

Aluko, Olajide. "African Response to External Intervention in Africa since Angola." *African Affairs* 80.319 (1981): 159–179.

Annan, Kofi. "Two Concepts of Sovereignty." *The Economist* 352.8137 (1999): 49–50.

Antoniazzi, Chiara Tea. "Land, Natural Resources, and Environmental Protection in the Juba Peace Agreement." *African Conflict and Peacebuilding Review* 12.2 (2022): 133–150.

Autesserre, Séverine. *The Trouble with the Congo*. New York: Cambridge University Press, 2010.

Babatunde, Abosede Omowumi. "Environmental Insecurity and Poverty in the Niger Delta: A Case of Ilaje." *African Conflict & Peacebuilding Review* 7.2 (2017): 36–59.

Bah, Abu Bakarr. "Ethnic Conflicts and Management Strategies in Bulgaria, Sierra Leone and Nigeria." Programme on Ethnic and Federal Studies Monograph New Series, no. 3. Ibadan, Nigeria: John Archers Publishers, 2003.

———. "Changing World Order and the Future of Democracy in Sub-Saharan Africa." *Proteus: A Journal of Ideas* 21.1 (Spring 2004): 3–12.

———. *Breakdown and Reconstitution: Democracy, the Nation-State, and Ethnicity in Nigeria*. Lanham, MD: Lexington Books, 2005.

———. "Democracy and Civil War: Citizenship and Peacemaking in Côte d'Ivoire." *African Affairs* 109.437 (2010): 597–615.

———. "State Decay and Civil War: A Discourse on Power in Sierra Leone." *Critical Sociology* 37.2 (2011): 199–216.

———. "State Decay: A Conceptual Frame for Failing and Failed States in West Africa." *International Journal of Politics, Culture, and Society* 25.1–3 (2012): 71–89.

———. "The Contours of New Humanitarianism: War and Peacebuilding in Sierra Leone." *Africa Today* 60.1 (2013): 3–26.

———. "People-Centered Liberalism: An Alternative Approach to International State-Building in Sierra Leone and Liberia." *Critical Sociology* 43.7–8 (2017): 989–1007.

Bah, Abu Bakarr (ed.). *International Security and Peacebuilding: Africa, the Middle East, and Europe*. Bloomington: Indiana University Press, 2017.

——— (ed.). "African Agency in New Humanitarianism and Responsible Governance." In *International Security and Peacebuilding: Africa, the Middle East, and Europe*, 148–169. Bloomington: Indiana University Press, 2017.

——— (ed.). *Post-conflict Institutional Design: Peacebuilding and Democracy in Africa*. London: Zed Books, 2020.

Bah, Abu Bakarr, and Ibrahim Bangura. "Landholding and the Creation of Lumpen Tenants in Freetown: Youth Economic Survival and Patrimonialism in Postwar Sierra Leone." *Critical Sociology* 49.7–8 (2023): 1289–305.

Bah, Abu Bakarr, and Nikolas Emmanuel. *International Statebuilding in West Africa: Civil Wars and New Humanitarianism in Sierra Leone, Liberia, and Côte d'Ivoire*. Bloomington: Indiana University Press, forthcoming, 2024.

———. "Positive Peace and the Methodology of Costing Peacebuilding Needs: The Case of Burundi." *Administrative Theory & Praxis* 43.3 (2020): 299–318.

Bah, Abu Bakarr, and Margaret Nasambu Barasa. "Indigenous Knowledge and the Social Construction of Patriarchy: The Case of the Bukusu of Kenya." *Critical Sociology* 49.2 (2023): 217–232.

Bayart, Jean-François. *The State in Africa: The Politics of the Belly*. Cambridge, MA: Polity, 2009.

Beck, Ulrich. *What Is Globalization?* Cambridge, MA: Polity, 2000.

Beck, Ulrich, Natan Sznaider, and Rainer Winter (eds.). *Global America? The Cultural Consequences of Globalization*. Liverpool: Liverpool University Press, 2003.

Beevers, Michael D. "Governing Natural Resources for Peace: Lessons from Liberia and Sierra Leone." *Global Governance* 21.6 (2015): 227.

Benjaminsen, T. A., and B. Ba. "Farmer-Herder Conflicts, Pastoral Marginalisation and Corruption: A Case Study from the Inland Niger Delta of Mali." *Geographical Journal* 175.1 (2009): 71–81.

Biel, Melha Rout. "IGAD and Regional Actors in the South Sudan Crisis: A Tale of Interests and Influence." *African Conflict and Peacebuilding Review* 11.2 (2021): 85–103.

Boutros-Ghali, Boutros. "An Agenda for Peace: Preventive Diplomacy, Peacemaking and Peacekeeping." *International Relations* 11.3 (1992): 201–218.

Branchesi, Jacopo, and Francesco de Rosa. "Economic Prospects and Challenges for Sudan after the Juba Peace Agreement: The Role of Development Endeavors in Promoting Peacebuilding and Community Stabilization in Darfur." *African Conflict and Peacebuilding Review* 12.2 (2022): 216–240.

Bratton, Michael, and Nicholas Van de Walle. *Democratic Experiments in Africa: Regime Transitions in Comparative Perspective*. New York: Cambridge University Press, 1997.

Buzan, Barry, and Ole Wæver. *Regions and Powers: The Structure of International Security*. New York: Cambridge University Press, 2003.

Chabal, Patrick, and Jean-Pascal Daloz. *Africa Works: The Political Instrumentalization of Disorder*. London: James Currey, 1998.

Charbonneau, Bruno. "Dreams of Empire: France, Europe, and the New Interventionism in Africa." *Modern & Contemporary France* 16.3 (2008): 279–295.

Collins, Patricia Hill. *Black Feminist Thought: Knowledge, Consciousness, and the Politics of Empowerment*. New York: Routledge, 2002.

Commission on Human Security. *Human Security Now*. New York: United Nations, 2003.

Davidson, Basil. *The Black Man's Burden: Africa and the Curse of the Nation-State*. New York: Times Press, 1993.

Davis, John (ed.). *Terrorism in Africa: The Evolving Front in the War on Terror*. Lanham, MD: Lexington Books, 2012.

Duffield, Mark. *Global Governance and the New Wars: The Merging of Development and Security*. London: Zed Books, 2014.

Ellis, Stephen. *The Mask of Anarchy: The Destruction of Liberia and the Religious Dimension of an African Civil War*. New York: New York University Press, 2006.

Fanon, Frantz. *The Wretched of the Earth*. New York: Grove Press, 1963.

Fofana, Umaru, and Cooper Inveen. "Freetown in Shock after Dozens Killed in Sierra Leone Protests," August 11, 2022, https://www.reuters.com/world/africa/six-police-officers-killed-sierra-leone-protests-police-head-2022-08-11.

Friedman, Thomas L. *The World Is Flat: A Brief History of the Twenty-first Century*, updated and expanded ed. New York: Farrar, Straus and Giroux, 2006.

Giulianotti, Richard, and Roland Robertson. "The Globalization of Football: A Study in the Glocalization of the 'Serious Life.'" *The British Journal of Sociology* 55.4 (2004): 545–568.

———. "Glocalization, Globalization and Migration: The Case of Scottish Football Supporters in North America." *International Sociology* 21.2 (2006): 171–198.

Herbst, Jeffrey. "War and the State in Africa." *International Security* 14.4 (1990): 117–139.

Jackson, Robert H., and Carl Gustav Rosberg. *Personal Rule in Black Africa: Prince, Autocrat, Prophet, Tyrant*. Berkeley: University of California Press, 1982.

Kaldor, Mary. *New and Old Wars: Organised Violence in a Global Era*. New York: John Wiley & Sons, 2013.

Kelsen, Hans. "Collective Security and Collective Self-Defense under the Charter of the United Nations." *The American Journal of International Law* 42.4 (1948): 783–796.

Kjeldgaard, Dannie, and Søren Askegaard. "The Glocalization of Youth Culture: The Global Youth Segment as Structures of Common Difference." *Journal of Consumer Research* 33.2 (2006): 231–247.

Köhler, Bettina, and Markus Wissen. "Glocalizing Protest: Urban Conflicts and the Global Social Movements." *International Journal of Urban and Regional Research* 27.4 (2003): 942–951.

Kupchan, A. Charles, and Clifford A. Kupchan. "The Promise of Collective Security." *International Security* 20.1 (1995): 52–61.

Ladan, Usman. "Transnational Terrorism Revisited: Is Boko Haram an al-Qaeda Affiliate?" *African Conflict and Peacebuilding Review* 12.1 (2022): 105–126.

Le Billon, Philippe. "Angola's Political Economy of War: The Role of Oil and Diamonds, 1975–2000." *African Affairs* 100.398 (2001): 55–80.

Little, Douglas. "Cold War and Colonialism in Africa: The United States, France, and the Madagascar Revolt of 1947." *Pacific Historical Review* 59.4 (1990): 527–552.

Lynch, Gabrielle. "Negotiating Ethnicity: Identity Politics in Contemporary Kenya." *Review of African Political Economy* 33.107 (2006): 49–65.

Mailafia, Obed O. *Europe and Economic Reform in Africa: Structural Adjustment and Economic Diplomacy*. New York: Routledge, 2005.

Marfo, Samuel, Halidu Musah, and Dominic DeGraft Arthur. "Beyond Classical Peace Paradigm: A Theoretical Argument for a Glocalized Peace and Security." *African Journal of Political Science and International Relations* 10.4 (2016): 47–55.

Mazrui, Ali A. "The Blood of Experience: The Failed State and Political Collapse in Africa." *World Policy Journal* 12.1 (1995): 28–34.

McFalls, Laurence. "Benevolent Dictatorship: Sovereign Authority and Humanitarian War." In *Contemporary State of Emergency: The Politics of Military and*

Humanitarian Intervention, ed. Didier Fassin and Mariella Pandolfi, 317–34. Brooklyn: Zone Books, 2010.

Mills, C. Wright. "The Promise." *The Sociological Imagination* (1959): 3–24. http://people.uncw.edu/levyd/soc105/Mills,%20the%20Promise.PDF.

Minter, William. *Apartheid's Contras: An Inquiry into the Roots of War in Angola and Mozambique.* Johannesburg: Witwatersrand University Press, 1994.

Musah, Abdel-Fatau. "Privatization of Security, Arms Proliferation and the Process of State Collapse in Africa." *Development and Change* 33.5 (2002): 911–933.

Njoku, Emeka Thaddues. "Merchants of Terror: Neo-patrimonialism, Counterterrorism Economy, and Expansion of Terrorism in Nigeria." *African Conflict and Peacebuilding Review* 10.2 (2020): 83–107.

Nwankpa, Michael. "Understanding the Local-Global Dichotomy and Drivers of the Boko Haram Insurgency." *African Conflict and Peacebuilding Review* 10.2 (2020): 43–64.

Osaghae, Eghosa E. "The Ogoni Uprising: Oil Politics, Minority Agitation and the Future of the Nigerian State." *African Affairs* 94.376 (1995): 325–344.

Oyebade, Adebayo, and Abiodun Alao (eds.). *Africa after the Cold War: The Changing Perspectives on Security.* Trenton, NJ: Africa World Press, 1998.

Paris, Roland. *At War's End: Building Peace after Civil Conflict.* New York: Cambridge University Press, 2004.

Prunier, Gérard. "Rebel Movements and Proxy Warfare: Uganda, Sudan and the Congo (1986–99)." *African Affairs* 103.412 (2004): 359–383.

———. *Africa's World War: Congo, the Rwandan Genocide, and the Making of a Continental Catastrophe.* New York: Oxford University Press, 2008.

Putnam, Robert D. "Diplomacy and Domestic Politics: The Logic of Two-Level Games." *International Organization* 42.3 (1988): 427–60.

Ramadane, Mahamat. "About 50 People Killed in Chad Protests, Government Says." Reuters, October 20, 2022, https://www.reuters.com/world/africa/chad-police-fire-tear-gas-pro-democracy-protests-2022-10-20.

Reno, William. *Corruption and State Politics in Sierra Leone.* New York: Cambridge University Press, 1995.

Roark, James L. "American Black Leaders: The Response to Colonialism and the Cold War, 1943–1953." *African Historical Studies* 4.2 (1971): 253–270.

Robertson, Roland. "Globality and Modernity." *Theory, Culture & Society* 9.2 (1992): 153–161.

———. "Globalisation or Glocalisation?" *Journal of International Communication* 1.1 (1994): 33–52.

———. "Glocalization: Time-Space and Homogeneity-Heterogeneity." *Global Modernities* 2.1 (1995): 25–44.

Robertson, Roland, and Kathleen E. White. "What Is Globalization." In *The Blackwell Companion to Globalization,* ed. George Ritzer, 54–66. New York: Wiley, 2007.

Schwab, Peter. "Cold War on the Horn of Africa." *African Affairs* 77.306 (1978): 6–20.

Shubin, Vladimir Gennadevich. *The Hot "Cold War": The USSR in Southern Africa.* London: Pluto Press, 2008.

Steger, Manfred B. *The Rise of the Global Imaginary: Political Ideologies from the French Revolution to the Global War on Terror.* New York: Oxford University Press, 2008.

Tang, Shipping. *The Social Evolution of International Politics*, online ed. Oxford: Oxford University Press, 2013. https://doi.org/10.1093/acprof:oso/9780199658336.001.0001.

Taylor, Ian. "What Fit for the Liberal Peace in Africa?" *Global Society* 21.4 (2007): 553–566.

Thachuk, Kimberley, and Karen Saunders. "Under the Radar: Airborne Arms Trafficking Operations in Africa." *European Journal on Criminal Policy and Research* 20.3 (2014): 361–378.

Turner, Matthew D., et al. "Livelihood Transitions and the Changing Nature of Farmer-Herder Conflict in Sahelian West Africa." *The Journal of Development Studies* 47.2 (2011): 183–206.

United Nations General Assembly and Security Council. "Report of the Panel on United Nations Peace Operations" (A/55/305 S/2000/809), August 21, 2000 (Brahimi Report). https://peacekeeping.un.org/sites/default/files/a_55_305_e_brahimi_report.pdf.

United Nations Peacekeeping. "Where We Operate." United Nations, accessed November 7, 2023, https://peacekeeping.un.org/en/where-we-operate.

Varin, Caroline. "No Opportunity Lost: The ISWAP Insurgency in the Changing Climate of Lake Chad Region." *African Conflict and Peacebuilding Review* 10.2 (2020): 141–157.

Vlassenroot, Koen, and Hans Romkema. "The Emergence of a New Order? Resources and War in Eastern Congo." *Journal of Humanitarian Assistance* 28 (2002): 24–39.

Waltz, Kenneth "Reflections on Theory of International Politics: A Response to My Critics." In *Neorealism and Its Critics*, ed. Robert Keohane, 322–46. New York: Columbia University Press, 1986.

Webber, M. "Soviet Policy in Sub-Saharan Africa: The Final Phase." *The Journal of Modern African Studies* 30.1 (1992): 1–30.

Wyss, Marco. "The Gendarme Stays in Africa: France's Military Role in Côte d'Ivoire." *African Conflict & Peacebuilding Review* 3.1 (2013): 81–111.

Zolberg, Aristide R. "Patterns of National Integration." *The Journal of Modern African Studies* 5.4 (1967): 449–467.

———. "The Structure of Political Conflict in the New States of Tropical Africa." *American Political Science Review* 62.1 (1968): 70–87.

Chapter 1

African Realities and Knowledge Production

Conceptions of Civil Wars, International Interventions, and State Building

ABU BAKARR BAH AND NIKOLAS EMMANUEL

Africa's position in the literature as well as within knowledge production in the field of international relations (IR) has generally been problematic because of the continent's perceived marginalization. In the case of IR theory more specifically, the topic of this apparent marginalization has been more than something of a controversy for rather some time, to say the least. Yet, in more recent years, questions have arisen about the assumedly deep, "unbridgeable" divide between IR theory and input from the African continent. Quite a lengthy list of scholarship has emerged on the matter, which will be discussed in the next several pages. This literature includes works on Africa's place in the world as well as in IR scholarship. All of these works are very relevant to the core issues that have been going on in Africa as well as in a global context. In particular, issues of civil wars, international interventions for humanitarian and security interests, and the nature and trajectory of the state have been central to the African experiences and international relations as a whole. Yet some see a disconnect between African IR and mainstream

IR. This chapter addresses these issues through the lens of IR to provide deeper insights on them, in addition to contributing to the wider body of knowledge in the field. Undoubtedly, IR has given significant attention to African issues. Knowledge about Africa has also neatly dovetailed with the conceptual and theoretical contributions of this body of work. Although this assumption has not been completely agreed upon across the scholarship.

Perhaps a basic question that needs a bit of clarification before we delve into Africa's place in IR knowledge production is how and why African knowledge is marginalized. Africa's marginalization in IR is part of the wider political and economic marginalization that Africa has been experiencing in the global system. Carl Death provides two important reasons to explain the marginalization of Africa in IR. As he points out, "IR theorists have sometimes regarded Africa as peripheral either because its states were seen as weak and it lacked genuine 'Great Powers' able unilaterally to shape world politics, or because it was assumed to be behind the rest of the world (and particularly America and Europe) on a progressive trend toward civilization, democracy, and modernity."[1] Death captures both the academic and nonacademic factors in Africa's marginalization. Academically, social scientific knowledge production has been dominated by Western universities, research centers, and publishing outlets. As Patricia Collins shows in her Afrocentric epistemology, the works of Black scholars face systematic barriers that hinder their publication by major Western journals and publishing houses that dominate contemporary social and scientific knowledge production.[2] This academic marginalization intersects with Africa's other forms of marginalization in the global economic and political order. Indeed, colonialism, economic dependency, and political and military interventions are all manifestations of the marginalization of Africa.[3] Not surprisingly, African countries have often been referred to as Third World, and at best as developing and part of the Global South. Clearly, academia is not separate from the system of Western domination toward Africa, but it has been an integral part of it. As Death and Collins rightly note, the link between the everyday world and academia is real.

This chapter focuses on African cases as well as the broader issues that arise from them and the challenges they face in their relations with the world at large. We demonstrate that Africa's international relations are connected to and in many ways very similar to those of the rest of the world. Along these lines, it does not make sense to relegate African cases to the sidelines in the international system. Our argument centers on the fact that African realities are important parts of the puzzle in the development of IR theory, but they have also been fertile ground for knowledge production on issues such as security and governance in Africa, as well as in the rest of the world. Throughout history, Africa has not just reflected global trends and theoretical debates but has also shaped and advanced them. Accordingly, it can be argued that perhaps some of the most groundbreaking developments and challenges in IR theory have come from African realities. This fact can help push IR theory. Opening up IR to consider the histories of the world outside North America and Europe provides exciting opportunities to push the discipline in new directions. This work shows that in a clearly dualistic manner, IR theory can help us understand a variety of phenomena in Africa and beyond. Inversely, it can be argued that the history and realities emerging from the African continent can help us improve IR theory and provide the discipline with exciting opportunities for change that can better capture a broader and clearer understandings of reality. African realities should therefore be at the center of building IR as a field, not just as being illustrative cases that are occasionally applied to existing theories that are almost exclusively developed outside the continent. When focusing on the developing world, scholarly discussions through the years have overly focused on the effectiveness, capacity, strategies, and political will of external interveners in civil wars to establish peace, much to the detriment of the role(s) of domestic actors in peacebuilding. Along these lines, we aim to provide a crucial bridge between the domestic and the international most critically in an African context. This internal-external interaction cannot be ignored, because the boundaries between domestic affairs and international relations are never clear-cut. This is why we place our focus on the theoretical synergy between the domestic and the international, in Africa and beyond.

Accordingly, one of the principal lines of inquiry in the literature on this topic asks about what role do the realities emerging from the continent play in knowledge production, notably in IR scholarship, as well as in the way we conceptualize common issues such as war, international intervention, peace, and the state. Following this, alongside the likes of Dunn and Shaw, much of the recent literature asks how Africa is situated in the pages of IR theory.[4] Are African realities at the center or on the sidelines of the discipline? Some see a mismatch between African realities and the development of IR theory. That is to say, numerous scholars hold the position that Africa is primarily viewed as being a marginal player in international politics and thus is frequently sidelined by IR research in general.[5] As Death notes, this marginality is connected to Africa's wider marginalization in the global order.[6]

Regardless of all of the talk of Africa playing only a marginal role, there exists a deeper desire among many African IR scholars to "demonstrate the centrality of the experience of the continent to every theoretical approach to IR."[7] Furthermore, Lemke indicates that "African international relations are an especially important part of the puzzle.... [The] goal is to ... improve existing international relations research designs so that Africa and the developing world more generally no longer go missing."[8] This aspiration is also advanced by Death when he remarks that "it has always been recognized that global events and structures like colonialism and independence, the Cold War and the new world order after the fall of the Berlin Wall, the economic and cultural globalization of contemporary capitalism, and the War on Terror, have profoundly shaped African politics and international relations. Research in this area has not just reflected global trends and theoretical debates, but has also shaped and advanced them."[9]

Accordingly, much of the recent African IR literature echoes this clear connection between realities on the continent and on IR theoretical development as a whole. As Sophie Harman and William Brown have rightly noted, this way of seeing Africa can help bring forward opportunities for new theorizing in IR.[10] They "reject the notion that there is an unbridgeable divide between the study of Africa and IR; considerable work remains to realize the potential that each holds for the development of the other."[11] African realities can also be seen as fertile ground for reassessing IR theory more generally. On the other hand, some see clear shortcomings in IR theory as it relates to Africa and to elsewhere in the developing world.[12] This has all led to the emergence of something of an "Africanist critique" of IR theory, clearly a part of a larger movement of post-Western IR theorizing.[13] However, it is probably more accurate to follow Lemke's line of reasoning when he points out that "there is no one Africanist critique" of IR.[14] Instead, there are many of them.

Additionally, as Harman and Brown indicate, there exists a paradox around Africa's place in IR.[15] On the one hand, the continent occupies a rather peripheral position in the discipline, which is dominated by its overarching focus on great powers.[16] On the other hand, some of the perhaps most innovative developments in IR have arguably been coming from the actualities and the opportunities as well as the challenges emanating from the African continent. The lasting impact of colonialism, proxy wars, emerging security threats, weak state contagion, humanitarian intervention, piracy, resource-fueled conflicts, and the like can all be seen as concepts in African politics that have challenged and changed knowledge production, as well as the practice of IR, not to mention policymaking more generally.

As this chapter shows, Africa's international relations issues are connected to and in many ways very similar to those of the rest of the planet and hardly merit being thought of as being sidelined. While some may say that the African continent has potentially been historically pushed to the edges of mainstream IR, if not ignored completely, it has increasingly been the focus of significantly rich empirical research across a variety of key issues in the discipline, like those mentioned above. We would even go so far as to agree with Taylor and Williams, who emphasize the centrality of African processes in IR in pointing out that the continent "has been unavoidably entangled in the ebb and flow of events and changing configurations of power."[17] And as will be pointed to later in this section, this is nothing new and should not be surprising.

AFRICAN REALITIES AND THEORY DEVELOPMENT

In key IR debates—between viewing the world through realist, liberal, constructivist, or more critical lenses—African politics are present, if not front and center. Africa-inspired IR is dominated by the dichotomies of conflict and cooperation, authority and resistance, self-interest and social justice. While some view the African continent as being highly marginal in global politics and more specifically in IR scholarship, others such as Death agree with Taylor and Williams and rightly argue that the various actors on the continent have always been at the center of international relations—from the scourge of the slave trade, to precolonial global interactions, to imperialism and colonial domination, to independence, to the emergence of the Cold War, to the new world order after the fall of the Berlin Wall, to the economic and cultural globalization of contemporary capitalism, and to the recent War on Terror.[18] All these historical events and eras have left deep marks on both African politics and international relations, and it is unimaginable to separate the two from these processes and overall theoretical development.

Clearly, the African continent has historically been a product of international politics, while also being conductive of it. Yet, perhaps more important for the question of knowledge production in IR, Death succinctly argues that "African studies specialists have played a major role in challenging and revising some of the supposed 'timeless truths' of IR," such as the central role of the state in the international system, the role of international anarchy, the mistake of "black boxing" the state in international relations, and so on.[19] Furthermore, William Brown argues that IR reduces "the complexity of the world in order to highlight certain important features.... They rely on conceptual abstractions such as 'state' and 'anarchy' to refer to real aspects of the world but in a necessarily imperfect, generalized way."[20] The historic use of such abstract and generic concepts in IR based on histories from the developed countries has failed to capture African realities, such as the issue of patrimonialism.[21] Changing this can help push IR theoretical development in new directions.

Others have gone further and argued that it is necessary to reexamine some of the basic assumptions and concepts of the core theoretical lens of a discipline that many see as overly centered on scholarship about and produced in North America or Europe.[22] Opening up IR to meet the histories of the world outside North America and Europe will clearly provide us with exciting opportunities to push the discipline in new directions. Along these lines, efforts like that of the *Oxford Research Encyclopedia of International Studies,* a joint collaboration between Oxford University Press and the International Studies Association, have emerged that aim to create a continually updated digital space to develop cutting-edge research on a wide variety of issues, including those discussed here. Africa has arisen as an area of interest in this effort.[23] This helps theoretical development and its application in the policymaking realm as well.

That is to say, some may even go so far as to indicate that Africa is of central relevance to the future development of contemporary IR theory.[24]

Nonetheless, while there are some mismatches between IR theory and commonly understood African realities that are perhaps warranted, we believe that clearly there are a wide number of opportunities to be seized in which the African continent can help inspire contemporary IR theory in new and exciting directions, such as in the study of conflicts and migration.[25] Furthermore, contemporary IR theory is not irrelevant in helping to explain Africa's international relations, and vice versa.[26] However, as Harmon and Brown note, "Bringing Africa in from the margins of how we think about international relations also requires a broader engagement with issue-specific research and greater reflection on what such empirical research says about international relations and the assumptions and concepts used to explain it."[27] The hope is that all of this can encourage further theoretical innovation, knowledge production, and a better understanding of the contributions that Africa is making in contemporary IR theory, as well as that of IR on Africa.

Interestingly, one particular concept has emerged in the forefront of the effort to bring Africa more centrally into IR—that is, the reality of colonialism. As we know, the two prominent historical IR theoretical approaches, those of realism and liberalism, trace their origins back to the two basic yet opposing ideas of conflict and cooperation.[28] However, Death does not see IR theory moving forward and incorporating African realities by exploring only the ideas of conflict or cooperation.[29] In addition to the "Cs" in conflict or cooperation, Death sees another "C," that of colonialism, as being central to IR. He argues that colonialism is crucial to pushing IR in new directions by taking Africa into clearer consideration. As he indicates,

> African engagements with world politics did not begin with colonial encounters, and trade, conflict, and the exchange of people and ideas go back well beyond the formal structures of colonialism. However, it was the so-called "Scramble for Africa" in the nineteenth century as European powers divided the continent into what they thought resembled "modern" territories and boundaries, and carved up colonial possessions to fuel global imperial projects, that created some of the most profound and long-lasting structures of African international politics. The Berlin Conference of 1884–5 encapsulates the interplay of conflict and cooperation in international politics. Bismarck orchestrated European diplomacy to avoid outright war, but in so

doing inaugurated decades of colonial and postcolonial conflict in Africa. Whereas the architects of empire saw Africa as the setting for the spread of "Christianity, Civilization, and Commerce," a more appropriate "three Cs" might be conflict, cooperation, and colonialism.[30]

This work also shows that in a clearly dualistic manner, IR theory can help us understand a variety of phenomena in Africa and beyond. Inversely, it can be argued that the history and realities emerging from the African continent can help us improve IR theory and provide the discipline with exciting opportunities for change that can better capture a broader and clearer understanding of reality. African realities should be therefore at the center of building IR as a field, not just as being illustrative cases that are occasionally applied to existing theory that are almost exclusively developed outside the continent.

That is to say that along with Harman and Brown, "we reject the notion that there is an unbridgeable divide between the study of Africa and IR."[31] The only question for us is how to do it better—in a way that reinforces the interconnections and mainstreams the works of Africanists and African scholars. Each holds an immense amount of potential in the development of the other. Interestingly, along these lines, there has been a shift in Africa's place in IR literature in recent years. Africa's absence from IR is less marked as the twenty-first century has progressed, although much more needs to be done. This can be illustrated by examining the evolution in the various academic pieces citied in the beginning of this section. For this to be a productive endeavor, however, we need to address problems of knowledge production itself, as seen through a more critical and, perhaps more centrally, a more African lens.

COLONIAL PATTERNS OF KNOWLEDGE PRODUCTION AND POLICYMAKING

Colonialism has not only left a deep impression on people, or scarred Africa's geography, but also profoundly affected knowledge production and policymaking concerning the continent—something that has been going on for far too long. In addition, those in the camp that follow this line of reasoning have provided the strongest arguments about re-evaluating Africa's (not to mention all of the Global South's) position in the existing body and production of IR theory. Bhambra et al. make an interesting argument in a 2020 *Foreign Policy* article, pointing out that a "reckoning is long overdue within the academic discipline of international relations (IR). . . . Mainstream IR has not been entirely honest about its ideological or geographic origins. . . . IR must come to terms with the erasure of the roles non-Western political actors and societies have played in shaping global affairs."[32]

Similarly, Baaz and Verweijen hold that the core concepts in IR "are shaped by a long history of colonialism and racism."[33] This is not an end in itself, just that these understandings need to be remembered when we try to transform the way we view African realities and their relation to IR theory development. Based on the extant literature, it is important to ask three crucial questions: (1) How devastating were the waves of European colonialism? (2) How significant was the impression left on the state-building processes across the African continent? (3) How have international relations in the postcolonial era been affected by the long period of colonial domination? Holistically, these points tend to be ignored in the mainstream IR theoretical literature. Furthermore, for some, IR theory is inherently imperialist and colonial in its orientation toward Africa and the rest of the world primarily outside of Europe and North America. According to such an analysis, IR theory takes as its basis the need to "civilize" or "change" Africa in a way that fits into Western ideas about society and the Westphalian state, notably in politics and international interaction.[34]

The aim of such a coloniality approach in IR is to address issues of race and the impact of imperialism in knowledge production within the discipline, as well as with other social sciences and humanities.[35] The desire with this line of inquiry is to probe new ways of conceptualizing the colonial legacies in IR generally and on Africa more specifically.[36] Achille Mbembe (perhaps the leading scholar on the theoretical development and application of the topic), in *On the Postcolony*, powerfully argues that the process of colonization, as well as having been subjected to it, has had a tremendous impact on the nature of power and politics more generally in Africa.[37] Mbembe examines the sociological, anthropological, historical, and philosophical issues of power and subjectivity in Africa through coloniality. As he points out, Africa has been a political, social, and cultural space where the markers of neocolonialism continue to shape the application of power and African subjectivities—within Africa and in Africa's interaction with the rest of the world. This subjectivity links not only to political and economic power but also to the knowledge domination we see in IR. Furthermore, Karen Tucker argues that efforts to address race and imperialism "have framed the distortions and exclusions of mainstream IR in relation to a 'colonial matrix of power' that reproduces colonial forms of domination in international politics and contributes to ongoing Eurocentrism in the discipline."[38] Sabelo Ndlovu-Gatsheni has directly taken up this issue of epistemological coloniality in African studies, which includes IR. As he has argued, colonialism and decolonization are evolving phenomena and cannot be "treated as past formations and movements."[39] Ndlovu-Gatsheni exposes the complexities of decolonizing knowledge about Africa by examining various radical intellectual turns in the study of Africa, such as Afro nationalism, Afro-Marxist political economy, postcolonial feminism, and resurgent decolonial interventions. Despite all of these, he finds that there is still a hegemonic and well-funded Africanist enterprise serving the cognitive empire that shapes knowledge about Africa in the global economy of knowledge.[40] Despite these limitations, Ndlovu-Gatsheni notes the importance of the ongoing struggle to decolonize knowledge about Africa and the need for epistemic freedom. This endeavor requires confronting the global economy of knowledge, understanding the politics of knowledge production and imperialism, and centering the contributions of African intellectuals. In IR, this would require both the mainstreaming of African cases and experiences as well as the works of African scholars in the field. Even more, the role and character of African universities and knowledge production institutions more broadly would need to be redefined, especially in relation to the global economy of knowledge.[41] How can this problem of the legacy of colonial domination be overcome? Coloniality of IR can also be viewed as a resource for scholars seeking ways to critique and reconstruct IR theory as discussed in the previous section.[42] However, more importantly for our endeavors, we need to ask what understanding/impact does a coloniality approach have on international military intervention, postwar peacebuilding, and state building? Neta Crawford's work looks at these questions and includes the impact of colonialism in her research on humanitarian intervention. As Crawford points out, the "debates about humanitarian intervention are in many ways a continuation of arguments about colonialism."[43] Along the lines of Mbembe, Ndlovu-Gatsheni, Tucker, and Crawford, it can be argued that IR theory in Africa, not ignoring other parts of the globe, has clear and even very deep colonial roots. Clearly, the key elements of statehood such as defined territorial boundaries, a central government, and state security apparatus that controls the legitimate use of violence across its territory were established according to the Weberian idea of the Westphalian state during colonial rule.[44] However, colonial states were not conceived as cohesive cultural units that could be transformed into nations.[45]

As numerous studies of African states show, the state is essentially a problematic amalgamation of various ethnic groups and regional entities. As Abu Bakarr Bah summed up the problem in his study of Nigeria, "From the perspective of nation-state building and democratization, the legacies of colonialism are truly paradoxical. While on the one hand, colonialism defined the territory and established the key political and economic institutions of the country, colonial rule worked against the integration of the various peoples that constitute Nigeria and created unbalanced structural and institutional arrangements that promoted conflict among the various ethnic groups in the country."[46] Across Africa, the colonial agenda undermined nationhood rather than promote it. The colonial territories were amalgamations of people of diverse cultures who were pitted against one another for access to and the strategic control of state resources. It is clear that the legacies of colonial rule have had a more than significant impact not only on the process of, but also on our conceptualization of, conflict, peacebuilding, and state building in Africa, as well as beyond. Here, nonetheless, our study seeks to push forward the discourse on African states, without forgetting their colonial and neocolonial baggage, onto their contemporary moral and security connectedness to the international community.

THE DOMESTIC AND THE INTERNATIONAL IN CIVIL WARS, PEACEBUILDING, AND STATE BUILDING

Civil wars, by far, are the primary type of warfare on the planet and have been so for the past several decades. They are a particularly brutal and extremely costly type of warfare, both in terms of the loss of human lives and of overall economic destruction. Increasingly, these wars have been dubbed new wars precisely because of their brutality and deviation from the wars in Western countries during the late 1800s and early 1900s.[47] Civil wars affect societies far beyond the termination of the war itself—frequently setting development back decades and leaving indelible scars between societal groups ripped apart by the violence. Worse yet, war recurrence is extremely common—that is to say, peace after civil war rarely endures beyond a few years after termination of the violence. This is the reason that countries such as Liberia, Sierra Leone, Côte d'Ivoire, Mali, Libya, Democratic Republic of the Congo, Burundi, and Somalia have attracted so much international attention, leading to major peacekeeping, peacemaking, and state-building efforts aided significantly by a variety of actors from the international community. Yet, for much of its postcolonial history the African continent has been united around the idea of sovereignty, refusing outside interference in internal politics. However, this has to some extent changed in recent years. Paradoxically, as Ricardo Soares de Oliveira and Harry Verhoeven point out, "a continent that might once have been described as the world's most sovereigntist has thus, intriguingly, become highly tolerant, and even encouraging, of military intervention."[48]

Before continuing, let us consider what brings about violent intrastate conflicts and why the international community seems so ready to intervene. Civil wars break out because of deeply complex constellations of causes. No single factor explains it all. Specific conditions are not deterministic; and a particular circumstance or group of circumstances may lead to the outbreak of violent conflict in one society but not in another. This is what makes comprehending civil wars, including their commencement, their duration, and their termination, so difficult. However, the social sciences are not without potential explanations. The literature points to five central theoretical groups of arguments relating to the causes of civil war: structural (weak/collapsed states, differing levels of regional growth, rapid population growth, etc.); political (bad leadership, poor governance, shifting balance of ethnic power, scapegoating, outbidding, etc.);[49] economic (greed/grievance arguments, poor economic performance potentially leading to heightened rebel recruitment, high dependence on primary commodity exports, geography capable of sustaining the population);[50] social psychological (relative deprivation, sense/fear of group inadequacy or inferiority);[51] and situational (ethnic/group security dilemma).[52]

So the outbreak of each civil war is most likely due to a unique and complex grouping of causes. This makes any overarching theoretical generalization extremely difficult to be applicable to specific cases. That said, we see state decay as a key element that frequently leads to civil war in a wide number of tangible scenarios. This concept is generally the result of a combination of three closely related elements: (1) the brittle domestic political structures that fail to facilitate intergroup bargaining, (2) the failure of political leadership, and (3) the residual effects of the international political and economic environment. Overall, state decay is the bankrupting of the state and a rupture in the production of goods and services as a result of high-level state mismanagement and corruption, frequently compounded by adverse international economic conditions.[53] State decay is a key factor that leads to civil war, as illustrated in cases such as those of Sierra Leone, Liberia, Côte d'Ivoire, Mali, and Somalia, to name a few. Accordingly, we hold that scholarly discussions across the years have overly focused on the effectiveness, capacity, strategies, and political will of external interveners in civil wars to establish peace, much to the detriment of the role(s) of domestic actors in peacebuilding.[54] A good illustration of this is the case of Côte d'Ivoire, where domestic actors and issues were at the center of the peace process, along with significant international involvement.[55]

It is crucial to point out here that peacebuilding and state building are not simply domestic matters alone, as most evident in postwar reconstruction efforts.[56] Somewhat misguidedly, most traditional IR scholars "treat individual nation-states as sovereign systems whose internal politics can be safely ignored."[57] However, international politics and external intervention play crucial roles in domestic politics, and inversely intrastate politics also deeply mark the role of the international community. That said, while all politics are clearly local, as they say, they are also strongly influenced by international elements. This means that the state and its internal policymaking processes have been wrongly "black boxed" and ignored in traditional IR theory for some time. This is something that African IR has rightly picked up on, perhaps better than traditional IR. Structural realists see "states as if they were black boxes: they are assumed to be alike, save for the fact that some states are more or less powerful than others."[58] This assumption apparently misses the true reality of the importance of domestic politics in international politics, and vice versa.

Studies on Africa enter inside the "black box" of the policymaking process, showing its connectivity to and interplay with the external international community. Because the state is a defined political, economic, and social space that is tied to the international system, state decay in countries such as Sierra Leone, Liberia, Côte d'Ivoire, and Mali can be gauged by examining their internal and external political, economic, and social development trajectories. Internal factors require attention whenever we set out to explain policy responses to international stimuli.[59] Even Kenneth Waltz hedged his bets by indicating that someone "may one day fashion a unified theory of internal and external politics," until which time, however, this theoretical separation need "not bother us unduly."[60] Clearly, we agree with the literature that argues for the interdependence and complex interplay of domestic and international politics. It is impossible to untangle them in a glocalized situation.

Works on Africa often show that reducing explanations of security issues to either exclusively domestic or international stimuli can be misleading. Clearly, civil wars, peacebuilding, and state building are not simply domestic matters alone. One also has to consider important international elements, with external interventions being potentially necessary and ideally guided by the principles of new humanitarianism and people-centered liberalism.[61] By weaving together the concepts as well as the realities of state decay along with the dynamics of international interventions and complex postwar reconstructions effort in Africa, it is possible to bridge the domestic and the international, especially in African security issues.[62]

This internal-external synergy cannot be ignored. Simply seeing the state as a black box to be pushed aside in traditional IR theory has been more or less eclipsed or at least turned on its head in more recent IR theorizing.[63] A number of IR scholars have been studying causal links between domestic structures and foreign policy for some time and call for a closer relationship between comparative politics and IR for some time now.[64] Death quite succinctly argues that "research on African politics shows how the boundaries between domestic affairs and international relations are never clear-cut. . . . International and transnational power relations have always shaped African domestic politics, and domestic interests and ideas structure world politics. . . . International and domestic structures and actors interact and relate to each other."[65] Actors involved in these processes are pushed and pulled in multiple directions as understood in the literature on Robert Putnam's two-level game in which state agents are constantly and simultaneously negotiating with internal and external actors as they try to make policy decisions, while looking to try to benefit the interests of all the key stakeholders at the same time.[66]

Recent African IR, like that mentioned above, has increasingly opened up the black box of the state as wrongly portrayed in traditional IR theory. Accordingly, state policy formation is clearly shown as an exchange between domestic and international actors interacting together in policy formation. This is a clear strength and an exciting innovative factor showing how African realties can clearly contribute to the development of IR theory as a whole, as discussed earlier. The continent has shown that it can help explain concepts and ideas that more mainstream and traditional IR theory is not always very good at.

Before concluding, it is important to reiterate that there exists a lacuna in the literature evaluating the theoretical tools with which to think about how state building in war-torn countries takes place in a nexus between domestic capacity (the state's leaders and other domestic political and economic actors, along with ordinary citizens) and international actors. As such, it is important to connect the literatures on security, democracy, and international development—at the nexus between the domestic and international levels. One of the primary contributions of African cases to the general literature and debates is showing the international aspects of peacebuilding and state building. While the core issues of human security, governance, poverty, and so on are domestic, the efforts to resolve them are truly international. As such, African cases make valuable contribution to the debates on IR theory, the international system as a whole, and the role of international actors in the developing countries. All this is done in a way that recognizes the importance of domestic factors and their implications for the state and relations among different communities, especially in matter of human rights and security. Indeed, Africa has a role to play in the development of IR theory. In actuality, as has been argued above, the continent has always been central to these processes. Our ability to see the important role that African realties are playing and the perception that this role has been sidelined can be changed only with engaged scholarship that is willing to take on the core issues in IR theoretical development and challenge them, especially through the contributions of African scholars along with Africanists.

A central problem that emerges from the IR literature concerns the marginalization of African knowledge and the implications of that for the advancement of the subfield. This problem requires not only the decolonization of the knowledge production system in the field but also rigorous and persistent efforts to make studies on African experiences and issues rich in theory so that they can be more than mere case studies. Certainly, no single work can fix these problems. However, the discussion here is a small but an important step in using African experiences with civil wars and international interventions to make a broader theoretical contribution to issues of state building and the interaction of the domestic and the international in our understanding of the state, civil wars, and international humanitarian and security action.

As the literature shows, colonialism is a viable entry point for an African contribution to IR. Colonialism is not just a bygone historical phenomenon but a lasting dialectical legacy in the political and economic realities of African states. The discourse on colonialism can tap into both the historical and policy problems faced by African states and the system of knowledge production in IR and related fields. Following Death's three "Cs" in IR,[67] works on Africa tackle the issue of colonialism at three levels, namely: the historical level, policy level, and epistemological level. At the historical level, the African works often trace the genesis of the African state and the challenges of state building to the colonial roots of the state. At the policy level, they examine the variety of factors and contexts that necessitate and lead to robust international interventions in countries such as Sierra Leone, Liberia, Mali, Libya, and Côte d'Ivoire and the continued role of the international community in the postwar reconstruction efforts. The historical and policy realities of colonialism dovetail with colonialism in the epistemological sense in that African knowledge about its political and economic issues have to be tied to the Western system of knowledge in order for it to be truly visible at the global level. African experiences and knowledge about the political and economic realities of African countries have to be anchored in mainstream theories and methodologies as we know them in IR and related fields. Works on Africa can tackle this epistemological angle of colonialism by asserting the importance of African experiences in theory building and by mainstreaming the works of African scholars. Collectively, the historical and the policy issues of colonialism can lead to robust concepts of security, international intervention, and state building that expose the dialectics of colonialism—in its old and new forms—through notions of state decay, new humanitarianism, and people-centered liberalism. State decay is a vivid manifestation of the problems of colonization in the historical sense. The failures of African states are deeply rooted in the states' colonial past. At the same time, Africa's relations with the rest of the world, especially Western powers, have moved past orthodox colonialism. Rather, the uneven relation is wrapped in varying forms of humanistic moralities and savvy political and economic interests that facilitate and shape Africa's relations with the rest of the world. Both the doctrines of new humanitarianism and people-centered liberalism are fine examples of the unorthodox colonial relations that are often described as neocolonialism, domination, exploitation, and dependency—colonialism in the policy sense. African works can capture this epistemological angle to colonialism by developing concepts that connect to established IR theories while at the same time enriching those concepts and showing how African experience can benefit theory development in IR and related fields.

In the end, works on African security issues are about the Africa cases as well as the broader issues that challenge the relation between African countries and the world at large, especially the great powers. The nature and trajectory of the African state has become an issue to be solved and for the international community to learn from. Civil wars are not mere domestic or purely humanitarian issues. They are also matters of regional and international security that go well beyond the African continent. As such, the conditions of the African states are a constant source of policy experimentation and a gold mine for testing, perfecting, and expanding theory. The whole international military and humanitarian intervention enterprise has emerged as a fertile ground for experimenting with state building—be it in the form of neoliberal policies or the human development approach. This phenomenon has presented challenges and opportunities for better theorization of the state and security, and for understanding the right place of the state in contemporary political, economic, and social issues in Africa and globally.

NOTES

1. Carl Death, "An Introduction to Africa and the World," in *The African Affairs Reader: Key Texts in Politics, Development, and International Relations*, ed. Nic

Cheeseman, Lindsay Whitfield, and Carl Death (New York: Oxford University Press, 2017), 279.

2. Patricia Hill Collins, *Black Feminist Thought: Knowledge, Consciousness, and the Politics of Empowerment* (New York: Routledge, 2022).

3. Ali A. Mazrui, *Africa's International Relations: The Diplomacy of Dependency and Change* (New York: Routledge, 2019); Frantz Fanon, *The Wretched of the Earth*, ed. Jean-Paul Sartre, trans. Constance Farrington (New York: Grove Press, 1963); Michael Bratton and Nicholas Van de Walle, *Democratic Experiments in Africa: Regime Transitions in Comparative Perspective* (New York: Cambridge University Press, 1997); Ian Taylor and Paul Williams (eds.), *Africa in International Politics: External Involvement in the Continent* (New York: Routledge, 2004).

4. Kevin C. Dunn and Timothy M. Shaw, *Africa's Challenge to International Relations Theory* (New York: Palgrave, 2001).

5. William Brown, "Africa and International Relations: A Comment on IR Theory, Anarchy and Statehood," *Review of International Studies* 32.1 (2006): 119–143; Scarlett Cornelissen, Fantu Cheru, and Timothy M. Shaw, *Africa and International Relations in the 21st Century* (New York: Palgrave Macmillan, 2015).

6. Death, "An Introduction to Africa and the World."

7. Dunn and Shaw, *Africa's Challenge*, xi.

8. Douglas Lemke, "African Lessons for International Relations Research," *World Politics* 56.1 (2003): 116.

9. Death, "An Introduction to Africa and the World," 280.

10. Sophie Harman and William Brown, "In from the Margins? The Changing Place of Africa in International Relations," *International Affairs* 89.1 (2013): 69–87.

11. Harman and Brown, "In from the Margins?," 70.

12. Brown, "Africa and International Relations."

13. Arlene B. Tickner and Ole Wæver (eds.), *International Relations Scholarship around the World* (New York: Routledge, 2009).

14. Douglas Lemke, "Intra-national IR in Africa," *Review of International Studies* 37 (2011): 49–70.

15. Harman and Brown, "In from the Margins?"

16. John Mearsheimer, *The Tragedy of Great Power Politics* (New York: Norton, 2014).

17. Taylor and Williams, *Africa in International Politics*, i.

18. Death, "An Introduction to Africa and the World."

19. Death, 280.

20. Brown, "Africa and International Relations," 124.

21. Abu Bakarr Bah and Ibrahim Bangura, "Landholding and the Creation of Lumpen Tenants in Freetown: Youth Economic Survival and Patrimonialism in Postwar Sierra Leone," *Critical Sociology* 49.7–8 (2023): 1289–305; Abu Bakarr Bah and Margaret Nasambu Barasa, "Indigenous Knowledge and the Social Construction of Patriarchy: The Case of the Bukusu of Kenya," *Critical Sociology* 49.2 (2023): 217–232; Robert H. Jackson and Carl Gustav Rosberg, *Personal Rule in Black Africa: Prince, Autocrat, Prophet, Tyrant* (Berkeley: University of California Press, 1982).

22. Tickner and Wæver, *International Relations Scholarship*; Arlene Tickner, "Seeing IR Differently: Notes from the Third World," *Millennium* 32.2 (2003): 295–324; also see Pinar Bilgin, "Thinking Past 'Western' IR?," *Third World Quarterly* 29.1 (2008): 5–23.

23. *Oxford Research Encyclopedia of International Studies*, https://oxfordre.com/internationalstudies/page/about.

24. Tandeka C. Nkiwane, "Africa and International Relations: Regional Lessons for a Global Discourse," *International Political Science Review* 22.3 (2001): 279–290.

25. Abu Bakarr Bah and Nikolas Emmanuel, "Migration Cooperation between Africa and Europe: Understanding the Role of Incentives," *Oxford Research Encyclopedia of International Studies* (2022): https://doi.org/10.1093/acrefore/9780190846626.013.735.

26. Harmon and Brown, "In from the Margins?," 73–74.

27. Harmon and Brown, 87.

28. Michael C. Williams, "Why Ideas Matter in International Relations: Hans Morgenthau, Classical Realism, and the Moral Construction of Power Politics," *International Organization* 58.4 (2004): 633–665.

29. Death, "An Introduction to Africa and the World," 281.

30. Death, 281.

31. Harmon and Brown, "In from the Margins?," 70.

32. Gurmineder K. Bhambra et al., "Why Is Mainstream International Relations Blind to Racism? Ignoring the Central Role of Race and Colonialism in World Affairs Precludes an Accurate Understanding of the Modern State System," *Foreign Policy*, July 3, 2020, https://foreignpolicy.com/2020/07/03/why-is-mainstream-international-relations-ir-blind-to-racism-colonialism/.

33. Maria Baaz and Judith Verweijen, "Confronting the Colonial: The (Re)production of 'African' Exceptionalism in Critical Security and Military Studies," *Security Dialogue* 49.1–2 (2018): 69.

34. Cornelissen et al., "Introduction: Africa and IR in the 21st Century," 1; also see Karen Tucker, "Unraveling Coloniality in International Relations: Knowledge, Relationality, and Strategies for Engagement," *International Political Sociology* 12.3 (2018): 215–232.

35. Robbie Shilliam, "Race and Racism in International Relations: Retrieving a Scholarly Inheritance," *International Politics Reviews* 8 (2020): 152–195.

36. Swati Parashar and Michael Schulz, "Colonial Legacies, Postcolonial 'Selfhood' and the (Un)doing of Africa," *Third World Quarterly* 42.5 (2021): 867–881.

37. Achille Mbembe, *On the Postcolony* (Berkeley: University of California Press, 2001).

38. Tucker, "Unraveling Coloniality."

39. Sabelo J. Ndlovu-Gatsheni, "The Cognitive Empire, Politics of Knowledge and African Intellectual Productions: Reflections on Struggles for Epistemic Freedom and Resurgence of Decolonisation in the Twenty-First Century," *Third World Quarterly* 42.5 (2021): 896.

40. Sabelo J. Ndlovu-Gatsheni, "Intellectual Imperialism and Decolonisation in African Studies," *Third World Quarterly* (2023): https://doi.org/10.1080/01436597.2023.2211520.

41. Ndlovu-Gatsheni, "The Cognitive Empire."

42. Tucker, "Unraveling Coloniality," 216; Melody Fonseca, "Global IR and Western Dominance: Moving Forward or Eurocentric Entrapment?," *Millennium* 48.1 (2019): 45–59.

43. Neta Crawford, *Argument and Change in World Politics: Ethics, Decolonization, and Humanitarian Intervention* (New York: Cambridge University Press, 2002), 400.

44. Max Weber, *Max Weber: Essays in Sociology,* trans. and ed. H. H. Gerth and C. Wright Mills (New York: Routledge, 2009); Charles Tilly, "Reflections on the History of European State-Making," in *The Formation of National States in Western Europe,* ed. Gabriel Ardant and Charles Tilly (Princeton, NJ: Princeton University Press, 1975); Mahmood Mamdani, *Citizen and Subject: Contemporary Africa and the Legacy of Late Colonialism* (Princeton, NJ: Princeton University Press, 1996).

45. Basil Davidson, *The Black Man's Burden: Africa and the Curse of the Nation-State* (New York: Times Press, 1993).

46. Abu Bakarr Bah, *Breakdown and Reconstitution: Democracy, the Nation-State, and Ethnicity in Nigeria* (Lanham, MD: Lexington Books, 2005), 29.

47. Mary Kaldor, *New and Old Wars: Organized Violence in a Global Era* (Stanford, CA: Stanford University Press, 1999); Abu Bakarr Bah, "The Contours of New Humanitarianism: War and Peacebuilding in Sierra Leone," *Africa Today* 60.1 (2013): 3–26.

48. Ricardo Soares de Oliveira and Harry Verhoeven, "Taming Intervention: Sovereignty, Statehood and Political Order in Africa," *Survival* 60.2 (April–May 2018): 7.

49. Abu Bakarr Bah, "State Decay: A Conceptual Frame of Failing and Failed States in West Africa," *International Journal of Politics, Culture, and Society* 25.1 (2012): 71–89; William Reno, *Corruption and State Politics in Sierra Leone* (New York: Cambridge University Press, 2008); Robert H. Bates, *When Things Fell Apart: State Failure in Late-Century Africa* (New York: Cambridge University Press, 2008).

50. Paul Collier and Anke Hoeffler "On the Incidence of Civil War in Africa," *The Journal of Conflict Resolution* 46.1 (2002): 13–28.

51. Charles Tilly, *From Mobilization to Revolution* (Reading, PA: Addison-Wesley, 1978); Donald L. Horowitz, *Ethnic Groups in Conflict* (Berkeley: University of California Press, 1985).

52. Barry R. Posen, "The Security Dilemma and Ethnic Conflict," *Survival* 35.1 (1993): 27–47; David A. Lake and Donald Rothchild, "Containing Fear: The Origins and Management of Ethnic Conflict," *International Security* 21.2 (1996): 41–75.

53. Bah, "State Decay"; Reno, *Corruption and State Politics in Sierra Leone*; Bates, *When Things Fell Apart*; Patrick Chabal and Jean-Pascal Daloz, *Africa Works: Disorder as Political Instrument* (Bloomington: Indiana University Press, 1999); Nic Cheeseman, *Democracy in Africa: Successes, Failures, and the Struggle for Political Reform* (New York: Cambridge University Press, 2015).

54. Simon Chesterman, *Just War or Just Peace? Humanitarian Intervention and International Law* (New York: Oxford University Press, 2002); Michael Doyle and

Nicholas Sambanis, *Making War and Building Peace: United Nations Peace Operations* (Princeton, NJ: Princeton University Press, 2006); Roland Paris, *At War's End: Building Peace after Civil Conflict* (New York: Cambridge University Press, 2004); Stephen John Stedman, Donald Rothchild, and Elizabeth M. Cousens (eds.), *Ending Civil Wars: The Implementation of Peace Agreement* (Boulder, CO: Lynne Rienner Publishers, 2003).

55. Abu Bakarr Bah, "Democracy and Civil War: Citizenship and Peacemaking in Côte d'Ivoire," *African Affairs* 109.437 (2010): 597–615.

56. Abu Bakarr Bah and Nikolas Emmanuel, "Positive Peace and the Methodology of Costing Peacebuilding Needs: The Case of Burundi," *Administrative Theory & Praxis* 42.3 (2020): 299–318; Abu Bakarr Bah (ed.), *Post-conflict Institutional Design: Peacebuilding and Democracy in Africa* (London: Zed Books, 2020).

57. Paul E. Peterson, "The President's Dominance in Foreign Policy," *Political Science Quarterly* 109 (Summer 1994): 228.

58. Mearsheimer, *The Tragedy of Great Power*, 78; also see B. I. Finel, "Black Box or Pandora's Box: State Level Variables and Progressivity in Realist Research Programs," *Security Studies* 11.2 (2001): 187–227.

59. John Kurt Jacobsen, "Review: Are All Politics Domestic? Perspectives on the Integration of Comparative Politics and International Relations Theories," *Comparative Politics* 29.1 (1996): 93–115; Peter Gourevitch, "The Second Image Reversed: The International Sources of Domestic Politics," *International Organization* 31 (1978): 881–912.

60. Kenneth Waltz, "Reflections on Theory of International Politics: A Response to My Critics," in *Neorealism and Its Critics*, ed. Robert E. Keohane (New York: Columbia University Press, 1986), 340.

61. Bah, "The Contours of New Humanitarianism"; Abu Bakarr Bah, "People-Centered Liberalism: An Alternative Approach to International State-Building in Sierra Leone and Liberia," *Critical Sociology* 43.7–8 (2017): 989–1007.

62. Abu Bakarr Bah and Nikolas Emmanuel, *International Statebuilding in West Africa: Civil Wars and New Humanitarianism in Sierra Leone, Liberia, and Côte d'Ivoire* (Bloomington: Indiana University Press, forthcoming, 2024).

63. Lemke, "Intra-national IR."

64. Jacobsen, "Review: Are All Politics Domestic?"

65. Death, "An Introduction to Africa and the World," 281.

66. Robert D. Putnam, "Diplomacy and Domestic Politics: The Logic of Two-Level Games," *International Organization* 42.3 (1988): 427–460.

67. Death, "An Introduction to Africa and the World," 281.

BIBLIOGRAPHY

Baaz, Maria, and Judith Verweijen. "Confronting the Colonial: The (Re)production of 'African' Exceptionalism in Critical Security and Military Studies." *Security Dialogue* 49.1–2 (2018): 57–69.

Bah, Abu Bakarr. *Breakdown and Reconstitution: Democracy, the Nation-State, and Ethnicity in Nigeria*. Lanham, MD: Lexington Books, 2005.

———. "Democracy and Civil War: Citizenship and Peacemaking in Côte d'Ivoire." *African Affairs* 109.437 (2010): 597–615.

———. "State Decay: A Conceptual Frame of Failing and Failed States in West Africa." *International Journal of Politics, Culture, and Society* 25.1 (2012): 71–89.

———. "The Contours of New Humanitarianism: War and Peacebuilding in Sierra Leone." *Africa Today* 60.1 (2013): 3–26.

———. "People-Centered Liberalism: An Alternative Approach to International State-Building in Sierra Leone and Liberia." *Critical Sociology* 43.7–8 (2017): 989–1007.

Bah, Abu Bakarr (ed.). *Post-conflict Institutional Design: Peacebuilding and Democracy in Africa*. London: Zed Books, 2020.

Bah, Abu Bakarr, and Ibrahim Bangura. "Landholding and the Creation of Lumpen Tenants in Freetown: Youth Economic Survival and Patrimonialism in Postwar Sierra Leone." *Critical Sociology* 49.7–8 (2023): 1289–305.

Bah, Abu Bakarr, and Nikolas Emmanuel. "Positive Peace and the Methodology of Costing Peacebuilding Needs: The Case of Burundi." *Administrative Theory & Praxis* 42.3 (2020): 299–318.

———. "Migration Cooperation between Africa and Europe: Understanding the Role of Incentives." *Oxford Research Encyclopedia of International Studies* (2022). https://doi.org/10.1093/acrefore/9780190846626.013.735.

———. *International Statebuilding in West Africa: Civil Wars and New Humanitarianism in Sierra Leone, Liberia, and Côte d'Ivoire*. Bloomington: Indiana University Press, forthcoming, 2024.

Bah, Abu Bakarr, and Margaret Nasambu Barasa. "Indigenous Knowledge and the Social Construction of Patriarchy: The Case of the Bukusu of Kenya." *Critical Sociology* 49.2 (2023): 217–232.

Bates, Robert H. *When Things Fell Apart: State Failure in Late-Century Africa*. New York: Cambridge University Press, 2008.

Bhambra, Gurmineder K., Yolande Bouka, Randolph B. Persaud, Olivia U. Rutazibwa, Vineet Thakur, Duncan Bell, Karen Smith, Toni Haastrup, and Seifudein Adem. "Why Is Mainstream International Relations Blind to Racism? Ignoring the Central Role of Race and Colonialism in World Affairs Precludes an Accurate Understanding of the Modern State System." *Foreign Policy*, July 3, 2020. https://foreignpolicy.com/2020/07/03/why-is-mainstream-international-relations-ir-blind-to-racism-colonialism/.

Bilgin, Pinar. "Thinking Past 'Western' IR?" *Third World Quarterly* 29.1 (2008): 5–23.

Bratton, Michael, and Nicholas Van de Walle. *Democratic Experiments in Africa: Regime Transitions in Comparative Perspective*. New York: Cambridge University Press, 1997.

Brown, William. "Africa and International Relations: A Comment on IR Theory, Anarchy and Statehood." *Review of International Studies* 32.1 (2006): 119–143.

Chabal, Patrick, and Jean-Pascal Daloz. *Africa Works: Disorder as Political Instrument*. Bloomington: Indiana University Press, 1999.

Cheeseman, Nic. *Democracy in Africa: Successes, Failures, and the Struggle for Political Reform.* New York: Cambridge University Press, 2015.

Chesterman, Simon. *Just War or Just Peace? Humanitarian Intervention and International Law.* New York: Oxford University Press, 2002.

Collier, Paul, and Anke Hoeffler. "On the Incidence of Civil War in Africa." *The Journal of Conflict Resolution* 46.1 (2002): 13–28.

Collins, Patricia Hill. *Black Feminist Thought: Knowledge, Consciousness, and the Politics of Empowerment.* New York: Routledge, 2022.

Cornelissen, Scarlett, Fantu Cheru, and Timothy M. Shaw. *Africa and International Relations in the 21st Century.* Basingstoke, UK: Palgrave Macmillan, 2015.

Crawford, Neta. *Argument and Change in World Politics: Ethics, Decolonization, and Humanitarian Intervention.* New York: Cambridge University Press, 2002.

Davidson, Basil. *The Black Man's Burden: Africa and the Curse of the Nation-State.* New York: Times Press, 1993.

Death, Carl. "An Introduction to Africa and the World." In *The African Affairs Reader: Key Texts in Politics, Development, and International Relations,* ed. Nic Cheeseman, Lindsay Whitfield, and Carl Death, 279–289. New York: Oxford University Press, 2017.

Doyle, Michael, and Nicholas Sambanis. *Making War and Building Peace: United Nations Peace Operations.* Princeton, NJ: Princeton University Press, 2006.

Dunn, Kevin C., and Timothy M. Shaw. *Africa's Challenge to International Relations Theory.* New York: Palgrave, 2001.

Fanon, Frantz. *The Wretched of the Earth.* Edited by Jean-Paul Sartre. Translated by Constance Farrington. New York: Grove Press, 1963.

Finel, B. I. "Black Box or Pandora's Box: State Level Variables and Progressivity in Realist Research Programs." *Security Studies* 11.2 (2001): 187–227.

Fonseca, M. "Global IR and Western Dominance: Moving Forward or Eurocentric Entrapment?" *Millennium* 48.1 (2019): 45–59.

Gourevitch, Peter. "The Second Image Reversed: The International Sources of Domestic Politics." *International Organization* 31 (1978): 881–912.

Harman, Sophie, and William Brown. "In from the Margins? The Changing Place of Africa in International Relations." *International Affairs* 89.1 (2013): 69–87.

Horowitz, Donald L. *Ethnic Groups in Conflict.* Berkeley: University of California Press, 1985.

Jackson, Robert H., and Carl Gustav Rosberg. *Personal Rule in Black Africa: Prince, Autocrat, Prophet, Tyrant.* Berkeley: University of California Press, 1982.

Jacobsen, John Kurt. "Review: Are All Politics Domestic? Perspectives on the Integration of Comparative Politics and International Relations Theories." *Comparative Politics* 29.1 (1996): 93–115.

Kaldor, Mary. *New and Old Wars: Organized Violence in a Global Era.* Stanford, CA: Stanford University Press, 1999.

Lake, David A., and Donald Rothchild. "Containing Fear: The Origins and Management of Ethnic Conflict." *International Security* 21.2 (1996): 41–75.

Lemke, Douglas. "African Lessons for International Relations Research." *World Politics* 56.1 (2003): 114–138.

———. "Intra-national IR in Africa." *Review of International Studies* 37 (2011): 49–70.

Mamdani, Mahmood. *Citizen and Subject: Contemporary Africa and the Legacy of Late Colonialism.* Princeton, NJ: Princeton University Press, 1996.

Mazrui, Ali A. *Africa's International Relations: The Diplomacy of Dependency and Change.* New York: Routledge, 2019.

Mbembe, Achille. *On the Postcolony.* Berkeley: University of California Press, 2001.

Mearsheimer, John. *The Tragedy of Great Power Politics.* New York: Norton, 2014.

Ndlovu-Gatsheni, Sabelo J. "The Cognitive Empire, Politics of Knowledge and African Intellectual Productions: Reflections on Struggles for Epistemic Freedom and Resurgence of Decolonisation in the Twenty-First Century." *Third World Quarterly* 42.5 (2021): 882–901.

———. "Intellectual Imperialism and Decolonisation in African Studies." *Third World Quarterly* (2023). https://doi.org/10.1080/01436597.2023.2211520.

Nkiwane, Tandeka C. "Africa and International Relations: Regional Lessons for a Global Discourse." *International Political Science Review* 22.3 (2001): 279–290.

Parashar, Swati, and Michael Schulz. "Colonial Legacies, Postcolonial 'Selfhood' and the (Un)doing of Africa." *Third World Quarterly* 42.5 (2021): 867–881.

Paris, Roland. *At War's End: Building Peace after Civil Conflict.* New York: Cambridge University Press, 2004.

Peterson, Paul E. "The President's Dominance in Foreign Policy." *Political Science Quarterly* 109 (Summer 1994): 215–234.

Posen, Barry R. "The Security Dilemma and Ethnic Conflict." *Survival* 35.1 (1993): 27–47.

Putnam, Robert D. "Diplomacy and Domestic Politics: The Logic of Two-Level Games." *International Organization* 42.3 (1988): 427–60.

Reno, William. *Corruption and State Politics in Sierra Leone.* New York: Cambridge University Press, 2008.

Shilliam, Robbie. "Race and Racism in International Relations: Retrieving a Scholarly Inheritance." *International Politics Reviews* 8 (2020): 152–195.

Soares de Oliveira, Ricardo, and Harry Verhoeven. "Taming Intervention: Sovereignty, Statehood and Political Order in Africa." *Survival* 60.2 (April–May 2018): 7–32.

Stedman, Stephen John, Donald Rothchild, and Elizabeth M. Cousens (eds.). *Ending Civil Wars: The Implementation of Peace Agreement.* Boulder, CO: Lynne Rienner Publishers, 2003.

Taylor, Ian, and Paul Williams (eds.). *Africa in International Politics: External Involvement in the Continent.* New York: Routledge, 2004.

Tickner, Arlene. "Seeing IR Differently: Notes from the Third World." *Millennium* 32.2 (2003): 295–324.

Tickner, Arlene B., and Ole Waever (eds.). *International Relations Scholarship around the World.* New York: Routledge, 2009.

Tilly, Charles. "Reflections on the History of European State-Making." In *The Formation of National States in Western Europe*, ed. Gabriel Ardant and Charles Tilly, 3–83. Princeton, NJ: Princeton University Press, 1975.

——. *From Mobilization to Revolution*. Reading, PA: Addison-Wesley, 1978.

Tucker, Karen. "Unraveling Coloniality in International Relations: Knowledge, Relationality, and Strategies for Engagement." *International Political Sociology* 12.3 (2018): 215–232.

Waltz, Kenneth. "Reflections on Theory of International Politics: A Response to My Critics." In *Neorealism and Its Critics*, ed. Robert Keohane, 322–346. New York: Columbia University Press, 1986.

Weber, Max. *Max Weber: Essays in Sociology*, trans. and ed. H. H. Gerth and C. Wright Mills. New York: Routledge, 2009.

Williams, Michael C. "Why Ideas Matter in International Relations: Hans Morgenthau, Classical Realism, and the Moral Construction of Power Politics." *International Organization* 58.4 (2004): 633–665.

Chapter 2

Proscription Regimes and the Internationalization of National Security Threats

Countering Terrorism in Nigeria

FOLAHANMI AINA

The Nigerian state has been confronted with multiple national security threats in recent times. These threats have mostly emanated from violent non–state actors (VNSAs), some of which are affiliated with regional and international terrorist organizations such as al-Qaeda and the Islamic State. Some of these VNSAs include Boko Haram and its breakaway factions Ansaru, and the Islamic State in West Africa Province. Others include the activities of organized criminal gangs known as armed bandits. According to the United Nations Development Programme, the nefarious activities of Boko Haram led to the deaths of more than 350,000 people between 2009 and 2021, in addition to the displacement of more than 2.2 million people.[1] Similarly, according to the Armed Conflict Location and Event Data Project, the number of deaths from the criminal activities of armed bandits was 2,600 in 2021 alone.[2] The situation has resulted in the forced displacement of more than a million people into the Republic of Niger as refugees. While this chapter focuses on Boko Haram, its affiliates, and armed bandits, other groups include the Iranian-backed Shiite group Islamic Movement of Nigeria and the secessionist Indigenous People of Biafra group. The study seeks to provide an answer to the question of how the proscription of local terrorist groups as national security threats contributes toward the internationalization of local terrorist groups. Proscription in a way feeds into the glocalization of security, especially the War on Terror.

In response to domestic threats to its national security, the Nigerian state has deployed a combination of both kinetic and nonkinetic responses, which have not necessarily brought a complete end to the threats. Kinetic measures are understood to include militaristic approaches to addressing insecurity while nonkinetic measures are nonmilitaristic approaches to addressing insecurity. Some of the nonkinetic measures adopted by the Nigerian state include negotiations, peace talks, and amnesty, as well as other efforts targeted at suppressing VNSAs by banning motorcycles and shutting down telecommunications services in some of the affected areas. Kinetic measures, on the other hand, have included utilizing the state's coercive apparatus to deter VNSAs such as carrying out multiple military campaigns, which are often intelligence driven. Going a step further beyond these efforts, the Nigerian state has proscribed VNSAs as terrorists, thereby legitimizing the use of force against them. This proscription regime, as a national security policy decision, has tended to internationalize what were initially home-grown domestic terrorist groups. This has been manifested through the kinds of international support Nigeria has since attracted through the sale and transfer of advanced military weaponry, as well as increased security force assistance. In addition, it has also attracted regional and other foreign military interventions such as the case with the Multinational Joint Task Force in the Lake Chad Basin region, France's pivot to Niger, and the US establishment of a drone base in Niger.

This chapter argues that the glocalization of local terrorist groups through proscription has had significant adverse unintended consequences for the prosecution of the War on Terror. Notably, proscription has led to the overmilitarization of the terrorist-induced conflicts at the expense of addressing the underlying socioeconomic, political, and environmental factors that drive political violence. Also, proscription has led to increased military spending at the expense of development initiatives. In addition, its implications for the criminalization of dissent and self-determination have in some instances led to an escalation of the activities of VNSAs and their facelessness. All of these results evoke questions about the interconnections between the domestic and external factors in Nigerian security that cannot be reduced to domestic terrorism or to global terrorism. In many ways, it seems that Nigerian security has glocal features. Indeed, there have been concerns that the proscription of VNSAs could potentially result in the use of unsuitable military strategies against them and in some instances the profiling of certain ethnic groups. Furthermore, the rebranding of organized criminal groups as terrorists makes negotiating with them difficult.[3] Overall, the internationalization of national security threats through proscription portends serious implications for the prospects of peace and security in Nigeria. This is particularly so as it reinforces the glocalization of threats beyond national borders. By examining the proscription regime through a glocalized security lens, the chapter contributes to the literature on VNSAs in Nigeria. Notably, it points to the way efforts to combat VNSAs are internationalized even when their core grievances are domestic. Such is the case with the selective and delayed internationalization and proscription of violent herdsmen as terrorists.

GLOCALIZED SECURITY: NATIONAL SECURITY THREATS, COUNTERTERRORISM, AND PROSCRIPTION REGIMES

States are primarily concerned with ensuring their own survival within the international system. This concern could be from internal or external threats emanating from terrorist groups that undermine their national security. It is imperative to note that definitions of national security over the years have been mostly confined to traditional structural-realist approaches that are less accommodating of other approaches that derive utility in values and norms such as constructivism, as Ronald Kreb has argued.[4] A state's national security refers to a condition whereby its survival is primarily guaranteed against threats. To a large extent, the framing of threats by states is reflective of the extent to which they perceive the threats.[5] For instance, Suthaharan Nadarajah argues that terrorism proscription by the West reflects situational interpretations of the contexts and dynamics within which West-led interventions for global stability—equated with liberal order—are pursued.[6] While a significant body of work exists on the designation of terrorist groups, it is imperative to first provide a conceptual clarification on some of the key terms used in the discourse on the subject matter.

A terrorist group, as defined by Brian Phillips, is a subnational political organization that uses terrorism.[7] This study adopts the same definition, given its broad categorization. Terrorist groups are therefore subnational political entities, often driven by a political ideology, that utilize acts of terror directed at the state with the intent of causing change in their favor. Terrorist organizations have therefore been described as a prototypical threat.[8] Lee Jarvis defines terrorism as a specific set of violence conducted by non–state actors against civilians to communicate something to an external audience.[9] He further contends that the dominant approach to the terrorism discourse is one that has come under scrutiny, which makes its understanding more contested than we think.[10] Non–state groups/actors refer to entities within the political system that do not constitute formal state representation but yield significant influence as well as pressure on the state, such as terrorists, in this context. As Abu Bah rightly notes, non–state actors are different from state actors in that the latter refers to states and intergovernmental organizations, whereas the former is mostly adopted as a generalization for international nongovernmental organizations and civil society. Notably, violent non–state actors are distinct from civil non–state actors.[11] This study centers on violent non–state actors, such as the terrorists, secessionists, and armed bandits in Nigeria.

In response to terrorist groups, states often attempt to discredit them through designation, which is usually followed by labels such as "proscribed," "listed," "blacklisted," "outlawed," and "banned."[12] The two most common terms are "designation" and "proscription," which are often used interchangeably. Dating as far back as 1887, proscription began in the United Kingdom, specifically in Northern Ireland when it was applied to the Irish National League, and it has evolved over time in response to the changing conflict context.[13] Nathan Rasiah defines proscription as the process by which organizations believed by the government to be associated with terrorism are criminalized.[14] This definition implies a correlation between proscription and counterterrorism, as governments attempt to discredit the activities of terrorist groups. As Sophie Haspeslagh argues, a potential impact of proscription is that it affects the peace process, particularly with regard to third-party efforts aimed at engaging with these groups.[15]

These concerns over violent non–state actors make the academic study of proscription, which has not received adequate attention, even more important. This is particularly significant when considered within the broader framework of its interconnectedness to the counterterrorism and national security discourse—also herein understood as glocalized security. Glocalized security reflects the intersectionality between domestic and external grievances and interests within the context of countries that are affected by extreme violence and wars. It therefore provides an impetus toward understanding how the interconnectedness of domestic and external matters results in the production of new war dynamics, thereby requiring substantial domestic reforms and the recalibration of external interests in order to attain sustainable peace. This entails considering the peculiarities of domestic realities on the ground against a blanket approach toward neoliberal constructs of governance and the rule of law in addressing conflicts. As Roland Robertson rightly notes, glocalization's conceptual advantage is in its general theorization of globalization, thereby facilitating the thoroughness of the discourse on various problems differentiating between the global and the local.[16]

Lee Jarvis and Tim Legrand offer four reasons why scholarly attention should be accorded to proscription. According to them, the first is related to the extremely wide use of the power of proscription. The second has to do with its historical lineage, while the third is attributed to the significant implications of proscription on political life, and the fourth is that the relevance and effectiveness of the power of proscription against terrorism are not yet established.[17] Arguing elsewhere, both scholars contend that the limited attention on proscription has mostly focused on the causal question of what proscription does rather than what is made possible by it.[18]

Proscription has been defined by Vicki Sentas as a counterterrorism technique that involves listing or designating non–state actors as terrorist organizations, whereby individuals and populations associated with armed non–state actors are targeted for disruption, stigmatization, and prosecution.[19] Echoing this line of thought, Daniel Kirkpatrick notes that proscription is a central pillar of counterterrorism.[20] Counterterrorism can be defined as the interventions of the state aimed at degrading and denying terrorist groups the freedom of action, mostly through the use of force. Despite the use of proscription as a counterterrorism tool, it remains unclear what the impact of this framing is on terrorist violence.[21] In fact, one study reveals that terrorist groups which have been proscribed are not only more violent and better equipped, but they also tend to leverage other international terror networks.[22] This has the potential effect of negating the very reason for their proscription in the first place, which among other things is intended at derailing their operations.

The post-9/11 world, which birthed the Global War on Terror, has made the proscription of terrorist groups increasingly popular.[23] This has been accompanied by the attendant consequence of lacking consistency.[24] Terrorism proscription is therefore inherently political. As Chi Zhang notes, the political nature of proscription is reflected in the inconsistency associated with the criteria for inclusion as a terrorist group.[25] Given that terrorist groups adopt various tactics when inflicting acts of terror on their chosen targets, Mirna El Masri and Brian Philips argue that the more consequential the target that is being attacked by terrorist groups or organizations, the higher the likelihood of designating the terrorist group or organization in question as terrorists.[26] An explanation for this can be found in the prevarication of political decision-makers as a result of their ethnic and religious identities and affiliations to some of these groups.

However, designation could also be attributed to other factors beyond the result of attack methods, such as a US policy diffusion which implies designation that is shaped by the choice of the United States in designating Islamist groups, for instance.[27] In China, for example, which adopts the double-track system of terrorism proscription, it has been argued that owing to the political and symbolic nature of terrorism designation and proscription, it is difficult for the government to ascertain the balance between effectiveness of designation and judicial justice.[28]

But on certain occasions, states may be inclined to de-proscribe terrorist groups. For instance, this could be because of the need to ensure that the rationale behind proscription is not disconnected from the possibility of illegality or for macro-political reasons such as an attempt at fostering political inclusion as argued by Clive Walker.[29] Following the framing of national security threats by states, the proscription of terrorist organizations by nation-states reflects a complex web of dynamics that often extends beyond national borders. On this, Sentas argues that the operations and effects of proscription are organized through transnational cooperation, and as such they involve complex interaction of other diverse listing regimes.[30]

In problematizing the issues around national security threats, counterterrorism, and proscription regimes, this study adopts the securitization theory. The securitization theory is useful in providing context and understanding on the emergence and evolution of counterterrorism policy as it relates to national security while considering the transnational nature of threats posed by proscribed terrorist groups. The foundations of the securitization theory can be found in the works of Buzan et al., who approach it from the perspective of its intersubjectivity and social constructivism, thereby arguing that security occurs when an issue poses an existential threat to a designated referent object, which could be the state, government, territory, and society.[31] This theory offers useful insights in understanding the foundations upon which glocalized security rests. This is particularly so given that the identification and subsequent framing of a threat by the state potentially sets the premise upon which its internationalization occurs.

This identification and framing of threats as an approach to security is what underpins the Copenhagen School of thought on the subject. As Angela Bourne notes, the Copenhagen School of thought draws on the poststructuralist tradition, whereby the social power of language plays a role in the social world, whereas the sociological perspective considers securitization within the broader ambience of changing political culture, public opinion, or international politics.[32] Lee Jarvis and Tim Legrand make an important observation on the theoretical anchor of securitization, noting that while an issue may qualify as securitized, the response of an audience to a securitizing move might initially fall between acquiescence and opposition, or consent and resistance.[33] In addition, they offer an important theoretical contribution through the conceptualization and analysis of logics of inquiry in the form of questions, taking the particular case of parliamentarians in the United Kingdom.[34] These questions cover justification, explanation, elaboration, clarification, and scope.[35] They therefore argue that the role of questions within the security discourse is useful toward ascertaining the empirical and conceptual exploration of audience participation in security politics.[36]

The Challenges of Proscription

While the proscription of terrorist groups as a counterterrorism policy has its advantages, such as the ability to rally public support against a perceived threat, the proscription of terrorist groups could expand the power asymmetry between states and violent non–state actors.[37] This asymmetry empowers hardliners while also reducing the prospects of a perceived mutually harmful stalemate.[38] While the proscription of terrorist groups could potentially reduce terrorist attacks, its effect is mostly felt within younger terrorist groups without sponsors rather than within older ones.[39]

Brian Phillips offers a counter-argument which suggests that the designation of terrorist groups significantly affects them in a number of ways, including putting a constraint on their funding sources and enhancing international counterterrorism cooperation against them.[40] This likely impedes their operations. He, however, acknowledges that while designation could reduce the ability to carry out attacks by terrorist groups, the impact on such groups is dependent on the contexts in which they operate.[41] This position is similarly echoed by Craig Forcese and Kent Roach, who liken the listing of terrorist groups to "yesterday's law," in addition to being problematic and offering marginal utility.[42] Considering the importance of time and temporality, Marieke de Goede points to a significant flaw of proscription. Notably, decisions on proscription are informed by urgent yet unspecified security threats, which implies that they are not necessarily responsive to a specified attack that is imminent.[43] As such, proscription measures constitute significant implications for democratic engagement in contemporary societies.[44] Adding to the broader debate on proscription regime, a recent study by Yusutaka et al. shows a negative association between terrorist designation and terrorist attacks, with the former having an effect on the latter only in an earlier period.

Furthermore, the proscription of terrorist groups affects alternative peace routes by placing legal constraints on engagement, thereby reducing trust, polarizing intergroup relations, and affecting the incentives of third parties to engage in negotiations.[45] To this end, it has been argued that by design, proscription seeks to protect the state's legitimacy rather than to stop political violence.[46] Proscription may therefore be a way by which the state justifies its response to the material reality of political violence. However, its semiosis reflects the construction of power relations that legitimizes the state while de-legitimizing other competing political forces.[47]

As the world becomes increasingly globalized, events in one place could potentially have disruptive effects in other places. This has been the case with the wave of terrorism across the globe, especially considering their transnational nature. To this end, the proscription of domestic terrorist groups could potentially internationalize perceived national security threats. This often results in foreign states' including proscribed groups in another country in their own lists of proscribed entities. With countries across the globe establishing connections between terrorism in other places and terrorism within their own borders, they tend to corroborate the validity of the glocalized security thesis. This also offers opportunities for cooperation in mitigating these threats. As Brian argues, fighting terrorism is far more effective when countries cooperate.[48] Using the example of the Tigers of Tamil Eelam and the Sri Lankan state, Nadarajah and Sriskandarajah note that the characterization of the conflict as a form of terrorism by the state has not only affected its evolution; it also serves to further the strategic aims of the state within the domestic and international spheres.[49] This demonstrates the important role of framing perceived threats and the potential consequences, which might include protracted conflict, as proscription tends to diminish the prospects of conflict resolution.

HISTORY OF PROSCRIPTION IN NIGERIA

Faced with multiple national security threats since 1970, Nigeria has responded in different ways, including proscription. The legal framework upon which Nigeria's proscription regimes lie is derived from the Terrorism (Prevention) Act (TPA), which was passed into law in 2011.[50] TAP was amended in 2013, resulting in the Terrorism (Prevention) (Amendment) Act 2013 (TPAA).[51] TPAA Section 1(2) defines terrorism as a premeditated act carried out with malice and which may result in damage or harm to a country or international organization and is intended to compel, intimidate, destabilize, destroy, influence, and coerce a government, its constitution, its economy, and its international organization. The amended act goes on to state that these may also include violent attacks against individuals, kidnapping, destruction of public facilities, hijacking and diversion of public transport systems, unauthorized manufacturing, possession or movement of conventional and nonconventional weapons, and arson aimed at endangering human life, in addition to other acts recognized and prohibited by other international conventions to which Nigeria has adhered. According to section 2 of TPAA, an organization of two or more persons involved in promoting or collaborating to prepare the acts laid out in Section 1(2)(3) of the TPA, which are terrorist acts, qualifies to be proscribed. TPAA does not target single individuals for proscription, based on these provisions.

TPAA clearly indicates the process by which proscription is done, through a chain of command that begins with the attorney general and ends with the approval of the president. Afterward, a proscription application is then filed with a judge for the purpose of declaring any such group or organization as being proscribed. TPAA places significant power on the executive arm of government, particularly the president, in addition to not clearly spelling out the yardstick adopted when designating proscribed groups, thereby permitting room for abuse of power.[52] Following the enactment of TPAA, the Nigerian state has since gone on to proscribe some groups that it perceives to be a threat to the country's national security. Some of these groups include Jamāʾat Ahl as-Sunnah lid-Daʾwah waʾl-Jihād (also known as Boko Haram). By extension, this also includes Jamaʾatu Ansarul Muslimina Fi Biladis Sudan (Ansaru), which is the first breakaway faction of Boko Haram. In addition, there is the Islamic State in West Africa Province (ISWAP), which is the second breakaway faction of Boko Haram; the Indigenous People of Biafra (IPOB); Islamic Movement in Nigeria (IMN); and armed bandits (including the Yan Bindiga and the Yan Taʾadda groups).

Some of the factors that have given rise to the proscribed groups include socioeconomic grievances over issues such as poverty, socioeconomic inequality, high unemployment rates, and high rates of illiteracy.[53] Other factors include weak state institutions, political marginalization, poor governance, and ecological problems.[54] These factors, though local, are not peculiar to Nigeria. These problems are also seen in other fragile states across the globe, which points to the glocalized nature of some of these threats.[55] A few examples across Africa include Cameroon, Chad, and Niger in the Lake Chad Basin, as well as Burkina Faso and Mali in the Sahel region. These cases of Boko Haram, IPOB, IMN, and armed

Proscription Regimes and the Internationalization of National Security Threats 65

bandits reveal Nigeria's experience with proscription. They demonstrate the nature of the threats to national security as well as the nature of proscription as a counterterrorism policy response.

Boko Haram/ISWAP and Ansaru

The Boko Haram terrorist group is known as Jamā'at Ahl as-Sunnah lid-Da'wah wa'l-Jihād (JASJ) in Arabic, meaning "People Committed to the Prophet's Teaching and Jihad."[56] JASJ has gone by several names in the past, such as Yusuffiya during the period of 2004 to 2009.[57] Boko Haram's early origins can be traced back to 2003 in northeast Nigeria under the leadership of Muhammed Ali.[58] The activities of the group began to pose a serious threat to Nigerian national security when its preaching (*dawa*) took on an extremist posture. This led to the arrest of its leader at the time, Muhammed Yusuf (the son of Ali), by Nigerian security forces in 2009. Yusuf would later die in police custody the same year.[59] A new leader, in the person of Abubakar Shekau, a protégé of Yusuf, would emerge.[60] The Nigerian state has responded to the threat posed by Boko Haram (and its breakaway factions Ansaru and ISWAP) by launching multiple military campaigns against it in the north and the Lake Chad Basin region, in addition to proscribing the group and its associates on May 24, 2013.[61]

Boko Haram has been responsible for attacks on government institutions, kidnappings, suicide bombings, exploitation, and sexual violence and abuse against women and girls. Notably, Boko Haram is believed to have kidnapped more than 2,000 women and girls, most of whom have been used as sexual slaves, intelligence gatherers, recruiters, and fighters.[62] Some of the weaponry used by the group includes mortars, improvised explosive devices, and vehicle borne improvised explosive devices. Boko Haram's political ideology is driven by its desire to establish an Islamic caliphate in Nigeria, ruled by Sharia law.[63] Boko Haram, which gained notoriety when it kidnapped 276 schoolgirls from their school in Chibok, Borno state, in 2014,[64] has been affiliated with al-Qaeda, a foreign terrorist organization (FTO), since its formation.

As Boko Haram evolved, it was confronted with internal tensions over issues of doctrine. This led to its first breakaway in 2011 by a faction known as Ansarul Muslimina Fi Biladis Sudan, popularly known as Ansaru. Ansaru fighters were originally militants who had split from Boko

Haram and subsequently trained by al-Qaeda in the Islamic Magrib (AQIM).[65] This new group was led by Abubakar Kambar.[66] Ansaru gained popularity internationally for launching a deadly attack on the United Nations building in Nigeria's capital city, Abuja, in 2011.[67] Ansaru went underground for about a decade but recently re-emerged in the northwest and north central regions of Nigeria. The group has always maintained its allegiance to al-Qaeda, and in 2022 it affirmed connections with AQIM.[68]

In 2015, the Shekau-led faction of Boko Haram pledged its allegiance to the Islamic State and adopted the name Islamic State in West Africa Province (ISWAP).[69] This move led to the appointment of a new leader by the Islamic State caliph in the person of Abu Musab.[70] This implied that Shekau was demoted as leader of ISWAP. No longer comfortable with the group's doctrines, Shekau would go on to lead JASJ, making ISWAP essentially Boko Haram's second breakaway faction. With the death of Shekau in May 2021, JASJ has mostly confined its operations to the Lake Chad Basin region.[71] In what appears to be one of its deadliest attacks in recent times, JASJ launched an assault on Lake Chad's Bohoma Peninsula that lasted more than seven hours and claimed the lives of nearly a hundred soldiers, with more than fifty others injured.[72]

The Indigenous People of Biafra

Following its independence from the United Kingdom in 1960, the Nigerian state began its arduous journey of nation building. Accommodating the views of divergent interest groups posed a challenge, given Nigeria's complex ethnic composition. The Igbos in the southern part of the country held the view that their concerns over marginalization had fallen on deaf ears and as such they had decided to pursue a secessionist objective—the creation of an independent Biafran Republic—a decision which did not sit well with Nigeria's military junta at the time, which had assumed power after a series of coups and counter-coups.[73] The failure of regionalism/federalism to address the Igbos' grievances could be attributed to the absence of an elite consensus around an integrated model that was attuned with Nigeria's broader national identity at the time.[74]

Perceiving this decision as a direct threat to Nigeria's sovereignty and its national security, the Nigerian state moved to prevent the secession after the separatists, led by Lt. Col. Emeka Odumegwu-Ojukwu, formally declared the Biafran state on May 30, 1967. This led to a bloody civil war from 1967 to 1970, resulting in huge casualties on both sides. An estimated fifty thousand to three million people lost their lives.[75] This was in addition to a severe humanitarian crisis during the civil war that was caused by hunger and starvation.[76] At the end of the war, the Igbos remained part of the Nigerian state, but the clamor for an independent state was only temporarily buried. Postwar efforts intended at addressing these grievances were largely unsuccessful, particularly on the part of subsequent military regimes. However, since the return to democracy in 1999, under Nigeria's Fourth Republic, attempts have been made toward addressing these grievances through Nigeria's federal character principle, a constitutional provision that seeks to ensure equal representation of Nigeria's major ethnic groups in federal governance.[77]

Secessionist agitations have gained momentum in recent times, under Nigeria's Fourth Republic, which began with Ralph Nwazurike, the leader of the Movement for the Actualization of the Sovereign State of Biafra, as well as the Indigenous People of Biafra (IPOB), led by Nnamdi Kanu in the southern region, calling for an independent Biafran state. This has posed a serious threat particularly to Nigeria's national security given that IPOB's paramilitary wing, the Eastern Security Network, has been responsible for the death of many innocent Nigerians across the region. In addition, the activities of IPOB have attracted international attention. IPOB was formally proscribed by the Nigerian state as a terrorist organization on September 20, 2017.[78] This effectively rendered the activities of the group illegal and constituting acts of terror on Nigerian soil. Since the group's proscription, the Nigerian state has responded to the threat posed by IPOB mostly by using kinetic measures, involving military campaigns such as Operation Phyton Dance II.

Islamic Movement of Nigeria

Northern Nigeria is home to a significant number of Muslims. The dominant Hausa tribe in northern Nigeria is predominantly Muslim. Islam continues to yield significant influence across the region. The Islamic Movement of Nigeria (IMN), which began in the 1980s, is a Shiite religious organization, led by Sheikh Ibrahim Zakzaky, seeking to establish an Islamic state in Nigeria. It is inspired by the Iranian Revolution of

1979, which overthrew the Shah. IMN originated in Zaria, Kaduna state, and has mostly adopted nonviolent means in the pursuit of its objectives. IMN has since pledged allegiance to the late Ayatollah Khomeini, who continues to yield considerable influence over the group. IMN considers itself an independent government on Nigerian soil, in addition to recognizing its leader, Sheikh Zakzaky, as the only legitimate source of authority in Nigeria, since it considers the Nigerian government corrupt. This constitutes a direct affront to Nigeria's sovereignty and by extension its national security. IMN is also known to have branches and administrative structures across Nigeria, in addition to its own schools and hospitals in northern Nigeria.[79] The group was proscribed in July 2019.

Unlike Boko Haram, which opposes Western education, IMN's leadership has encouraged its members to pursue Western education. However, IMN's political ideology of replacing Nigeria's secular state with an Islamic state is perceived as a direct threat to national security. Despite its nonviolence posture, some of its protests have turned violent. In 2014, during a raid by Nigerian security forces on Husainiyah Baqiyatullah, IMN's spiritual base, thirty-four members of the group were killed, in addition to three of Zakzaky's sons and his elder sister.[80] A more recent example was during what has come to be known as the Zaria Massacre, when IMN members clashed with the Nigerian military, resulting in the killing of at least 348 civilians.[81] Zakzaky was arrested in 2015 and charged with murder by the Kaduna state government.[82]

IMN was proscribed in 2019 following a violent protest in Abuja demanding the release of Zakzaky by IMN members. The protest resulted in the death of one police officer, a journalist, and eleven protesters.[83] The proscription of IMN implies that the organization is designated a terrorist group and its activities are deemed illegal. The group has sought to challenge its proscription in court. IMN has also received some support from within and outside of Nigeria in its effort to overturn its proscription. Notably, the Catholic cardinal of Abuja, Cardinal John Onaiyekan, has condemned the ban on IMN.[84] Also, protests have been held in Tehran, the Iranian capital, demanding the release of Zakzaky and former Iranian president Hassan Rouhani is reported to have reached out to President Muhammadu Buhari, a Sunni Muslim, to convey his concerns after the killings that occurred during Zakzaky's arrest in 2015.[85]

Armed Bandits

Banditry, as in many other parts of the world, has existed in Nigeria for a long time. However, the origins of contemporary armed banditry in Nigeria have been traced to 2011 following significant transnational movement into Nigeria. Kungiyar Gayu, the first of these bandit organizations, emerged in northwest Nigeria's Zamfara state under its notorious leader, Buharin Daji. Kungiyar Gayu's primary goal was to fight off perceived social injustice against Fulani pastoralists in the form of exploitation, deprivation, and extortion. In that sense, the group fought to foster the social welfare and security of Fulani pastoralists. Kungiyar Gayu's activities were initially limited to Zamfara state but would later include Kaduna and Sokoto states in the northwestern region.[86]

By 2016, Kungiyar Gayu had taken on a more transnational posture, expanding to include other groups like the Tuaregs of Mali, Chad, and Niger Republic, as well as fighters from other neighboring countries.[87] Kungiyar Gayu has been accused of indiscriminate killings, kidnappings, theft, and sexual violence. Nigeria's armed banditry–induced conflicts in the north have their roots in the region's prevalent farmer-herder crisis.[88] The crisis has further taken on the form of a multidimensional crisis bearing the hallmarks of petty and sophisticated crimes, including armed robbery, pillage of villages, kidnappings for ransom, and illegal gold mining.[89] Given the threat posed by Kungiyar Gayu, the Nigerian government launched military operations against the groups, most notably Operation Sharan Daji, which was launched in 2016. The leader of Kungiyar Gayu, Buharin Daji, was killed in 2018, but splinter armed banditry groups soon emerged in northwest Nigeria, especially in the states of Kaduna, Katsina, and Sokoto.[90] Armed bandits have been growing in numbers, with an estimate of more than 30,000 fighters across the northern region.[91] It is estimated that in each of the mostly affected states, there are about three hundred armed bandit groups with more than a hundred camps spread across the troubled regions.[92] The activities of armed bandits have resulted in significant loss of lives and a brewing humanitarian crisis in the region.[93] Armed bandits were responsible for the deaths of about 8,000 people between 2011 and 2019 alone.[94] In addition, around 1 million people have been displaced in Nigeria as of 2022.[95] Another 11,500 have also been displaced in neighboring Niger Republic as a result of the heinous activities of armed bandits.[96] Armed banditry has become a real national security problem for Nigeria and the region. On November 29, 2021, the Nigerian government proscribed armed bandits, including Kungiyar Gayu, Yan Bindiga, and the Yan Ta'adda.[97] By this proscription, the activities of these groups are considered by the Nigerian state to be acts of terrorism and illegality.

GLOCALIZED SECURITY AND THE INTERNATIONALIZATION OF TERRORISM: THREATS AND CONSEQUENCES

Terrorism remains a significant challenge affecting the national security of the Nigerian state. This is evident in the multiple military operations being carried out across the country. However, terrorism has remained unabated. Beyond the human costs in the form of loss of lives and the destruction of property as well as the financial costs through increased military spending, terrorism caused by Boko Haram and armed banditry in the country has conflagrated and spread into neighboring countries, such as those in the Lake Chad Basin region and the Sahel region. In Nigeria, the most affected states by the activities of Boko Haram/ISWAP are the northeast states of Borno, Adamawa, and Yobe (known as the BAY states). This, however, is not to say that Boko Haram does not carry out attacks in other parts of the country, as it has done in the northwest and north central regions. Ansaru has mostly carried out its operations in the northwest region, particularly around the Birnin Gwari area of Kaduna state.

In response to the transnational threat posed by Boko Haram and its breakaway factions, Ansaru and ISWAP, the Multinational Joint Task Force (MNJTF) was established by member states of the Lake Chad Basin region, which includes Cameroon, Chad, Niger, and Nigeria. The Benin republic, even though not part of the Lake Chad Basin region, is also a member of the MNJTF, which was initiated in late 2014. MNJTF, which has a force of eight thousand, is supported by the European Union and the African Union and overseen by the Lake Chad Basin Commission. MNJTF reflects the glocalized nature of the various terrorism threats not only to Nigeria but also to other countries in the region. Given that most of the Lake Chad Basin region countries are endowed with natural resources critical to the global economy, more powerful external actors have also taken keen interest in the security situation in the region and see terrorism as a transnational threat. As terrorism caused by the activities of Boko Haram and its affiliates continues in Nigeria, its ripple effects are seen not only on Nigeria's national security but on regional security as well. Between 2013 and 2014, Boko Haram consolidated its hold on the Lake Chad Basin, taking advantage of cross-border trade, criminal networks, and religious ties to Islamic schools in Maiduguri. It expanded its operations in the region, resulting in more pillage, kidnappings, and revenge attacks as it recruited more people and promoted its extremist ideology.[98] Despite Boko Haram's expansion across the region, Nigeria continues to be the most affected when compared with other countries. This could be attributed to the fact that the Sambisa Forest, whence Boko Haram launches most of its attacks, is in Nigeria.

Acknowledging the transnationality of the threat posed by Boko Haram to regional stability, the affected countries have deployed troops to fight Boko Haram. However, that has made those states targets for Boko Haram attacks, which began to escalate in 2014. Other international partners who have a stake in the region's security and stability have shown bilateral support toward the MNJTF. This support has come from countries such as the United States, the United Kingdom, and France.[99] The involvement of these external actors reveals the increasing internationalization of the crisis posed by terrorism across the region as evident in the various jihadi terrorist groups in the Sahel region affiliated with al-Qaeda or the Islamic State. Despite the occasional competition that exists among these groups, they pose a danger for Nigeria and the other affected states as their cross-border activities and collaboration increase.

Another issue of growing concern has been the threat posed by armed bandits in Nigeria, who have now been designated as terrorists. Although the terrorists operate mostly in the northwest and north central regions, the proximity of Kaduna's borders to Niger Republic has meant that these terrorist groups are bound to exploit existing socioeconomic and potentially political cleavages along that corridor. Despite being designated as terrorists, they have appeared to be driven mostly by economic opportunism rather than by an underlying political ideology. The humanitarian crisis caused by armed banditry already bears serious consequences for neighboring Niger Republic, as pointed out earlier, which could constitute increased pressure on its social amenities and facilities with the rise in the influx of displaced persons. Niger Republic remains one of the poorest countries in the West African subregion.

There are also growing concerns about the potential relationship between armed bandits and jihadi terrorist groups in Nigeria, a situation that has serious consequences on national and regional security. For instance, armed bandits are reported to have purchased sophisticated weaponry from jihadist terrorists, and they also receive training on how to use the weapons.[100] The acquisition of weaponry by armed bandits from jihadist terrorists further contributes to the destabilization of the already troubled region. There is also the likelihood that given the concerns of their strategic interests in the region over Boko Haram, major powers (e.g., the European Union, the United States, the United Kingdom, and France) will become more vested in providing additional military support to Nigeria. The French decision to move its military operation to Niger after France was asked to leave Mali puts France in the crosshairs of Boko Haram and the armed bandits.[101] The African Union has also expressed worry over the growing threat of armed banditry and the potential of supporting an expanded military campaign.[102]

While African conflicts are conflicts that occur on African soil, the factors that fuel them, the actors that direct them, and the means through which they are fought extend far beyond Africa. Beyond vested external interests in these conflicts, most of which are deeply rooted in forces of global liberal governance, there are also other Africans, best described as conflict entrepreneurs, such as those in the diaspora, who stand to benefit from these conflicts politically, economically, and socially. An example is Simon Ekpa, a Nigerian of Igbo origin, who was arrested in Finland in connection with his role in the nefarious activities of IPOB.

Hidden Consequences of Proscription

Generally, Nigeria has internationalized the threats posed by home-grown terrorism. Proscription of terrorist groups has consequences, consequences that could be both intentional and unintentional. Nigeria's role as a regional hegemon and its status as a strategic regional ally to world powers mean that major powers will take a keen interest in its affairs. This is especially so when these threats have consequences on the national security interests of other countries. From a democracy standpoint, Nigeria's counterterrorism policy of proscriptions is problematic because by labeling and making illegal the activities of groups such as IMN and IPOB, Nigeria is stifling the fundamental rights of its citizens. However, the Nigerian state is compelled to act in the overall interest of ensuring the safety and security of its citizens.

One of the consequences of Nigeria's proscription of VNSAs has been an open invitation to external actors, thereby making them increasingly involved in Nigeria's fight against domestic terrorism. These external actors could potentially seek a physical presence close by the theaters of operations under the guise of providing military support, which could pose a challenge to Nigeria's sovereignty. An example of this was the United States' construction of an air base in Agadez, Niger,[103] after first establishing a drone base in Dirkou. These bases give the United States an extra footing in the affairs of Niger.[104] Another case is the French involvement in Mali in ways that overstepped the wishes of the Malian people. The closer external actors are to Nigeria, the higher the likelihood that they will interfere in the country's internal affairs, including on how it should fight terrorism. An example of this has been the United States' expression of concerns over allegations of human rights abuses and violations leveled against the Nigerian military.[105]

Proscription also breeds overdependence on external actors for the supply of sophisticated weaponry required to execute Nigeria's war against terrorist groups. A notable example was the delay, based on policy disagreements, in the delivery of twelve A-29 Super Tucano fighter jets bought from the United States in 2017; the jets were not delivered until 2021.[106] Nigeria is also dependent on China, from which it purchased military equipment in 2021, such as VT-4 (MBT-3000) main battle tanks and SH-5 105 mm self-propelled howitzers.[107] In 2019, Nigeria bought a significant amount of weapons, which included thirty-five main battle tanks, twenty-five Typhoon MRAPS (mine-resistant, ambush-protected vehicles), ten Spartan armored personnel carriers, twenty armored guard booths, five armored mine-clearing vehicles, fifty troop-carrying vehicles, forty Buffalo vehicles, four ships, 182 rigid hull inflatable and Epenal boats, twenty-five fixed-wing aircraft, and twelve helicopters.[108] Nigeria also purchased eight unmanned aerial vehicles (UAVs).[109] This overdependency on sophisticated weaponry to prosecute the war on proscribed terrorist groups feeds into the Nigerian militarization. Proscription also leads to increased military aid to Nigeria, which perpetuates the war. External military aid also comes with a requirement to implement security-sector reforms that are appealing to external actors.

The internationalization of Nigeria's national security threats through proscription of terrorist groups has also attracted the international humanitarian-aid regime into Nigeria, most notably the United Nations, the World Bank, and the European Union. For instance, IPOB has done a lot to internationalize against the federal government of Nigeria its agitations and allegations of human rights abuses. While this might be helpful in the short to medium term, it also creates conditions for external actors to promote their policy agendas and in some cases use Nigeria as an experimentation ground. The aid regime often masks domestic grievances that lead to terrorism, leaving them unsolved. In the process, proscribed groups become further emboldened as they gain additional international exposure and visibility that help them drive recruitment, gain resources, acquire weapons, and connect with foreign terrorist organizations.

THE FUTURE OF PROSCRIPTION REGIMES IN NIGERIA

The activities of home-grown violent non–state actors such as Boko Haram, Ansaru, ISWAP, and armed bandits operating within Nigeria have had devastating consequences on peace and security, not only in Nigeria but regionally and beyond as well. This problem has necessitated a regional response such as the establishment of the MNJTF. As part of Nigeria's response to national security threats, it has chosen to proscribe terrorist groups with the intent of making their activities illegal. This has also resulted in the glocalization of these security threats, thereby attracting global attention and action to combat them. The proscription of terrorist groups, especially Boko Haram, by the Nigerian state signaled Nigeria's commitment to the Global War on Terror, despite the push and resistance by the Christian Association of Nigeria and the Nigerian Supreme Council for Islamic Affairs on the need to label Boko Haram a terrorist group.

While proscription has provided the Nigerian state with the means to pursue military campaigns against terrorist groups, it has also resulted in the internationalization of security threats and possible solutions at the expense of more home-grown solutions that could address the domestic causes of terrorism. This has led to overdependence on foreign weaponry, problematic military aid, external political interference, excessive spending on arms, and humanitarian dependency. At the same time, terrorist groups are becoming emboldened and are developing new capacities.

The central argument in this chapter is that proscription as a counterterrorism policy response does not necessarily serve to deter domestic terrorist groups, as their nefarious activities tend to continue unabated even after proscription. The chapter adds the Nigeria case to studies that point in this direction. Terrorism proscription is often neglected in the broader studies of terrorism. The Nigerian proscription regime points to the limitations of proscription in the fight against extreme political violence, which is often proscribed and labeled as global terrorism without taking into account the local and domestic causes of extreme political violence. All of this is done through a novel conceptual frame of glocalized security to accentuate the interconnections between the domestic and external aspects to the Nigerian security problem.

NOTES

1. Taylor Hanna, David K. Bohl, Mickey Rafa, and Jonathan D. Moyer, *Assessing the Impact of the Conflict on Development in North East Nigeria* (Abuja: United Nations Development Programme, 2021), https://www.ng.undp.org/content /nigeria/en/home/library/human_development/assessing-the-impact-of -conflict-on-development-in-north-east-ni.html; International Organization for Migration, "Displacement Tracking Matrix Nigeria North-East Zone," UN Migration, International Organization for Migration, Global Data Institute Displacement Tracking Matrix, 2022, https://dtm.iom.int/reports/nigeria-%E2 %80%94-north-east-%E2%80%94-displacement-dashboard-39-december-2021 (page discontinued).

2. Olajumoke, Ayandele and Curtis Goos, "Mapping Nigeria's Security Crisis: Players, Targets and Trends," Armed Conflict Location & Event Data, May 20, 2021, https://acleddata.com/2021/05/20/mapping-nigerias-kidnapping-crisis -players-targets-and-trends/.

3. Sophie Haspeslagh, "The Mediation Dilemma of (Not) Talking to Terrorists," *Swiss Political Science Review* 26.4 (2020): 506–526.

4. Ronald Krebs, "The Politics of National Security," in *The Oxford Handbook of International Security*, ed. Alexandra Gheciu and William C. Wohlforth (Oxford: Oxford University Press, 2018).

5. Mirna El Masri and Brian J. Philips, "Threat Perception, Policy Diffusion, and the Logic of Terrorist Group Designation," *Studies in Conflict and Terrorism* (2021): 1–25.

6. Suthaharan Nadarajah, "The Tamil Proscriptions: Identities, Legitimacies and Situated Practices," *Terrorism and Political Violence* 30.2 (2018): 278–297.

7. Brian J. Phillips, "What Is a Terrorist Group? Conceptual Issues and Empirical Implications," *Terrorism and Political Violence* 27.2 (2015): 225–42.

8. Angela K. Bourne, "Securitization and the Proscription of Terrorist Organisations in Spain," *Terrorism and Political Violence* 30.2 (2018): 318–335.

9. Lee Jarvis, "Terrorism, Counter-terrorism, and Critique: Opportunities, Examples and Implications," *Critical Studies on Terrorism* 12.2 (2019): 339–358.

10. Jarvis, 349.

11. Abu Bakarr Bah, "Civil Non–state Actors in Peacekeeping and Peacebuilding in West Africa," *Journal of International Peacekeeping* 17 (2013): 313–336.

12. El Masri and Philips, "Threat Perception."

13. Daniel Kirkpatrick, "Proscribing the Past or De-proscribing the Future: A Genealogy and Critical Discourse Analysis of Proscription in the North of Ireland, 1887–2017," *Critical Studies on Terrorism* 12.2 (2019): 317–338.

14. Nathan Rasiah, "Reviewing Proscription under the Terrorism Act 2000," *Judicial Review* 13.3 (2008): 187–190.

15. Sophie Haspeslagh, "'Listing Terrorists': The Impact of Proscription on Third-Party Efforts to Engage Armed Groups in Peace Processes—a Practitioner's Perspective," *Critical Studies on Terrorism* 6.1 (2013): 189–208.

16. Roland Robertson, "Globalisation or Glocalisation," *The Journal of International Communication* 1.1 (2012): 33–52.

17. Lee Jarvis and Tim Legrand, "The Proscription or Listing of Terrorist Organisations: Understanding, Assessment, and International Comparisons," *Terrorism and Political Violence* 30.2 (2018): 199–215.

18. Lee Jarvis and Tim Legrand, "Legislating for Otherness: Proscription Powers and Parliamentary Discourse," *Review of International Studies* 42 (2016): 558–574.

19. Vicki Sentas, "Terrorist Organisation Proscription as Counterinsurgency in the Kurdish Conflict," *Terrorism and Political Violence* 30.2 (2018): 298–317.

20. Kirkpatrick, "Proscribing the Past," 317–338.

21. Rebecca H. Best and Simanti Lahiri, "Hard Choices, Soft Targets: Terror Proscription and Strategic Targeting Decisions of FTO," *International Interactions* 47.6 (2021): 955–985.

22. Best and Lahiri, 955.

23. Haspeslagh, "Listing Terrorists," 1–40.

24. El Masri and Philips, "Threat Perception."

25. Chi Zhang, "The Double-Track System of Terrorism Proscription in China," *Terrorism and Political Violence* 33.3 (2021): 505–526.

26. El Masri and Philips, "Threat Perception," 6.

27. El Masri and Philips.

28. Zhang, "The Double-Track System," 519.

29. Clive Walker, "'They Haven't Gone Away You Know': The Persistence of Proscription and the Problems of Deproscription," *Terrorism and Political Violence* 30.2 (2018): 236–258.

30. Sentas, "Terrorist Organisation Proscription."

31. Barry Buzan, Ole Wæver, and Jaap de Wilde, *Security: A New Framework for Analysis* (Boulder, CO: Lynne Rienner, 1998); Thierry Balzacq, *Securitization Theory* (Abingdon, UK: Routledge, 2011).

32. Bourne, "Securitization and the Proscription of Terrorist Organisations in Spain," 322.

33. Lee Jarvis and Tim Legrand, "'I Am Somewhat Puzzled': Questions, Audiences and Securitization in the Proscription of Terrorist Organisations," *Security Dialogue* 48.2 (2017): 149–167.

34. Jarvis and Legrand, 151.

35. Jarvis and Legrand, 160.

36. Jarvis and Legrand, 162.

37. Ioana E. Matesan, "Ripeness in Negotiating with Proscribed Terrorist Groups," *Ethnopolitics* 22.2 (2022): 178–189.

38. Matesan, 178.

39. Best and Lahiri, "Hard Choices, Soft Targets," 955–985.

40. Brian J. Philips, "Foreign Terrorist Organisation Designation, International Cooperation, and Terrorism," *International Interactions* 45.2 (2019): 316–343.

41. Philips, 324.

42. Craig Forcese and Kent Roach, "Yesterday's Law: Terrorist Group Listing in Canada," *Terrorism and Political Violence* 30.2 (2018): 259–277.

43. De Marieke Goede, "Proscription's Futures," *Terrorism and Political Violence* 30.2 (2018): 336–355.

44. Goede, 348.

45. Matesan, "Ripeness in Negotiating," 197.

46. Kirkpatrick, "Proscribing the Past," 317.

47. Kirkpatrick, 219.

48. Philips, "Foreign Terrorist Organisation Designation," 337.

49. Suthaharan Nadarajah and Dhananjayan Sriskandarajah, "Liberation Struggle or Terrorism? The Politics of Naming the LTTE," *Third World Quarterly* 26.1 (2005): 87–100.

50. UNODC, *User's Guide to the Terrorism (Prevention) Act, 2011 (TAP) as Amended by the Terrorism (Prevention) (Amendment) Act, 2013 (TPAA)* (Nairobi: United Nations Office on Drugs and Crime, 2021), https://www.unodc.org/documents/nigeria//UNODC_Users_Guide_to_Terrorism.pdf.

51. UNODC, *User's Guide.*

52. E. U. Ejeh, A. I. Bappah, and Y. Dankofa, "Proscription of Terrorism in Nigeria: A Comparative Legal Study," *Commonwealth Law Bulletin* 46.3 (2020): 367–390.

53. James A. Piazza, "Poverty, Minority Economic Discrimination, and Domestic Terrorism," *Journal of Peace Research* 48.3 (2011): 339–353; Francis Stewart, "Horizontal Inequalities and Conflict: An Introduction and Some Hypotheses," in *Horizontal Inequalities and Conflict,* ed. Francis Stewart (London: Palgrave Macmillan, 2002); U. Solomon Ayegba, "Unemployment and Poverty as Sources and Consequence of Insecurity in Nigeria: The Boko Haram Insurgency Revisited,"

African Journal of Political Science and International Relations 9.3 (2015): 90–99; Freedom C. Onuoha, "The Islamist Challenge: Nigeria's Boko Haram Crisis Explained," *African Security Review* 19.2 (2010): 54–67.

54. Richard Jackson, "The State and Internal Conflict," *Australian Journal of International Affairs* 55.1 (2001): 65–81; Caitriona Dowd and Adam Drury, "Marginalization, Insurgency and Civilian Insecurity: Boko Haram and the Lord's Resistance Army," *Peacebuilding* 5.2 (2017): 136–152; Håvard Hegre and Håvard Mokleiv Nygård, "Governance and Conflict Relapse," *Journal of Conflict Resolution* 59.6 (2015): 984–1016; United Nations Development Programme, *Human Development Report 2016* (New York: United Nations Development Programme, 2016), https://hdr.undp.org/content/human-development-report-2016.

55. Bah, "Civil Non–state Actors."

56. BBC, "Who Are Nigeria's Boko Haram Islamist Group?," BBC, November 24, 2016, https://www.bbc.co.uk/news/world-africa-13809501.

57. BBC, "Who Are Nigeria's Boko Haram Islamist Group?"

58. BBC, "Who Are Nigeria's Boko Haram Islamist Group?," 1; Bulama Bukarti, "Revisiting the Beginning of Boko Haram," *War on the Rocks*, January 24, 2022, https://warontherocks.com/2022/01/revisiting-the-beginning-of-boko-haram/.

59. Andrew Walker, *What Is Boko Haram?*, Special Report 308 (Washington, DC: United States Institute of Peace, 2012), https://www.usip.org/sites/default/files/resources/SR308.pdf.

60. Jacob Zenn, *Unmasking Boko Haram: Exploring Global Jihad in Nigeria* (Boulder, CO: Lynne Reinner, 2020).

61. Federal Republic of Nigeria, "Terrorism (Prevention) (Proscription Order) Notice 2013," *Federal Republic of Nigeria Official Gazette* 100.34 (2013): https://www.cbn.gov.ng/out/2013/fprd/terrorism%20(prevention)%20(proscription%20order)%20notice,%202013.pdf.

62. Stig Jarle Hansen, *Horn, Sahel and Rift, Fault-Lines of the African Jihad* (Oxford: Oxford University Press, 2018); Amnesty International, *"Our Job Is to Shoot, Slaughter and Kill": Boko Haram's Reign of Terror in North-East Nigeria* (London: Amnesty International, 2015), https://www.amnesty.org.uk/files/amnesty_international_nigeria_-_bh_report_april_2015.pdf?VersionId=VABTKXoO9JB6VCeDPXg.jBfizyew_UuN.

63. Walker, *What Is Boko Haram?*

64. Nima Elbagir, "Witness to Terror: Nigeria's Missing Schoolgirls," CNN, May 15, 2014, http://edition.cnn.com/2014/05/15/world/nigeria-nima-elbagir-chibok/index.html.

65. Jacob Zenn, "Boko Haram's Conquest for the Caliphate: How Al Qaeda Helped Islamic State Acquire Territory," *Studies in Conflict & Terrorism* 43.2 (2020): 89–122.

66. Walker, *What Is Boko Haram?*

67. BBC, "Abuja Attack: Car Bomb Hits Nigeria UN Building," BBC, August 27, 2011, https://www.bbc.co.uk/news/world-africa-14677957.

68. ISS, "Ansaru's Comeback in Nigeria Deepens the Terror Threat," Institute for Security Studies, June 1, 2022, https://issafrica.org/iss-today/ansarus-comeback-in-nigeria-deepens-the-terror-threat.

69. BBC, "Nigeria's Boko Haram Pledges Allegiance to Islamic State," BBC, March 7, 2015, https://www.bbc.co.uk/news/world-africa-31784538.

70. Zenn, *Unmasking Boko Haram.*

71. ICG, "Behind the Jihadist Attack in Chad," International Crisis Group, April 6, 2020, https://www.crisisgroup.org/africa/central-africa/chad/derriere-lattaque-jihadiste-au-tchad.

72. ICG, "Behind the Jihadist Attack in Chad."

73. Eghosa E. Osaghae, "The Long Shadow of Nigeria's Military Epochs, 1966–79 and 1983–99," in *The Oxford Handbook of Nigerian Politics,* ed. Carl Levan and Patrick Ukata (Oxford: Taylor and Francis, 2018).

74. Rotimi Suberu, *Federalism and Ethnic Conflict in Nigeria* (Washington, DC: United States Institute of Peace, 2001).

75. Roy Doron, "The Nigerian Civil War and Its Legacies," in *The Oxford Handbook of Nigerian History,* ed. Falola Toyin and Matthew M. Heaton (Oxford: Taylor and Francis, 2022).

76. Obi Nwakanma, "The Nigerian Civil War and the Biafran Secessionist Revival," in Levan and Ukata, *The Oxford Handbook of Nigerian Politics.*

77. Suberu, *Federalism and Ethnic Conflict in Nigeria.*

78. Premium Times, "Nigerian Court Grants Injunction Proscribing IPOB," *Premium Times,* September 20, 2017, https://www.premiumtimesng.com/news/headlines/243750-nigerian-court-grants-injunction-proscribing-ipob.html.

79. Haruna Shehu Tangaza, "Islamic Movement in Nigeria: The Iranian-Inspired Shia Group," BBC, August 5, 2019, https://www.bbc.co.uk/news/world-africa-49175639.

80. Tangaza.

81. BBC, "Mass Graves for '300 Shia Nigerians' in Zaria," BBC, December 23, 2015, https://www.bbc.co.uk/news/world-africa-35168211.

82. Evelyn Okakwu, "Detained Nigeria Shiite Leader El-Zakzaky Charged with Murder," *Premium Times,* April 26, 2018, https://www.premiumtimesng.com/news/headlines/266353-detained-nigeria-shiite-leader-el-zakzaky-charged-with-murder.html.

83. Human Rights Watch, "Nigeria: Court Bans Shia Group," Human Rights Watch, July 30, 2019, https://www.hrw.org/news/2019/07/30/nigeria-court-bans-shia-group.

84. Tangaza, "Islamic Movement in Nigeria."

85. Tangaza.

86. Ahmed Rufa'i Murtala, "'I Am a Bandit': A Decade of Research in Zamfara State Bandit's Den" (presented at the Fifteenth University Seminar Series, Usman Danfodiyo University, Sokoto, Nigeria, September 9, 2021).

87. Murtala.

88. Adedeji Ademola, "The Growing Threat of Armed Banditry in North-West Nigeria," *Strife*, 2021, https://www.strifeblog.org/2021/01/08/the-growing-threat-of-armed-banditry-in-north-west-nigeria/ (site discontinued).
89. Ademola.
90. Murtala, "I Am a Bandit."
91. I. Muhammed Yaba, "Matawalle: There Are 30,000 Armed Bandits across the North," *Daily Trust*, April 2, 2021, https://dailytrust.com/matawalle-there-are-30000-armed-bandits-across-the-north.
92. Yaba.
93. France24, "Northwest Nigeria Facing 'Brewing Humanitarian Crisis,'" France24, July 10, 2021, https://www.france24.com/en/live-news/20211007-northwest-nigeria-facing-brewing-humanitarian-crisis.
94. ICG, "Violence in Nigeria's North West: Rolling Back the Mayhem," International Crisis Group, May 18, 2020, https://www.crisisgroup.org/africa/west-africa/nigeria/288-violence-nigerias-north-west-rolling-back-mayhem.
95. I. Hassan and J. Barnett, "Northwest Nigeria's Bandit Problem: Explaining the Conflict Drivers," Centre for Democracy and Development, 2022, https://cddwestafrica.org/wp-content/uploads/2022/04/Conflict-Dynamics-and-Actors-in-Nigerias-Northwest.pdf (page discontinued).
96. UNHCR, "Bandit Attacks Drive Nigerian Villagers to Flee to Niger," United Nations Higher Commissioner for Refugees, December 3, 2021, https://www.unhcr.org/uk/news/latest/2021/12/61a9d2844/bandit-attacks-drive-nigerian-villagers-flee-niger.html.
97. Ameh Ejekwonyilo, "Updated: Nigerian Govt Gazettes Declaration of Bandit Groups as Terrorists," *Premium Times*, January 5, 2022, https://www.premiumtimesng.com/news/headlines/504177-just-in-nigerian-govt-gazettes-declaration-of-bandit-groups-as-terrorists.html.
98. ICG, *What Role for the Multinational Joint Task Force in Fighting Boko Haram?* (Brussels: International Crisis Group, 2020), 1–2, https://www.crisisgroup.org/africa/west-africa/291-what-role-multinational-joint-task-force-fighting-boko-haram.
99. ICG, *What Role?*, 3.
100. Oluwole Ojewale, "The Increasing Nexus between Bandits and Terrorists in Nigeria's Northwest," LSE Firoz Lalji Institute for Africa, October 26, 2021, https://blogs.lse.ac.uk/africaatlse/2021/10/26/nexus-between-bandits-terrorists-nigeria-northwest-military-response-policy/; Punch, "Boko Haram Fighters Train Bandits in Anti-aircraft Gun Use—Military Sources," *Punch*, September 26, 2021, https://punchng.com/boko-haram-fighters-train-bandits-in-anti-aircraft-gun-use-military-sources/.
101. David Rich, "Niger Becomes France's Partner of Last Resort after Mali Withdrawal," France24, February 18, 2022, https://www.france24.com/en/africa/20220218-niger-becomes-france-s-partner-of-last-resort-after-mali-withdrawal.
102. African Union, "Chairperson of the African Union Commission Condemns the Killing by Armed Bandits in Northwest Nigeria," African Union, January 11, 2022, https://au.int/ar/node/41354.

103. Carla Babb, "US-Constructed Air Base in Niger Begins Operations," Voice of America, November 1, 2019, https://www.voanews.com/a/africa_us-constructed-air-base-niger-begins-operations/6178666.html.

104. John Campbell, "The Presence of Lethal U.S. Drones in Niger Is Expanding," Council on Foreign Relations, September 11, 2018, https://www.cfr.org/blog/presence-lethal-us-drones-niger-expanding.

105. Sani Tukur, "U.S. Warns Nigerian Military against Human Rights Abuses," *Premium Times*, May 19, 2013, https://www.premiumtimesng.com/news/134974-u-s-warns-nigerian-military-against-human-rights-abuses.html.

106. Valerie Insinna, "US Approves A-29 Super Tucano Sale to Nigeria," *Defense News*, August 3, 2017, https://www.defensenews.com/air/2017/08/03/us-approves-a-29-super-tucano-sale-to-nigeria/; Premium Times, "Nigerian Govt Takes Delivery of Final Batch of Tucano Jets," *Premium Times*, October 18, 2021, https://www.premiumtimesng.com/news/more-news/490528-nigerian-govt-takes-delivery-of-final-batch-of-tucano-jets.html.

107. Defence Web, "Nigerian Military Receives Tanks, Artillery from China," Defence Web, April 9, 2020, https://www.defenceweb.co.za/featured/nigerian-military-receives-tanks-artillery-from-china/.

108. Defence Web, "Nigerian Military Receives Tanks."

109. Singh Inder Bisht, "Nigeria Takes Delivery of Chinese Drones to Combat Insurgency, Armed Banditry," *The Defense Post*, November 10, 2020, https://www.thedefensepost.com/2020/11/10/nigeria-wing-loong-drones/.

BIBLIOGRAPHY

Ademola, Adedeji. "The Growing Threat of Armed Banditry in North-West Nigeria." *Strife* (blog), January 8, 2021. https://www.strifeblog.org/2021/01/08/the-growing-threat-of-armed-banditry-in-north-west-nigeria/ (site discontinued).

African Union. "Chairperson of the African Union Commission Condemns the Killing by Armed Bandits in Northwest Nigeria." African Union, January 11, 2022. https://au.int/ar/node/41354.

Amnesty International. *"Our Job Is to Shoot, Slaughter and Kill": Boko Haram's Reign of Terror in North-East Nigeria*. London: Amnesty International, 2015. https://www.amnesty.org.uk/files/amnesty_international_nigeria_-_bh_report_april_2015.pdf?VersionId=VABTKXoO9JB6VCeDPXg.jBfizyew_UuN.

Ayandele, Olajumoke, and Curtis Goos. "Mapping Nigeria's Security Crisis: Players, Targets and Trends." Armed Conflict Location & Event Data, May 20, 2021. https://acleddata.com/2021/05/20/mapping-nigerias-kidnapping-crisis-players-targets-and-trends/.

Ayegba, U. Solomon. "Unemployment and Poverty as Sources and Consequence of Insecurity in Nigeria: The Boko Haram Insurgency Revisited." *African Journal of Political Science and International Relations* 9.3 (2015): 90–99.

Babb, Carla. "US-Constructed Air Base in Niger Begins Operations." Voice of America, November 1, 2019. https://www.voanews.com/a/africa_us-constructed-air-base-niger-begins-operations/6178666.html.

Bah, Abu Bakarr. "Civil Non–state Actors in Peacekeeping and Peacebuilding in West Africa." *Journal of International Peacekeeping* 17 (2013): 313–336.

Balzacq, Thierry. *Securitization Theory*. Abingdon, UK: Routledge, 2011.

BBC. "Abuja Attack: Car Bomb Hits Nigeria UN Building." BBC, August 27, 2011. https://www.bbc.co.uk/news/world-africa-14677957.

———. "Mass Graves for '300 Shia Nigerians' in Zaria." BBC, December 23, 2015. https://www.bbc.co.uk/news/world-africa-35168211.

———. "Nigeria's Boko Haram Pledges Allegiance to Islamic State." BBC, March 7, 2015. https://www.bbc.co.uk/news/world-africa-31784538.

———. "Who Are Nigeria's Boko Haram Islamist Group?" BBC, November 24, 2016. https://www.bbc.co.uk/news/world-africa-13809501.

Best, Rebecca H., and Lahiri, Simanti. "Hard Choices, Soft Targets: Terror Proscription and Strategic Targeting Decisions of FTO." *International Interactions* 47.6 (2021): 955–985.

Bisht, Singh Inder. "Nigeria Takes Delivery of Chinese Drones to Combat Insurgency, Armed Banditry." *The Defense Post*, November 10, 2020. https://www.thedefensepost.com/2020/11/10/nigeria-wing-loong-drones/.

Bourne, Angela K. "Securitization and the Proscription of Terrorist Organisations in Spain." *Terrorism and Political Violence* 30.2 (2018): 318–335.

Bukarti, Bulama. "Revisiting the Beginning of Boko Haram." *War on the Rocks*, January 24, 2022. https://warontherocks.com/2022/01/revisiting-the-beginning-of-boko-haram/.

Buzan, Barry, Ole Wæver, and Jaap de Wilde. *Security: A New Framework for Analysis*. Boulder, CO: Lynne Rienner, 1998.

Campbell, John. "The Presence of Lethal U.S. Drones in Niger Is Expanding." Council on Foreign Relations, September 11, 2018. https://www.cfr.org/blog/presence-lethal-us-drones-niger-expanding.

Defence Web. "Nigerian Military Receives Tanks, Artillery from China." Defence Web, April 9, 2020. https://www.defenceweb.co.za/featured/nigerian-military-receives-tanks-artillery-from-china/.

Doron, Roy. "The Nigerian Civil War and Its Legacies." In *The Oxford Handbook of Nigerian History*, ed. Falola Toyin and Matthew M. Heaton, 399–421. New York: Oxford University Press, 2022.

Dowd, Caitriona, and Adam Drury. "Marginalization, Insurgency and Civilian Insecurity: Boko Haram and the Lord's Resistance Army." *Peacebuilding* 5.2 (2017): 136–152.

Ejeh, E. U, A. I. Bappah, and Y. Dankofa. "Proscription of Terrorism in Nigeria: A Comparative Legal Study." *Commonwealth Law Bulletin* 46.3 (2020): 367–390.

Ejekwonyilo, Ameh. "Updated: Nigerian Govt Gazettes Declaration of Bandit Groups as Terrorists." *Premium Times*, January 5, 2022. https://www.premiumtimesng.com/news/headlines/504177-just-in-nigerian-govt-gazettes-declaration-of-bandit-groups-as-terrorists.html.

Elbagir, Nima. "Witness to Terror: Nigeria's Missing Schoolgirls." CNN, May 15, 2014. http://edition.cnn.com/2014/05/15/world/nigeria-nima-elbagir-chibok/index.html.

El Masri, Mirna, and Brian J. Philips. "Threat Perception, Policy Diffusion, and the Logic of Terrorist Group Designation." *Studies in Conflict and Terrorism* (2021): 1–25.

Federal Republic of Nigeria. "Terrorism (Prevention) (Proscription Order) Notice 2013." *Federal Republic of Nigeria Official Gazette* 100.34 (2013). https://www.cbn .gov.ng/out/2013/fprd/terrorism%20(prevention)%20(proscription%20order) %20notice,%202013.pdf.

Forcese, Craig, and Kent Roach. "Yesterday's Law: Terrorist Group Listing in Canada." *Terrorism and Political Violence* 30.2 (2018): 259–277.

France24. "Northwest Nigeria Facing 'Brewing Humanitarian Crisis.'" France24, July 10, 2021. https://www.france24.com/en/live-news/20211007-northwest -nigeria-facing-brewing-humanitarian-crisis.

Goede, de Marieke. "Proscription's Futures." *Terrorism and Political Violence* 30.2 (2018): 336–355.

Hanna, Taylor, David K. Bohl, Mickey Rafa, and Jonathan D. Moyer. *Assessing the Impact of the Conflict on Development in North East Nigeria*. Abuja: United Nations Development Programme, 2021. https://www.ng.undp.org/content/nigeria/ en/home/library/human_development/assessing-the-impact-of-conflict-on -development-in-north-east-ni.html.

Hansen, Stig Jarle. *Horn, Sahel and Rift: Fault-Lines of the African Jihad*. Oxford: Oxford University Press, 2018.

Haspeslagh, Sophie. "'Listing Terrorists': The Impact of Proscription on Third-Party Efforts to Engage Armed Groups in Peace Processes—a Practitioner's Perspective." *Critical Studies on Terrorism* 6.1 (2013): 189–208.

———. "The Mediation Dilemma of (Not) Talking to Terrorists." *Swiss Political Science Review* 26.4 (2020): 506–526.

Hassan, I., and J. Barnett. "Northwest Nigeria's Bandit Problem: Explaining the Conflict Drivers." Centre for Democracy and Development, 2022. https:// cddwestafrica.org/wp-content/uploads/2022/04/Conflict-Dynamics-and -Actors-in-Nigerias-Northwest.pdf (page discontinued).

Hegre, Håvard, and Håvard Mokleiv Nygård. "Governance and Conflict Relapse." *Journal of Conflict Resolution* 59.6 (2015): 984–1016.

Human Rights Watch. "Nigeria: Court Bans Shia Group." Human Rights Watch, July 30, 2019. https://www.hrw.org/news/2019/07/30/nigeria-court-bans-shia -group.

ICG. "Behind the Jihadist Attack in Chad." International Crisis Group, April 6, 2020. https://www.crisisgroup.org/africa/central-africa/chad/derriere-lattaque -jihadiste-au-tchad.

———. "Violence in Nigeria's North West: Rolling Back the Mayhem." International Crisis Group, May 18, 2020. https://www.crisisgroup.org/africa/west-africa/ nigeria/288-violence-nigerias-north-west-rolling-back-mayhem.

———. *What Role for the Multinational Joint Task Force in Fighting Boko Haram?* Brussels: International Crisis Group, 2020. https://www.crisisgroup.org/africa/west -africa/291-what-role-multinational-joint-task-force-fighting-boko-haram.

Insinna, Valerie. "US Approves A-29 Super Tucano Sale to Nigeria." *Defense News*, August 3, 2017. https://www.defensenews.com/air/2017/08/03/us-approves-a-29-super-tucano-sale-to-nigeria/.

International Organization for Migration. "Displacement Tracking Matrix Nigeria North-East Zone." UN Migration, International Organization for Migration, Global Data Institute Displacement Tracking Matrix, 2022. https://dtm.iom.int/reports/nigeria-%E2%80%94-north-east-%E2%80%94-displacement-dashboard-39-december-2021 (page discontinued).

ISS. "Ansaru's Comeback in Nigeria Deepens the Terror Threat." Institute for Security Studies, June 1, 2022. https://issafrica.org/iss-today/ansarus-comeback-in-nigeria-deepens-the-terror-threat.

Jackson, Richard. "The State and Internal Conflict." *Australian Journal of International Affairs* 55.1 (2001): 65–81.

Jarvis, Lee. "Terrorism, Counter-terrorism, and Critique: Opportunities, Examples and Implications." *Critical Studies on Terrorism* 12.2 (2019): 339–358.

Jarvis, Lee, and Tim Legrand. "Legislating for Otherness: Proscription Powers and Parliamentary Discourse." *Review of International Studies* 42 (2016): 558–574.

———. "'I Am Somewhat Puzzled': Questions, Audiences and Securitization in the Proscription of Terrorist Organisations." *Security Dialogue* 48.2 (2017): 149–167.

———. "The Proscription or Listing of Terrorist Organisations: Understanding, Assessment, and International Comparisons." *Terrorism and Political Violence* 30.2 (2018): 199–215.

Kirkpatrick, Daniel. "Proscribing the Past or De-proscribing the Future: A Genealogy and Critical Discourse Analysis of Proscription in the North of Ireland, 1887–2017." *Critical Studies on Terrorism* 12.2 (2019): 317–338.

Krebs, Ronald. "The Politics of National Security." In *The Oxford Handbook of International Security*, ed. Alexandra Gheciu and William C. Wohlforth, 259–273. Oxford: Oxford University Press, 2018.

Lynch, Andrew, Nicola McGarrity, and George Williams. "The Proscription of Terrorist Organisations in Australia." *Federal Law Review* 37.1 (2019): 1–40.

Matesan, Ioana Emy. "Ripeness in Negotiating with Proscribed Terrorist Groups." *Ethnopolitics* 22.2 (2022): 178–189.

Nadarajah, Suthaharan. "The Tamil Proscriptions: Identities, Legitimacies and Situated Practices." *Terrorism and Political Violence* 30.2 (2018): 278–297.

Nadarajah, Suthaharan, and Dhananjayan Sriskandarajah. "Liberation Struggle or Terrorism? The Politics of Naming the LTTE." *Third World Quarterly* 26.1 (2005): 87–100.

Nwakanma, Obi. "The Nigerian Civil War and the Biafran Secessionist Revival." In *The Oxford Handbook of Nigerian Politics*, ed. Carl Levan and Patrick Ukata, 620–636. New York: Oxford University Press, 2018.

Ojewale, Oluwole. "The Increasing Nexus between Bandits and Terrorists in Nigeria's Northwest." LSE Firoz Lalji Institute for Africa, October 26, 2021. https://blogs.lse.ac.uk/africaatlse/2021/10/26/nexus-between-bandits-terrorists-nigeria-northwest-military-response-policy/.

Okakwu, Evelyn. "Detained Nigeria Shiite Leader El-Zakzaky Charged with Murder." *Premium Times*, April 26, 2018. https://www.premiumtimesng.com/news/headlines/266353-detained-nigeria-shiite-leader-el-zakzaky-charged-with-murder.html.

Onuoha, Freedom. "The Islamist Challenge: Nigeria's Boko Haram Crisis Explained." *African Security Review* 19.2 (2010): 54–67.

Osaghae, Eghosa E. "The Long Shadow of Nigeria's Military Epochs, 1966–79 and 1983–99." In *The Oxford Handbook of Nigerian Politics*, ed. Carl Levan and Patrick Ukata, 171–189. New York: Oxford University Press, 2018.

Phillips, Brian J. "Foreign Terrorist Organisation Designation, International Cooperation, and Terrorism." *International Interactions* 45.2 (2019): 316–343.

———. "What Is a Terrorist Group? Conceptual Issues and Empirical Implications." *Terrorism and Political Violence* 27.2 (2015): 225–242.

Piazza, James A. "Poverty, Minority Economic Discrimination, and Domestic Terrorism." *Journal of Peace Research* 48.3 (2011): 339–353.

Premium Times. "Nigerian Court Grants Injunction Proscribing IPOB." *Premium Times*, September 20, 2017. https://www.premiumtimesng.com/news/headlines/243750-nigerian-court-grants-injunction-proscribing-ipob.html.

Premium Times. "Nigerian Govt Takes Delivery of Final Batch of Tucano Jets." *Premium Times*, October 18, 2021. https://www.premiumtimesng.com/news/more-news/490528-nigerian-govt-takes-delivery-of-final-batch-of-tucano-jets.html.

Punch. "Boko Haram Fighters Train Bandits in Anti-aircraft Gun Use—Military Sources." *Punch*, September 26, 2021. https://punchng.com/boko-haram-fighters-train-bandits-in-anti-aircraft-gun-use-military-sources/.

Rasiah, Nathan. "Reviewing Proscription under the Terrorism Act 2000." *Judicial Review* 13.3 (2008): 187–190.

Rich, David. "Niger Becomes France's Partner of Last Resort after Mali Withdrawal." *France24*, February 18, 2022. https://www.france24.com/en/africa/20220218-niger-becomes-france-s-partner-of-last-resort-after-mali-withdrawal.

Robertson, Roland. "Globalisation or Glocalisation." *The Journal of International Communication* 1.1 (2012): 33–52.

Rufa'i Murtala, Ahmed. "'I Am a Bandit': A Decade of Research in Zamfara State Bandit's Den." Presented at the Fifteenth University Seminar Series, Usman Danfodiyo University, Sokoto, Nigeria, September 9, 2021.

Sentas, Vicki. "Terrorist Organisation Proscription as Counterinsurgency in the Kurdish Conflict." *Terrorism and Political Violence* 30.2 (2018): 298–317.

Stewart, Francis. "Horizontal Inequalities and Conflict: An Introduction and Some Hypotheses." In *Horizontal Inequalities and Conflict*, ed. Francis Stewart, 3–24. London: Palgrave Macmillan, 2002.

Suberu, Rotimi, *Federalism and Ethnic Conflict in Nigeria*. Washington, DC: United States Institute of Peace, 2001.

Tangaza, Haruna Shehu. "Islamic Movement in Nigeria: The Iranian-Inspired Shia Group." BBC, August 5, 2019. https://www.bbc.co.uk/news/world-africa-49175639.

Tominaga, Yasutaka, Chai-yi Lee, and Mengting Lyu. "Introducing a New Dataset on Designated Terrorist Organisations (DTO)." *Peace Research* 59.5 (2022): 756–766.

Tukur, Sani. "U.S. Warns Nigerian Military against Human Rights Abuses." *Premium Times*, May 19, 2013. https://www.premiumtimesng.com/news/134974-u-s-warns-nigerian-military-against-human-rights-abuses.html.

UNHCR. "Bandit Attacks Drive Nigerian Villagers to Flee to Niger." United Nations Higher Commissioner for Refugees, December 3, 2021. https://www.unhcr.org/uk/news/latest/2021/12/61a9d2844/bandit-attacks-drive-nigerian-villagers-flee-niger.html.

United Nations Development Programme. *Human Development Report 2016*. New York: United Nations Development Programme, 2016. https://hdr.undp.org/content/human-development-report-2016.

UNODC. *User's Guide to the Terrorism (Prevention) Act, 2011 (TPA) as Amended by the Terrorism (Prevention) (Amendment) Act, 2013 (TPAA)*. Nairobi: United Nations Office on Drugs and Crime, 2021. https://www.unodc.org/documents/nigeria//UNODC_Users_Guide_to_Terrorism.pdf.

Walker, Andrew. *What Is Boko Haram?* Special Report 308. Washington, DC: United States Institute of Peace, 2012. https://www.usip.org/sites/default/files/resources/SR308.pdf.

Walker, Clive. "'They Haven't Gone Away You Know': The Persistence of Proscription and the Problems of Deproscription." *Terrorism and Political Violence* 30.2 (2018): 236–258.

Yaba, I. Muhammed. "Matawalle: There Are 30,000 Armed Bandits across the North." *Daily Trust*, April 2, 2021. https://dailytrust.com/matawalle-there-are-30000-armed-bandits-across-the-north.

Zenn, Jacob. "Boko Haram's Conquest for the Caliphate: How Al Qaeda Helped Islamic State Acquire Territory." *Studies in Conflict & Terrorism* 43.2 (2020): 89–122.

———. *Unmasking Boko Haram: Exploring Global Jihad in Nigeria*. Boulder, CO: Lynne Reinner, 2020.

Zhang, Chi. "The Double-Track System of Terrorism Proscription in China." *Terrorism and Political Violence* 33.3 (2021): 505–526.

Chapter 3

Countering Violent Extremism through Community Policing in Likoni, Mombasa, Kenya

JOHN MWANGI GITHIGARO

Following the September 11, 2001, terrorist attacks on the United States (henceforth, 9/11), there has been a vigorous discourse on the Global War on Terror. In the immediate aftermath of the 9/11 terrorist attacks, cultural arguments emerged linking, in a misplaced fashion, Islam and violence.[1] The underlying discourse from the media and some scholars has been the tendency to interpret the concept of jihad with the prospects of violence. This ignores, however, the different variants of Islam and their associated practices. It is possible, however, that social actors have chosen to misinterpret religion in order to propagate violence. The immediate effect was to view or treat members of Muslim communities as terrorist suspects who need to be surveilled and curtailed.[2] The Global War on Terror discourse can be seen in the yet-unsettled idea of glocalization. The notion of glocality is framed as experiencing the global locally or through

I am indebted to the supports of the Next Generation Social Sciences in Africa fellowship and the African Peacebuilding Network fellowship at the Social Sciences Research Council, New York, which are supported by funds provided by the Carnegie Corporation of New York. These fellowships funded the fieldwork for this study.

local lenses. These experiences can be mediated by local power relations, cultural sensitivities, and geopolitical or geographical factors.[3] Glocalization in this context shall be applied in understanding not only how threats such as terrorism and violent extremism are debated locally but also which external influences have come to shape the attendant counterinterventions. This chapter situates approaches and interventions that speak in part to both the local and the international in the countering violent extremism (CVE) landscape. A running theme throughout the chapter is how the concept of community policing is being applied in counterterrorism efforts in Kenya, with a special focus on Mombasa.

The viewing or treatment of Muslims as terrorism suspects, and by extension the cultural argument that linked Islam with violence, became the vogue of analysis. This perspective was notably influenced by the clash of civilizations thesis advanced by Samuel Huntington, which has been criticized.[4] There is empirical evidence to suggest, however, that religion is not a significant predictor of the politically motivated violence often linked to Islam. Instead, the more acceptable links to political violence in the context of violent extremism tend to be placed in the realm of socioeconomic and political conditions in a country.[5]

Post-9/11, the immediate response by governments to political violence fit into the realm of counterterrorism. These included reactive measures focused on military means, tough antiterrorism legislation, and international cooperation, among other strategies to react to the threat of terrorism.[6] In the Kenyan context, all of these practices were visible after the 1998 attacks at the American Embassy in Nairobi. The state counterterrorism measures would lead over time to legislation (notably the Prevention of Terrorism Act 2012 and the Security Amendments Law 2014), the establishment of a specialized Anti-Terrorism Police Unit and the Kenya National Counter-Terrorism Center among other examples of measures.[7] Kenya's proximity to an unstable Somalia, the rise of the Al-Shabaab social movement, and a growing youth bulge in a tough economic environment, including a wide range of governance challenges such as lax border controls, have been touted as conducive factors leading to terrorist violence in Kenya.[8]

Whereas Kenya has mainly chosen to respond to the threats of terrorism by using military means such as the 2011 military incursion into Somalia and the subsequent inclusion into the African Union Mission in Somalia (AMISOM) contingent and presently the African Union Transition Mission in Somalia, there has been a notable shift in Kenya's response to terrorism. In mid-2016, Kenya launched a counter-violent extremism strategy that resulted in a notable shift in how violent extremism is to be dealt with. This strategy broadened the work of countering terrorism to soft power approaches beyond the traditional hard power militaristic strategies. This strategy speaks to the rise of soft power approaches that place various non–state actors as critical stakeholders in preempting violent extremism. Given that CVE is conceptualized within a peacebuilding role, a variety of non–state actors such as ad hoc community organizations, international NGOs, and local NGOs are engaged in multiple problem-solving roles.[9] Some of the non–state actors in Kenya engage in prevention work, but also in rehabilitation of and reintegration initiatives for former extremists, complementing the work of state actors. Kenya's national CVE strategy values non–state actors engaged in preventative interventions. For clarity, the emerging discourse of CVE is a paradigm shift from hard power militaristic reactive measures. Notably, it speaks to the use of noncoercive responses such as counternarratives and dialogue forums that aim to preempt violent extremism.

This study examines community policing in the counterterrorism domain. The central questions are as follows: In what ways are community policing deployed in the fight against terrorism? How receptive is the idea of counterterrorism at the community level? Overall, the study problematizes the opportunities and barriers that community policing presents in preventing terrorism. The study uses a qualitative approach. Data was collected through key informant interviews and focus group discussions. Notably, the study draws on twenty key informant interviews with security officials and local administrators in Likoni and Mombasa. It also draws on three focus group discussions (two with members of community policing and Nyumba Kumi structures and one with youth residents of Likoni). Each focus group discussion had an average of eight participants. The fieldwork was done in September and November 2016 and June 2017. Additional interviews were conducted in June 2018, September 2021, and April 2022. Thematic analysis and the use of secondary data were applied in the data analysis. The choice of the study site is informed by the current securitization of the coastal region of Kenya as a hotspot for recruitment into terrorist violence. This region has been linked to the presence of terror cells and established recruitment networks keen on mobilizing political violence.

CVE, COUNTERTERRORISM, AND GLOCALIZED SECURITY

CVE has become a catchphrase that has been applied in the context of preempting terrorist threats. Whereas there is yet to be a consensus on what it fully entails or does not entail, more-pragmatic views refer to it as a set of noncoercive measures to prevent terrorism. CVE is seen to involve, among other activities, counterradicalization. CVE is also more reflective as a field of policy practice as opposed to one of academic study. It is also a relatively new field, having emerged in the aftermath of the September 11, 2001, attacks on the United States. Whereas post-9/11 there was a focus on the use of coercive and hard power approaches (military means, use of force) to deal with the so-called terrorists, a CVE discourse altered that intervention. CVE remains critical of the use of force in dealing with the threats of terrorism. Rather, it calls for the use of softer and noncoercive responses aimed at preventing terrorism in the first place.[10] CVE is thus a departure from state counterterrorism approaches that engage in military means and use of tough legislation to deal with an ever-changing security landscape.[11]

This chapter draws not only from the counterterrorism and CVE discourses but also from the notion of glocalized security. Glocalized security in this chapter moves from a state-centric notion of security to the multiplicity of non–state actors, especially at the local level. In this sense, glocalized security fuses the local and national security concerns with the Global War on Terror.[12] Glocalization of security has been evident in Kenya's CVE landscape. There is the acknowledgment that security is no longer the sole preserve of the state. Instead, ensuring security is possible through an array of practices, including local approaches and the adaptation of international counterterrorism practices. As such, non–state actors have become important actors in CVE as they bring cultural and social capital that can complement the work of the state.[13] A community-policing approach to CVE also rests on the unconventional nature of violence as illustrated in the literature on new wars. New wars are no longer confined to state boundaries as they become glocal in nature.[14] It is in this context of the glocal turn that the shift from counterterrorism to CVE becomes very critical to Kenya's national security efforts.

The changing security landscape has led to a shift toward CVE. In the first place, hard counterterrorism measures have tended to be counterproductive as they alienate the very communities they are intended to serve and protect. For instance, they perpetrate various human rights violations, such as arbitrary arrests, forced disappearances, and the labeling of certain communities as risky ones that must be subjected to government surveillance. In the case of Kenya, Muslims and members of the Somali and coastal communities have been portrayed as security threats.[15] The larger implication of this is that stigmatized communities do not really cooperate with state security forces. Also, there have been growing calls to include community actors in the effort to prevent extreme violence. Notably, non−state actors, individuals, and communities are now being recognized as critical pillars in the CVE domain. In part, this demonstrates the changing nature of how security is governed.[16] CVE as a field of practice aims primarily at the prevention of radicalization that may lead to violent extremism. CVE preventative measures may include educational programs as well as working with a range of grassroots actors such as community and health workers to equip them with preventative interventions they can use in their localities.[17]

The idea of community involvement in CVE is increasingly being considered through a human security lens. By moving the focus of security from the statist lens, the debate on human security is considered important to locating the object of security. As such, the community, family, and non−state actors alongside the state play a role in guaranteeing human security. Depending on the local and the security contexts, communities' engagement with security actors such as the police is considered critical. Police engagement with the community can often create opportunities for dialogue in communities with high risks of youth radicalization's morphing into violent extremism. This can then create possibilities for an appreciative inquiry on what is ongoing in a community with regard to not only preventing violent extremism but also solving other social problems that can lead to radicalization.[18]

TERRORISM IN KENYA

Terrorism in Kenya, a growing phenomenon, can be traced to the mid-1990s. Terrorism was not always linked to Islamist-motivated violence. Initially, it was political violence against the government to protest marginalization. On the Kenyan coast, the rise of political violence was first traced to the activities of the Islamic Party of Kenya (IPK) in the early 1990s. Before the rise of the IPK, the Answar sect led by Sheikh Abdulaziz Rimo in Kwale, South Coast, prepared the stage for violent extremism on the Kenyan coast. This eventually spread to other parts of Kenya, albeit with connections to neighboring countries such as Tanzania.[19] Notably, the IPK and its ideologies were focused on speaking against the marginalization of Muslims in Kenya, especially on the coast. IPK, formed in 1992 and led by a fiery cleric, Sheikh Khalid Balala, set the stage for the rise of Islamic extremism in Kenya. IPK was deemed a security threat to the government and banned immediately, but some of the issues it agitated for later found resonance with violent extremist groups in the early 2000s.[20]

IPK raised several grievances, most notably marginalization of Muslims in government jobs and public institutions (including universities), lack of a university on the coast at the time, low level of development on the coast, and economic marginalization on the coast by up-country Christians. To the government, these kinds of grievances revived old fears and debates about the coast wanting to secede from Kenya.[21] It is some of these grievances that would be galvanized to form the Mombasa Republican Council, which is a movement agitating for the empowerment of Muslims on the coast of Kenya.[22] Recently, the council has been suspected of having links with Al-Shabaab.[23]

Global terrorism took root in Kenya during the 1990s with the setting up of al-Qaeda cells in eastern Africa. This resulted in the US Embassy bombings in Nairobi and Dar-es-Salaam in 1998, which were aimed primarily at Western interests. While the attacks were largely perpetrated by non–Kenyan citizens, they did point to some level of involvement by Kenyans. Previously, there was a terrorist bombing of the Norfolk Hotel in Nairobi on December 31, 1980, carried out by a Palestinian-linked actor, though Kenyans were complicit as well.[24] Since 1998, the Kenyan government, with the assistance of international partners, began to take the threats of terrorism seriously.[25] This led to intensified efforts to stabilize Somalia, which was believed to promote al-Qaeda sleeper cells in eastern Africa. Other government interventions included the establishment of the National Security Intelligence Service and a specialized counterterrorism police unit—the Anti-Terrorism Police Unit.

Also, anti-terror legislations were passed, such as the Prevention of Terrorism Act of 2012.[26]

In the mid-2000s, especially since 2007, terrorism threats on Kenya intensified as the Islamic Courts Union was ousted from Mogadishu in Somalia. A notable development was the recruitment of Kenyan youths into Al-Shabaab.[27] The initial motivation for youth recruitment into Al-Shabaab was to help drive Western forces occupying a Muslim nation (i.e., Somalia) under the frame of global jihad to defend a Muslim *ummah* (community of Muslims bound by religion) against external invaders. A significant event that affected terrorism in Kenya was the 2011 military incursion by Kenya into Somalia, dubbed Operation Linda Nchi. This initial unilateral military intervention by Kenya was principally meant to counter Al-Shabaab incursions into Kenya.[28] However, the Kenyan military intervention created a critical narrative conducive to radicalization, which Al-Shabaab and other terrorist groups exploited. The intervention was framed as a Christian invasion of Muslim lands, which radicalized people into jihadism. However, it is important to note the political angle of Al-Shabaab grievances, which are not necessarily compatible with Islamic teachings. Rather, radicalization should be seen largely as jihad narrative.[29]

COMMUNITY POLICING: ITS GENESIS AND NATURE

The concept of community policing, while contested in terms of definitions, draws from Anglo-American contexts in the 1980s. It was later exported to aid recipient countries by a host of actors such as international NGOs, donors, and private consultancy firms. Its intended aim is to police *with and for the community* rather than police the community. This implies that the police ought to be accountable and responsive to the citizens. The importation of community-policing models from the West to the African continent has been criticized on the basis that it has little regard for context. Whereas its goal is to entrench democratic policing, this policing model has to adapt to other local policing practices, existing power relations, and interests. The outcomes then tend to depart from the democratization of policing, which is often the goal of the international actors who popularize community policing.[30] Community policing was to create a platform from which citizens and the police would engage to enhance public safety. It has been touted as a policing model that would be engaged in proactive problem-solving responses as opposed to reactive actions. Developing strong relationships between the police and the community is a critical element of the community-policing model.[31] Overall, community policing rests on three principles: (1) focus on community building as a way to prevent crime, (2) collaborative decision-making and shared responsibility, and (3) small, independent, and autonomous police departments with strong connections to the community.[32] One of the most successful community-policing efforts in eastern Africa is the Tanzanian participatory policing model.

In Tanzania, community policing has been anchored on two planks. One is to improve public perceptions of the police and therefore enable intelligence gathering and cooperation with the Tanzania police force. The second is to encourage citizens to take responsibility for their security in what they call *Ulinzi Shirikishi* (i.e., participatory policing). The model has roots in *Sungu Sungu* (i.e., vigilantism) encouraged by the Chama cha Mapinduzi (Revolutionary Party). Sungu Sungu emerged in the 1980s as a response to a countrywide surge in violent crime in a context wherein state security agents were ineffective.[33] Among other crimes, cattle raiding was a big problem in rural communities. The response was to form village defense groups that assumed the name Sungu Sungu. The leadership, elected at the village level, comprised male elders skilled in traditional medicine. It also included able-bodied male residents armed with poisonous arrows to pursue cattle raiders. Village members contributed to the Sungu Sungu fund to support the vigilantes. Despite the brutality, Sungu Sungu was credited with reducing crime in Tanzania. The model was framed in the context of the self-reliance model of *Ujamaa*, which is Tanzania's version of socialism. In the Tanzanian context, community policing tied with tradition and became deeply localized.[34]

Kenya has been experimenting with community policing as a crime-prevention tool since the 2000s. The concept, while laden with ambiguities of what it means, has become popular as a tool for crime control across multiple contexts. It assumes that the police and those policed would consult on security needs and possible solutions. In Kenya, community policing became entrenched in the policing framework during the Kibaki presidency (2002–13).[35]

The National Police Service, previously called the Kenya Police Force (KPF), is primarily responsible for the maintenance of law and order. It is the institution that has been running the community-policing model since 2003. At independence in 1963, the KPF was transformed from a colonial police force to a regime-supporting police force. During the Daniel Moi administration (1978–2002), the KPF became associated with a wide range of human rights violations, such as detention of opposition figures without trials and abductions. The police force was additionally plagued by institutional corruption and nepotism while crime soared during the 1990s.[36] Overall, the police lacked public trust. These problems were compounded by state failure and the structural adjustment programs introduced during the 1990s. The state lost effective control as it resorted to state-sponsored violence. In some cases, state security agents worked with vigilante groups without official uniforms to harass perceived enemies of the regime. Eventually, the situation degenerated into politically driven ethnic violence (e.g., at the Rift Valley in 1992) and electoral violence (e.g., Likoni, Mombasa, in 1997).[37]

It was in this context of weakened state capacity that a bandit economy thrived with a host of security threats, such as robberies and carjackings. At the same time, there was a rise in ethnic-based urban vigilante groups such as Mungiki and the Kamjeshi. These groups fought to control streets, especially *matatu* (public transportation vans) transportation routes, often resulting in fatalities. In many of these street fights, the police would stand by without intervening, especially in areas controlled by the political opposition. Before the 2002 elections, police interventions were mostly limited to regime-friendly interests.[38] These problems necessitated the introduction of policing reforms to ensure effective and efficient policing. One of the progressive steps that the new National Rainbow Coalition government initiated was community policing. Community policing was meant to create a bottom-up style of policing focused on gaining the consent of the public.[39] The structure works at the police station level and is supposed in practice to uphold the tenets of public participation in the selection of members to the forum. The community-policing guidelines released by the National Police Service indicate that the representation at the community level should include youth, women, religious leaders, and the business community. During their monthly meetings, the committee members deliberate on security matters, offering a platform for information sharing, problem diagnosis, and strategies to improve local security.

The effectiveness of community policing in Kenya and in Mombasa has remained mixed. Evaluating it is hampered largely by trust deficits, inadequate resource allocation, and transparency gaps on how representatives are chosen. Addressing these kinds of challenges is critical to enhancing this citizen-centered policing model.

APPLICATION OF COMMUNITY POLICING TO COUNTERING TERRORISM

A key question in this study is the applicability of community policing to counterterrorism. In many ways, community policing has proved to be a useful model to enhance security. However, for it to be successful, there needs to be community trust and participation. In the study area, security is a glocal problem because of the domestic, regional, and global aspects of the radicalization into terrorism. Community policing itself has become a glocalized phenomenon. Under Kenya's counterterrorism policies, terrorism is an elevated form of crime. The elevation of acts of terrorism to crimes dovetails with the Global War on Terror (GWOT) discourse and policies. In line with CVE, community policing has been applied as a tool for preventing both "regular crimes" and terrorism. However, the application of community policing to counterterrorism can be difficult. Too often, it can be undermined by perceptions of the overpolicing of minority groups or lack of fair treatment. This undermines trust with the community and therefore jeopardizes cooperation and partnership with the police. In the context of the GWOT post-9/11, associating Islam with violence presents deep challenges for community engagement.[40] In addition, the use of community policing as a counterterrorism tool in border areas has been critiqued because of the mixed messages in terms of seeing terrorism as a home-grown problem or the result of Islamists' transnational networks.[41] To overcome the negative factors that undermine community-policing engagement in countering terrorism, analysts have called for a shift from a War on Terror policing to one that is founded on a criminal justice model. However, doing so would require genuine partnership and consultation between the police and the community.[42]

Since the 1998 US embassy bombings, Kenya has launched a series of policy interventions to reduce violent extremism. Initially, the state assumed a counterterrorism approach (anchored on hard power). This entailed reactive and punitive approaches in policing terrorism. Key counterterrorism initiatives included strengthening existing institutions such as the National Intelligence Service, creating new security forces such as the National Counter-Terrorism Center, establishing the Anti-Terrorism Police Unit (ATPU), and enacting legislation to prosecute terrorism suspects.[43] Since 2016, there has been a shift toward a complementary approach of relying on soft power in countering terrorism. This has been embedded in the National Countering Violent Extremism Strategy. This strategy considers community and citizen engagement to be a long-term approach that will promote resilience against terrorism. To this end, communities and a range of nongovernmental actors are seen as critical community partners.[44] Despite these changes, community policing as a counterterrorism tool is facing challenges.

One key problem is that a section of the Kenyan Muslim communities had been viewed as presenting terror threats. There are claims of human rights violations, such as arbitrary arrests, detentions, forced disappearances, and extraordinary renditions. All of these have created a distance between Muslim communities and the police.[45] Notably, the specialized ATPU has often been accused of human rights violations. Swoops and raids have been targeted at Muslim communities, especially after major terrorist attacks, such as the Westgate attack in September 2013. In April 2014, the government executed a security operation dubbed Operation Usalama Watch (*Usalama* means "safety" in Kiswahili) in Somali-dominated areas of Nairobi (i.e., Eastleigh and South C). Terrorism suspects, including Kenyan Somalis, were detained at the Kasarani Stadium, thereby reinforcing a narrative of state persecution of Kenyan Somalis. The linking of Kenyan Somali individuals with terrorism threats in this instance showed continuity with how they were viewed as suspects during the Shifta war (1963–67). Too often, they are framed as Al-Shabaab members. Operation Usalama Watch was actually plagued by corruption and improper detentions and harassment, which further drove a wedge between Kenyan Somalis and the Kenyan police.[46] Besides impacting negatively state-society relations, the scapegoating of ethnic Somalis in Kenya fed into the recruitment narratives of Al-Shabaab. Somali people's experiences with Usalama Watch were used to recruit for Al-Shabaab.[47] In other contexts, such as that of the UK, the PREVENT program, a counterterrorism approach of the UK government, has been similarly critiqued on the account that it has stereotyped Muslims as "suspect communities." In other words, Muslims perceive the range of counterterrorism initiatives, such as stop and search, house arrests, and so on, as largely targeted at their identity by uncritically linking them to terrorism threats.[48]

One of the key problems for community policing in CVE is apparent connection between the police and the US War on Terror programs. According to Alice Hills, USAID support for Kenyan police in the war on terrorism has produced unintended consequences. While it empowers the police force with capacity in counterterrorism, the police have been accused of violating Kenyan laws in marking arbitrary arrests and detention.[49] Under the GWOT, counterterrorism practices tend to use extralegal measures. In the study area of Likoni Sub-County in Mombasa, participants noted the ways in which community policing was applied in countering terrorism, notably through (1) information sharing, (2) collective problem solving, and (3) early warning mechanisms.

Information Sharing

One of the inputs of community policing in countering terrorism was information sharing, which was useful in preempting youth recruitment and radicalization. Study participants in Likoni observed that they regularly engaged in information sharing during monthly community-policing meetings. This perspective was gleaned from individual interviews and focus group discussions that included residents, security agencies, and local administrators. A local administrator in Mombasa inferred that interventions such as one at Nyumba Kumi (a ten-household security structure), which is part of the community-policing system, had information-sharing mandates in matters relevant to counterterrorism. As he observed, "There are several measures that we have put in place to deal with the threats of countering youth radicalization. One is engagement with the community through the Nyumba Kumi initiative and which is mainly about information sharing."[50] Participants observed that monthly community-policing meetings held in police stations often turned into avenues for counterterrorism crime mapping. Information sharing was not, however, limited to monthly meetings as members of community policing had access to senior police officials in addition to designated liaison officers at the police station level. Members of community policing would tap into community structures such as neighborhood watches that existed outside of the community-policing system to gather credible intelligence that they would share with the police. However, community-policing meetings that drew on a select number of community representatives also engaged with other closely related forms of crime, such as drug abuse. In terms of countering terrorism threats, information revolved around investigating potential terrorism suspects, youth disappearances, indoctrination suspects, and potential hideouts.

One interesting point is that community policing created an avenue for sharing information about potential terrorism suspects that needed further investigation, most often focusing on new entrants and strangers in the community. Community members would provide a description and location of potential suspects, while the police investigated the leads. Information on alleged youth disappearances was also investigated. It was noted that in 2016 and 2017 youths from Likoni had disappeared, with some of them communicating months later that they had joined Al-Shabaab or the Islamic State. These youths were suspected of moving to Somalia and Syria with the help of glocalized radicalization networks. Radicalization often connects to the GWOT discourses and perceived injustices such as discrimination in Kenya and the occupation of Muslim lands by Western powers. Having information on the so-called foreign travelers and returnees helps security agencies, particularly at border points, in conducting enhanced surveillance.[51]

Field accounts indicated that information shared in community-policing structures is used to dismantle indoctrination and recruitment networks at the community level. Community leads help the police apprehend potential suspects and raid training grounds. In Likoni, Salafis are prime suspects of indoctrination. Also, information is used to seek allies and do community sensitization. As one participant noted, "We are engaged in public sensitization on the threats of terrorism and how the public can take preventative measures, including sharing information on terror threats and suspects. Information sharing especially from the public is yet to be fully actualized."[52]

However, cooperation levels with the police depends on the trust level. Study participants were clear that cooperation was not always forthcoming. While on certain occasions when information sharing had worked, there existed several hurdles in the process. The youths, for instance, hardly trusted the police. As for the police, in their view the youths were broadly condemned as suspects who needed to be disciplined by the state. As one youth participant noted, "The youth in this area are associated with several crimes ranging from terrorism to robbery.... This has resulted in increased police presence and raids that unfairly target the youths as a reactive measure. This has in the meanwhile resulted in poor community relations."[53] Youths are often stopped by the police in their neighborhoods, which adds to the securitization and distrust of the police among the youths and the community at large.

Security officials reinforce a threat narrative that links the youths to terrorism threats on the coast of Kenya. As one police officer argued, "There is also the noncommitment by parents or guardians to give information to relevant government agencies for instance when their sons or daughters have disappeared to join terrorist organizations or have changed their mannerisms."[54] Security officers tend to blame guardians and parents for not taking full citizenship responsibilities by reporting their children to the police. However, such cooperation is difficult to get given the low trust levels between the community and the police. As one participant observed, "Some have good perceptions of police in the area but there are also those with negative perceptions of the police. Those who harbor negative perceptions could be those perhaps that consider the government including the police to be harassing them."[55] In addition to police harassment, the police are still considered to be corrupt and plagued with a culture of bribery. Even more problematic, trust levels had been complicated by community claims of youth disappearances and extrajudicial killings at the hands of the ATPU.[56] Some of the notorious ATPU officers were known by name and regularly mentioned in the study area. The residents often expressed displeasure at the heavy-handedness of the police in their communities in the name of counterterrorism.

Confidentiality is a key issue on whether community members would use the structures of community policing to share information on terrorism. Confidentiality had been breached several times and thus had had an impact on information sharing, which is critical for countering terrorism. As a local administrator mentioned, "Community policing and Nyumba Kumi are working but not at optimal levels with respect to countering violent extremism. The challenges lie with low levels of trust between the police and the community.... This distrust is mainly caused by the breach of confidentiality when crime information shared in confidence is leaked."[57] Similarly, a member of community policing in Likoni re-emphasized the negative repercussions brought about by confidentiality gaps. As a community member noted, "While information flow is important for community policing to work, we need to be given surety of our own safety."[58]

Overall, security officials are cognizant that their individual and collective actions contribute to mistrust at the community level. As such, they try to engage in confidence-building measures such as dialogue forums aimed at bridging the gaps between the public and the police. As a security official stated, "We are intent on improving community-police interactions through public *barazas* [public meeting place]. We are embracing this community-based model of policing by partnering with the community."[59] However, some community members remain apprehensive about cooperating with the police.

Collective Problem Solving and Early Warning Responses

Community policing is also seen as a way to engage in collective problem solving and create early warning responses. Collective problem solving involves members of the community-policing groups sharing with the police strategies and approaches they thought might preempt radicalization and related crimes. Study participants understood crime in both the local sense of regular crimes and in the regional and international terrorism frames. As such, solutions had both local and global dimensions. Community members could suggest preventative strategies to the police and other relevant government agencies in community-policing meetings. These included mapping out radicalization trends and related threats in their localities. Suggestions tended to include both practical and operational strategies for countering radicalization. Some of the practical interventions included awareness raising on active and responsible parenting. At the operational level, the places to target and individuals to watch out for would be raised in such meetings. As already noted, community policing requires genuine consultations and partnerships, which were often present in meetings.

Early warning response was also an important component of community policing in the study area. This mechanism was tied to flows of regular information between the community, the police, and local administrators in Mombasa County. Early warning response works through information flow from the members of the public to the security agencies. Some of the critical information used to determine the need for early response includes information gleaned from text messages, WhatsApp messages, phone calls, and visits to security facilities. A key element is quick responses to the information shared. The main priority is detecting individuals at risk of radicalization and understanding the radicalization process, especially at the neighborhood level. Risk factors and mitigation plans to counter radicalization are often discussed, and these can guide police response to threats. It would be critical for community-policing structures to receive feedback on the efficacy of the early warning mechanisms.

THE GLOCAL CHALLENGES TO APPLYING COMMUNITY POLICING IN COUNTERTERRORISM

Even though community policing has a lot of benefits, there are challenges in its application to counterterrorism. Part of the challenges relates to the fusion of local and global security issues through the terrorism frame. Notably, these challenges include the labeling of suspect communities, excessive securitization of terrorism threats, and fear of reprisal.

Labeling of Suspect Communities

The field findings in Likoni indicate that the treatment of Muslims as suspects had been hampering the cooperation of Muslims in the countering-radicalization domains. This created tensions between the community and the police. In Likoni, there was the overarching feeling of blanket condemnation of the Muslim community as responsible for terror threats. This perception had resulted from governmental discourses that framed radicalization as a Muslim problem. The effect of this securitization was the targeting of the Muslim identity in counterterrorism operations. As a participant notes, "When you are a Muslim, you are treated as a terrorist. . . . We need to change this perspective. . . . A Christian can also be radicalized and become a terrorist."[60]

Post-9/11 global security discourses tend to link Islam and Muslims with terrorist violence. This targeting reinforces government's perspective that Muslims are responsible for terrorism. In situating these threats, governments have sought to securitize Muslim identities. Securitization theory considers speech acts of government officials in framing a problem as existential threat to the state.[61] In the context of Western states and where comparisons can be drawn with Kenya, securitization theory enables a discourse of in(security) where governmental actions can be justified, even when they violate the rights of people. In the United Kingdom, which has been applying community policing since the 7/7 bombings in 2005, the model has been criticized for missing critical elements in the rise of Islamist terrorism and excessive focus on Muslim spaces, such as mosques. Critiques note that other spaces, such as prisons, internet cafés, and university campuses, are actually used for terrorist recruitment. In addition, there have been similar critiques of Islamophobic policing, which affects negatively community trust with security agencies. This has often created a backlash with the Muslim community, further alienating the community.[62]

Securitization of Youths

Securitization of youths by security agencies negatively affects cooperation. In Likoni, the youths often state that they would hardly trust police officers given the negative perceptions that were held of them by the police. Notably, the police often accused youths of crimes ranging from drug abuse, criminal gang activities, and joining terrorist organizations. While a section of the youths argued that some of the negative perceptions could be true, they argued against the blanket condemnation of youths as terror suspects.[63] Participants expressed that part of their minimized cooperation with the police had to do with the negative experiences they had had, including what they considered to be arbitrary arrests. Previous research in Kwale, Kenya, has documented similar youth experiences, including mass roundups, which further drive alienation and resentment toward law enforcement agents.[64]

The framing of the youths as a security threat breeds resentment to the police, which suffers from credibility issues related to corruption. As a security official stated:

> The perception of the police is largely negative. There is a perception already out there that the police are corrupt.... It is a perception out there but there are also real scenarios where police are participating in bribe-taking.

> Corruption, and especially to facilitate drug trafficking, has been rampant in the Coast region. Police are engaging in corruption to sort out their personal financial needs. The police have in certain instances also taken bribes to release suspects in their custody. . . . Drugs are being dumped here in Mombasa. . . . There are drug networks that have incorporated the police too. Given all these experiences, a section of the public would lose trust with the police and therefore hamper information sharing.[65]

Another police officer acknowledged the problems, arguing that the "police need to change their . . . approach to the public. We are trained to treat members of the public with dignity. We are servants, but when we come here, we change. Police are part of the community. . . . Trust and confidence are important in police work; good interaction yields actionable information and crime rates go down."[66]

Fear of Reprisal from Terrorist Networks

A major challenge to the use of community policy to counter terrorism is the fear of reprisal from terrorist networks. As one participant observed: "The community knows the already radical individuals, but they shy away from disclosing to authorities for fear of reprisals. If the radical groups were to discover that one has reported to the authorities, then one will be killed. This fear is impacting negatively on the information flow necessary for fighting terror."[67] In 2016, in the locality of Bongwe, on Kenya's south coast, three members of Nyumba Kumi were killed in an attack that was linked to Al-Shabaab. They were allegedly executed on the suspected claims of gathering intelligence against the group. There have also been related claims that some police officers are sympathizers of Al-Shabaab.[68]

From field accounts, a barrier to the effectiveness of community policing in preventing terrorism lies in confidentiality breaches, which significantly increase risks. Security officials are cognizant that confidentiality breaches have been hampering effective community policing. In one of the focus group discussions, a participant stated that "there is a need for the police to maintain confidentiality with crime information given by residents. If the source is leaked, and this has happened in several instances, then the community would be reluctant to share crime information with the police."[69]

STUDY IMPLICATIONS

Fieldwork findings in Likoni, Mombasa, have reinforced the value of trust in community policing. In many ways, the Kenyan authorities have uncritically blamed Kenya's terrorism problem on its minority Muslim population. The coastal Muslim population was securitized by the Moi administration as supporters of violent fundamentalism, especially after the 1998 US embassy bombings. As terror threats continued during the Kibaki administration (2002–13), the securitization of the Muslim identity increased through the creation of a range of counterterrorism organs. These included the creation of a specialized counterterrorism police force, the Kenya ATPU. Extraordinary renditions of terror suspects also happened during the Kibaki regime. International cooperation and domestic security interventions have been framed through the GWOT.[70] Kenyan police have generally been accused of being unaccountable in policing by security commentators and human rights actors. They observe that additional capacity such as counterterrorism skills would lead to unwanted consequences such as intimidation, corruption, and arbitrary arrests when it comes to information extraction.[71]

In revisiting the concept of glocalized security, this chapter has engaged with how the local and the global intersect in terms of security-threat conceptualization, but also the related responses. The chapter has demonstrated how an internationalized policing model, community policing, has been adapted from a general crime-control situation to a counterterrorism context, fusing it into the glocalized security mode of the War on Terror. Through glocalization, domestic threats have found resonance with the GWOT. In the process, community policing has been rendered very challenging both as an instrument of regular crime prevention and as a counterterrorism measure, largely because of the undermining of trust.

One of the key community-policing lessons from Likoni is the value of trust between the police and the community. The police would need to be transparent and do policing democratically by adhering to the rule of law. If the police gain the trust and legitimacy of the public, it will be easy for the citizens to engage with them constructively. In the Kenyan context, the nature of democratic policing is a work in progress given past repressive tendencies on the part of the police. The police in Kenya have been regularly accused of arbitrary arrests, mass roundups, and harassment, particularly in the counterterrorism domain.[72] All these undermine community policing and make the link between domestic issues and jihadi terrorism difficult to untangle in Kenya's security challenges. The glocalized security frame provides a useful lens through which to understand and address this challenge.

NOTES

1. Mahmood Mamdani, *Good Muslim, Bad Muslim: America, the Cold War and the Roots of Terror* (Kampala: Fountain Publishers, 2004).

2. Ahmed Umar, "Jihad Discourse and Its Reception among Sermon Listeners in Northern Nigeria," *African Conflict & Peacebuilding Review* 12.1 (2022): 1–26; Abu Bakarr Bah, "Racial Profiling and the War on Terror: Changing Trends and Perspectives," *Ethnic Studies Review* 29.1 (2006): 76–100.

3. Victor Roudometof, "Theorizing Glocalization: Three Interpretations," *European Journal of Social Theory* 19.3 (2016): 391–408.

4. Samuel Huntington, "The Clash of Civilizations?," *Foreign Affairs* 72.3 (1993): 22–49.

5. Süveyda Karakaya, "Religion and Conflict: Explaining the Puzzling Case of 'Islamic Violence,'" *International Interactions* 41.3 (2015): 509–538.

6. Edward Mogire and Kennedy Mkutu, "Counter-terrorism in Kenya," *Journal of Contemporary African Studies* 29.2 (2011): 473–491.

7. Oscar Mwangi, "The Dilemma of Kenya's New Counterterrorism and Asymmetric Warfare," *Peace Review* 29.3 (2017): 307–314.

8. John Githigaro, "An Assessment of Kenya's Counter-terrorism Responses in the Horn of Africa, Peacebuilding," in *Sub-Saharan Africa: African Perspectives*, ed. Samuel Kale Ewusi (Addis Ababa: University for Peace Africa Programme [UPEACE], 2015).

9. Abu Bakarr Bah, "Civil Non–State Actors in Peacekeeping and Peacebuilding in West Africa," *Journal of International Peacekeeping* 17.3–4 (2013): 313–336.

10. Shadon Harris-Hogan, Kate Barrelle, and Andrew Zammit, "What Is Countering Violent Extremism? Exploring CVE Policy and Practice in Australia," *Behavioral Sciences of Terrorism and Political Aggression* 8.1 (2016): 6–24.

11. Mogire and Mkutu, "Counter-terrorism in Kenya."

12. Samuel Marfo, Halidu Musah, and Arthur Dominic, "Beyond Classical Peace Paradigm: A Theoretical Argument for a 'Glocalized Peace and Security,'" *African Journal of Political Science and International Relations* 10.4 (2016): 47–55.

13. Bah, "Civil Non–State Actors in Peacekeeping."

14. Mary Kaldor, "In Defence of New Wars," *Stability: International Journal of Security and Development* 2.1 (2013): 2165–2627.

15. Jeremy Prestholdt, "Kenya, the United States, and Counterterrorism," *Africa Today* 57.4 (2011): 3–27.

16. Paul Higate and Mats Utas (eds.), *Private Security in Africa: From the Global Assemblage to the Everyday* (London: Zed Books, 2017).

17. Harris-Hogan et al., "What Is Countering Violent Extremism?"

18. Human Security Collective, "Community-Based Preventive and Remedial Measures to Prevent Violent Extremism: A Human Security Approach to Help Transform Conflicts, Improve Social Cohesion and Improve Local Security," *International Annals of Criminology* 56 (2018): 198–219.

19. Hassan Ndzovu, "Kenya's Jihadi Clerics: Formulation of a 'Liberation Theology' and the Challenge to Secular Power," *Journal of Muslim Minority Affairs* 38.3 (2018): 360–371; Andrew LeSage, "The Rising Terrorist Threat in Tanzania: Domestic Islamist Militancy and Regional Threats," *Strategic Forum* 288 (2014): 1–16.

20. Arye Oded, "Islamic Extremism in Kenya: The Rise and Fall of Sheikh Khalid Balala," *Journal of Religion in Africa* 26.4 (1996): 406–415.

21. Oded, "Islamic Extremism in Kenya."

22. Paul Goldsmith, *The Mombasa Republican Council Conflict Assessment: Threats and Opportunities for Engagement* (Nairobi: USAID, ACT, 2011).

23. Kennedy Mkutu, Martin Marani, and Mutuma Ruteere, *Securing the Counties: Options for Security after Devolution* (Nairobi: Center for Human Rights and Policy Studies, 2014).

24. Eric Otenyo, "New Terrorism: Toward an Explanation of Cases in Kenya," *African Security Review* 13.3 (2004): 75–84.

25. Otenyo.

26. Mogire and Mkutu, "Counter-terrorism in Kenya"; Juliet Kamau, "Is Counter-terrorism Counterproductive? A Case Study of Kenya's Response to Terrorism, 1998–2020," *South African Journal of International Affairs* 28.2 (2021): 203–231.

27. Stig Hansen, *Al-Shabaab in Somalia: The History and Ideology of a Militant Islamist Group* (London: C. Hurst, 2016).

28. International Crisis Group, *The Kenyan Military Intervention in Somalia: Africa Report 184* (Nairobi/Brussels: International Crisis Group, 2012).

29. Olivier Roy, *What Is the Driving Force behind Jihadist Terrorism? A Scientific Perspective on the Causes/Circumstances of Joining the Scene*, Speech at BKA Autumn Conference, November 18–19, 2015.

30. Charlotte Cross, "Community Policing and the Politics of Local Development in Tanzania," *Journal of Modern African Studies* 52.4 (2014): 517–540.

31. Peter Boettke, Jayme Lemke, and Liya Palagashvili, "Re-evaluating Community Policing in a Polycentric System," *Journal of Institutional Economics* 12.2 (2016): 305–325.

32. Boettke.

33. Cross, "Community Policing."

34. Cross.

35. Kenneth Omeje and John Githigaro, "The Challenges of State Policing in Kenya," *The Peace and Conflict Review* 7.1 (2012): 64–87.

36. Omeje and Githigaro.

37. Musambayi Katumanga, "A City under Siege: Banditry and Modes of Accumulation in Nairobi, 1991–2004," *Review of African Political Economy* 106 (2005): 505–520.

38. Katumanga.

39. Omeje and Githigaro, "The Challenges of State Policing in Kenya."

40. Kevin Dunn et al., "Can You Use Community Policing for Counter-terrorism? Evidence from NSW, Australia," *Police Practice and Research* 17.3 (2016): 196–211.

41. Jytte Klausen, "British Counter-terrorism After 7/7: Adapting Community Policing to the Fight against Domestic Terrorism," *Journal of Ethnic and Migration Studies* 35.3 (2009): 403–420.

42. Dunn et al., "Can You Use Community Policing for Counter-terrorism?"

43. Mogire and Mkutu, "Counter-terrorism in Kenya"; Oscar Mwangi, "The 'Somalinisation' of Terrorism and Counterterrorism in Kenya: The Case of Refoulement," *Critical Studies on Terrorism* 12.2 (2019): 298–316; Kamau, "Is Counter-terrorism Counterproductive?"

44. Government of Kenya, *National Strategy to Counter Violent Extremism* (Nairobi: Government of Kenya, 2016).

45. Mogire and Mkutu, "Counter-terrorism in Kenya"; Omeje and Githigaro, "The Challenges of State Policing in Kenya"; Kennedy Mkutu and Vincent Opondo, "The Complexity of Radicalization and Recruitment in Kwale, Kenya," *Terrorism and Political Violence* (2019), https://doi.org/10.1080/09546553.2018.1520700.

46. Sophia Balakian, "'Money Is Your Government': Refugees, Mobility, and Unstable Documents in Kenya's Operation Usalama Watch," *African Studies Review* 59.2 (2016): 87–111.

47. Paul Williams, "After Westgate: Opportunities and Challenges in the War against Al-Shabaab," *International Affairs* 90.4 (2014): 907–923.

48. Imran Awan, "'I Am a Muslim Not an Extremist': How the Prevent Strategy Has Constructed a 'Suspect' Community," *Politics & Policy* 40.6 (2012): 1158–1185.

49. Alice Hills, "Trojan Horses? USAID, Counter-terrorism, and Africa's Police," *Third World Quarterly* 27.4 (2006): 629–643.

50. Interview with local administrator, Mombasa, November 24, 2016.

51. Mercy Juma and John Githigaro, "Communities' Perceptions of Reintegration of Al-Shabaab Returnees in Mombasa and Kwale Counties, Kenya," *Journal for Deradicalization* 1.26 (2021): 71–109.

52. Interview with a male police officer, Mombasa, November 24, 2016.

53. Participant in a youth-only focus group discussion, Likoni, Mombasa, June 7, 2017.

54. Interview with a male police officer, Mombasa, November 24, 2016.

55. Interview with a police officer, Mombasa, November 24, 2016.

56. Mkutu and Opondo, "The Complexity of Radicalization."

57. Interview with a local administrator, Mombasa, June 7, 2017.

58. Interview with a member of community policing, Likoni, April 19, 2022.

59. Interview with a male security official, Mombasa, November 24, 2016.

60. Youth participant in a focus group discussion, Likoni, April 19, 2022.

61. Barry Buzan and Ole Wæver, "Macrosecuritisation and Security Constellations: Reconsidering Scale in Securitisation Theory," *Review of International Studies* 35.2 (2009): 253–276.

62. Klausen, "British Counter-terrorism After 7/7."
63. A common theme emphasized with a youth focus group discussion in Likoni, April 19, 2022.
64. Mkutu and Opondo, "The Complexity of Radicalization."
65. Interview with a senior security official, Likoni, Mombasa, November 24, 2016.
66. Interview with senior security official, male, Mombasa, September 10, 2021.
67. Interview with a security official, Likoni, November 24, 2016.
68. Mkutu and Opondo, "The Complexity of Radicalization."
69. Male participant in a focus group discussion, Likoni, Mombasa, June 7, 2017.
70. Prestholdt, "Kenya, the United States, and Counterterrorism"; Mogire and Mkutu, "Counter-terrorism in Kenya."
71. Hills, "Trojan Horses?"
72. Mkutu and Opondo, "The Complexity of Radicalization"; Omeje and Githigaro, "The Challenges of State Policing in Kenya."

BIBLIOGRAPHY

Anderson, David, and Jacob McKnight. "Kenya at War: Al-Shabaab and Its Enemies in Eastern Africa." *African Affairs* 111.454 (2014): 1–27.

Awan, Imran. "'I Am a Muslim Not an Extremist': How the Prevent Strategy Has Constructed a 'Suspect' Community." *Politics & Policy* 40.6 (2012): 1158–1185.

Bah, Abu Bakarr, "Racial Profiling and the War on Terror: Changing Trends and Perspectives." *Ethnic Studies Review* 29.1 (2006): 76–100.

———. "Civil Non–state Actors in Peacekeeping and Peacebuilding in West Africa." *Journal of International Peacekeeping* 17.3–4 (2013): 313–336.

Balakian, Sophia. "'Money Is Your Government': Refugees, Mobility, and Unstable Documents in Kenya's Operation Usalama Watch." *African Studies Review* 59.2 (2016): 87–111.

Boettke, Peter, Jayme Lemke, and Liya Palagashvili. "Re-evaluating Community Policing in a Polycentric System." *Journal of Institutional Economics* 12.2 (2016): 305–325.

Buzan, Barry, and Ole Wæver. "Macrosecuritisation and Security Constellations: Reconsidering Scale in Securitisation Theory." *Review of International Studies* 35.2 (2009): 253–276.

Cross, Charlotte. "Community Policing and the Politics of Local Development in Tanzania." *Journal of Modern African Studies* 52.4 (2014): 517–540.

Dunn, Kevin, et al. "Can You Use Community Policing for Counter-terrorism? Evidence from NSW, Australia." *Police Practice and Research* 17.3 (2016): 196–211.

Githigaro, John. "An Assessment of Kenya's Counter-terrorism Responses in the Horn of Africa." In *Peacebuilding in Sub-Saharan Africa: African Perspectives*, ed. Samuel Kale Ewusi, 161–193. Addis Ababa: University for Peace Africa Programme (UPEACE), 2015.

Goldsmith, Paul. *The Mombasa Republican Council Conflict Assessment: Threats and Opportunities for Engagement.* Nairobi: USAID, ACT, 2011.

Government of Kenya. *National Strategy to Counter Violent Extremism.* Nairobi: Government of Kenya, 2016.

Hansen, Stig. *Al-Shabaab in Somalia: The History and Ideology of a Militant Islamist Group.* London: C. Hurst, 2016.

Harris-Hogan, Shadon, Kate Barrelle, and Andrew Zammit. "What Is Countering Violent Extremism? Exploring CVE Policy and Practice in Australia." *Behavioral Sciences of Terrorism and Political Aggression* 8.1 (2016): 6–24.

Higate, Paul, and Utas, Mats (eds.). *Private Security in Africa: From the Global Assemblage to the Everyday.* London: Zed Books, 2017.

Hills, Alice. "Trojan Horses? USAID, Counter-terrorism, and Africa's Police." *Third World Quarterly* 27.4 (2006): 629–643.

Human Security Collective. "Community-Based Preventive and Remedial Measures to Prevent Violent Extremism: A Human Security Approach to Help Transform Conflicts, Improve Social Cohesion and Improve Local Security." *International Annals of Criminology* 56 (2018): 198–219.

Huntington, Samuel. "The Clash of Civilizations?" *Foreign Affairs* 72.3 (1993): 22–49.

International Crisis Group. *The Kenyan Military Intervention in Somalia: Africa Report 184.* Nairobi/Brussels: International Crisis Group, 2012.

Juma, Mercy, and John Githigaro. "Communities' Perceptions of Reintegration of Al-Shabaab Returnees in Mombasa and Kwale Counties, Kenya." *Journal for Deradicalization* 1.26 (2021): 71–109.

Kaldor, Mary. "In Defence of New Wars." *Stability: International Journal of Security and Development* 2.1 (2013): 2165–2627.

Kamau, Juliet. "Is Counter-terrorism Counterproductive? A Case Study of Kenya's Response to Terrorism, 1998–2020." *South African Journal of International Affairs* 28.2 (2021): 203–231.

Karakaya, Süveyda. "Religion and Conflict: Explaining the Puzzling Case of 'Islamic Violence.'" *International Interactions* 41.3 (2015): 509–538.

Katumanga, Musambayi. "A City under Siege: Banditry and Modes of Accumulation in Nairobi, 1991–2004." *Review of African Political Economy* 106 (2005): 505–520.

Klausen, Jytte. "British Counter-terrorism after 7/7: Adapting Community Policing to the Fight against Domestic Terrorism." *Journal of Ethnic and Migration Studies* 35.3 (2009): 403–420.

LeSage, Andrew. "The Rising Terrorist Threat in Tanzania: Domestic Islamist Militancy and Regional Threats." *Strategic Forum* 288 (2014): 1–16.

Mamdani, Mahmood. *Good Muslim, Bad Muslim: America, the Cold War and the Roots of Terror.* Kampala: Fountain Publishers, 2004.

Marfo, Samuel, Halidu Musah, and Arthur Dominic. "Beyond Classical Peace Paradigm: A Theoretical Argument for a 'Glocalized Peace and Security.'" *African Journal of Political Science and International Relations* 10.4 (2016): 47–55.

Mkutu, Kennedy, and Vincent Opondo. "The Complexity of Radicalization and Recruitment in Kwale, Kenya." *Terrorism and Political Violence* (2019). https://doi.org/10.1080/09546553.2018.1520700.

Mkutu, Kennedy, Martin Marani, and Mutuma Ruteere. *Securing the Counties: Options for Security after Devolution.* Nairobi: Center for Human Rights and Policy Studies, 2014.

Mogire, Edward, and Kennedy Mkutu. "Counter-terrorism in Kenya." *Journal of Contemporary African Studies* 29.2 (2011): 473–491.

Mwangi, Oscar. "The Dilemma of Kenya's New Counterterrorism and Asymmetric Warfare." *Peace Review* 29.3 (2017): 307–314.

———. "The 'Somalinisation' of Terrorism and Counterterrorism in Kenya: The Case of Refoulement." *Critical Studies on Terrorism* 12.2 (2019): 298–316.

Ndzovu, Hassan. "Kenya's Jihadi Clerics: Formulation of a 'Liberation Theology' and the Challenge to Secular Power." *Journal of Muslim Minority Affairs* 38.3 (2018): 360–371.

Oded, Arye. "Islamic Extremism in Kenya: The Rise and Fall of Sheikh Khalid Balala." *Journal of Religion in Africa* 26.4 (1996): 406–415.

Omeje, Kenneth, and John Githigaro. "The Challenges of State Policing in Kenya." *The Peace and Conflict Review* 7.1 (2012): 64–87.

Otenyo, Eric. "New Terrorism: Toward an Explanation of Cases in Kenya." *African Security Review* 13.3 (2004): 75–84.

Prestholdt, Jeremy. "Kenya, the United States, and Counterterrorism." *Africa Today* 57.4 (2011): 3–27.

Roudometof, Victor. "Theorizing Glocalization: Three Interpretations." *European Journal of Social Theory* 19.3 (2016): 391–408.

Roy, Olivier. "What Is the Driving Force behind Jihadist Terrorism? A Scientific Perspective on the Causes/Circumstances of Joining the Scene." Speech at BKA Autumn Conference, November 18–19, 2015.

Ruteere, Mutuma, and Marie Pommerolle. "Democratizing Security or Decentralizing Repression? The Ambiguities of Community Policing in Kenya." *African Affairs* 102 (2003): 587–604.

Umar, Ahmed. "Jihad Discourse and Its Reception among Sermon Listeners in Northern Nigeria." *African Conflict & Peacebuilding Review* 12.1 (2022): 1–26.

Williams, Paul. "After Westgate: Opportunities and Challenges in the War against Al-Shabaab." *International Affairs* 90.4 (2014): 907–923.

Chapter 4

Militarized Response to Domestic, Regional, and International Security Issues in Nigeria and Uganda

MICHAEL NWANKPA

The chapter interrogates the interplay between domestic and international elements that drive the militarized response of the Nigerian and Ugandan states to perceived and real security threats in the past two decades, particularly since the September 11, 2001 (hereafter 9/11), al-Qaeda attacks on the United States homeland. For more than two decades, but significantly since 9/11, African countries, including Nigeria and Uganda, have been battling the surge of terrorism, notably with terrorist groups such as Boko Haram and the Islamic State in West Africa Province in Nigeria and the Lord Resistance Army and the Allied Democratic Forces in Uganda, in addition to being engaged in other types of conflicts. With a shared history as former British colonies, both countries continue to face interethnic conflicts. Interethnic conflicts involve struggle for access to and control of resources and power among the plethora of ethnic groups within each country. Nigeria and Uganda also present natural resource–related conflicts, including pastoral conflict between herder and nonherder communities in the northern parts of each country. Interestingly, the conflicts in each country have produced wider economic, political, and security-related ramifications that extend beyond their territories. This has given rise to national, regional, and international concerns and responses. The governments of Nigeria and Uganda have adopted several responses, including negotiation, dialogue, and the use of force. A multifaceted response that recognizes the complexity of the security situation is undoubtedly the right approach. Yet the militarized response remains predominant in both cases. This chapter examines the impact of the Global War on Terror (GWOT) on the militarized approach adopted by the governments of Nigeria and Uganda. It assesses the consequences of the militarized responses on national, regional, and international security and, more importantly, considers whether the militarized reaction is (1) an effort to maintain the status quo or (2) a calculated attempt to deflect from good governance responsibilities, which is a more viable response for achieving a lasting solution. As such, the chapter addresses two critical questions. First, how does the GWOT influence the militarized approach by the Nigerian and Ugandan governments? Second, what are the consequences of the militarized responses to national, regional, and international security?

The chapter starts with a discussion of the globalized security landscapes. Next, it discusses the security situation (threats) in Nigeria and Uganda particularly in the past two decades. This is followed by an assessment of the GWOT and its influence on the militarized responses of the Nigerian and Ugandan governments and the security impacts. The issue is whether the militarized approach has reduced or exacerbated the security problems. The study draws upon secondary and primary data. The secondary data includes key literature and other relevant documents obtained from credible online and offline databases, including government websites. The primary data consists of semi-structured face-to-face interviews and one virtual interview conducted with key experts between 2013 and 2021, particularly relating to the Nigerian case study. Evidence from three key experts was particularly useful. I interviewed Baba Ahmed, a permanent secretary of the federal government of Nigeria, former gubernatorial candidate for Kaduna state, and former member of the 2013 Presidential Committee on Peaceful Resolution of Security Challenges in the North in 2014 in Kaduna state. In 2016, I interviewed Miliki, a human rights activist and national coordinator of the Partnership against Violent Extremism in Kogi state. In 2021, I conducted a virtual interview with retired Nigerian naval general Commodore Olawunmi. A face-to-face interview was practically impossible because of COVID-19-related travel restrictions.

THE GLOBALIZED SECURITY LANDSCAPE

The 9/11 terrorist attacks changed the topography of war and international security. The aftermath of the 9/11 terrorist attacks on the US homeland birthed a deep collective response to security signaled by the GWOT. Within the framework of the GWOT, the boundary between the local and global, and that between the internal and the external, became blurred.[1] Local conflicts became internationalized, and responses to dissents and oppositions became securitized. Indeed, 9/11 contributed hugely to the dynamic shift in contemporary war and the globalized response to it. However, the change really began in the decade before (1990–2000), when the almost half-century Cold War ended. Since the end of the Cold War, there have been some efforts to redefine the concept of war and conflict. Some scholars, like Mary Kaldor, contend that the end of the Cold War ushered in a new paradigm of war.[2] The new war is defined by low-intensity conflicts: internal or civil war. Here, Clausewitz's framework for explaining war is limited.[3] Unlike the "old wars" in which battles were fought and decided on the battlefield between standard armies, the new wars avoid battles and show different manifestations that are less conventional. These include old categorizations such as "wars between or among states [and new classifications such as] wars between a state and non-state forces outside the state, wars within states, and wars between or among non-state actors taking place outside of states."[4]

Interestingly, while the domestic space became the new theater of conflicts in the post–Cold War era, the international system remained intricately interwoven with local conflicts, shaping their course and trajectory.[5] In the new security landscape, states in the Global South are portrayed as threats to international peace and security because they lend themselves to exploitation by transnational terrorist and criminal networks that capitalize on their weaknesses, impoverishments, and disorder.[6] The entangling of international security with local conflicts lends itself to globalized security. Unlike the Cold War era, which was marked by "hard" security (such as nuclear weapons and balances of power between two major superpowers), post–Cold War security became characterized by soft security—terrorism, ethnic conflicts, and transnational crime.[7] More so, the consequences of the new wars, including forced mass displacement and refugees, reverberate outside the conflict area, threatening international peace and security. Such conflicts are thus seen to produce transnational security risks, which have resulted in collective security agreements at the global and regional levels between countries in the form of bilateral and/or multilateral partnerships. Collective responses have obscured the boundary between local and global security as well as upended traditional security roles of the police and the military, with the latter increasingly performing internal security duties that are ordinarily performed by the police.[8] Another notable change in the architecture of conventional security is the expansion of the "security governance" noted by the emergence and proliferation of non–state actors, including nongovernmental organizations, private militias, and security companies.[9]

This new security landscape requires a conceptual fusing of the global and the local in what has been dubbed "glocalization."[10] According to Robertson, the concept of glocalization offers itself as a more useful tool than globalization for disentangling the local and international. Globalization as a conceptual framework is considered limited in the way it attempts to homogenize and conflate global and local issues.[11] The integration and homogenization of cultures that globalization allows, although commendable at the superficial level, are most likely dangerous when we probe deeper into the predominant culture. Effectively, while globalization allows for cultural imperialism—that is, the suppression of other cultures (and, consequently, the elevation of others)—glocalization encourages a diffusion of cultures and ideas. Glocalization is the understanding of "globalisation as analytic boundaries, especially the spatial distinction between the global and the local, or that between universal and particular."[12] Glocalization therefore challenges the uniformity that the uncritical use of the term "globalization" presents. The presumption that globalization creates some form of singular interconnectedness that bridges different cultures is considered false.[13] Rather, the correct outlook is defined by the plurality of globalization (that is globalizations).[14] This is the perfect reflection of the binary and differential nature of the world that we live in.

Therefore, GWOT creates a problem in the way it tends to universalize, frame, and promote a particular problem and its responses.[15] The GWOT adopts the hegemonic tendencies of globalization.[16] The hegemonic tendency that is promoted is that of liberalism, particularly American liberalism. However, as Barry Buzan has rightly observed, the American liberalism that GWOT connotes and indirectly conveys will fail to take root because of many factors, including the illiberal approaches applied.[17] The predominant approach has been that of counterterrorism, which entails, in most cases, excessive and arbitrary use of force. As Kilcullen notes, the militarized approach is adopted because the GWOT is framed as a fight against a globalized Islamist insurgency.[18] As both Nigeria and Uganda (and many other cases) show, there is a need for a shift in approach toward soft, mostly counterinsurgency (rather than counterterrorism), responses. Counterinsurgency is suited to a glocalized response. The success of a glocalized approach will, however, depend on disaggregating target groups from links to global jihad.[19] While some groups deserve such labeling and linkage to the global jihad network, many other groups do not deserve to be tagged with global jihad. A glocalized response helps to avoid the generalized approach often applied in de-radicalization programs under the GWOT framework. It supports a personalized and specific approach to de-radicalization that takes account of each context and the different pathways toward radicalization.

THE STATE OF INSECURITY IN NIGERIA AND UGANDA

Over the past two decades, the security situations in Nigeria and Uganda have been increasingly dire. Although Nigeria and Uganda are practicing democracies notable in their adoption of constitutional democracy and periodic elections, authoritarian tendencies and characteristics are deeply entrenched in both countries. In Uganda, for instance, President Museveni has remained in power since 1986, when his National Resistance Movement/Army overthrew the government of Tito Okello. The elections in Uganda have been a farce at best. In Nigeria, although there have been regular successive transfers of power and change of government since it returned to democratic rule in 1999, the polity has remained highly militarized.[20]

Nigeria

Two years before 9/11, Nigeria returned to democratic rule after sixteen years (1983–99) of successive military regimes. Since 1999, Nigeria has maintained an uninterrupted democratic system of government. Nonetheless, Nigeria's democracy is fraught with great insecurities and instabilities. Virtually all the six geopolitical zones in Nigeria have either experienced or are currently experiencing violent conflicts. In the oil-rich Niger Delta, several hundreds of militant groups—including the umbrella militant group the Movement for the Emancipation of Niger Delta—engaged the Nigerian state in an armed struggle (2003–9) as they fought for control of the abundant oil resources in the region. In the predominantly Igbo southeast region, several groups, prominently the Movement for the Actualisation of the Sovereign State of Biafra (MASSOB; 1999–2012) and the Indigenous People of Biafra (IPOB) (2012–present), emerged demanding secession from the Nigerian state. In the Yoruba-dominated southwest, many interest groups, including the militant group O'Odua People's Congress, arose seeking an independent Yoruba nation and self-determination.[21] In the northern region of the country, extremist Islamist groups such as Boko Haram, with its splinter groups (Ansaru and ISWAP, Islamic State in West Africa Province) and other violent armed groups such as the Fulani militias (a loose network of hundreds of armed militia groups), have been terrorizing the region since 2000. Multiple conflicts threaten Nigeria's nascent democracy and political stability and in some cases extend the insecurity to the regional and international arenas.

For example, in the Igbo southeast, MASSOB, although largely peaceful in its approach, threatened Nigeria's sovereignty and territorial integrity by hoisting Biafran flags in different locations in the southeastern region and re-introducing Biafran passports and currency. MASSOB, like the other secessionist groups in the southeast, draws its inspiration from the ugly Nigeria-Biafra Civil War (1967–70), which led to the death of millions of Igbo people and the persistent political and economic marginalization of the Igbo people in Nigeria.[22] Since 2015, IPOB has become the face of agitation for secession of the Igbo people from the Nigerian state.[23] Like MASSOB's, IPOB's modus operandi has largely been nonviolent. These characteristics include mass protests and rallies; boycotting of elections; grounding of economic activities through sit-at-home orders; media propaganda, primarily through its London-based Radio Biafra, an online radio station that has been in existence since 2009; and demand for a referendum to decide Igbos' exit from the Nigerian state.

However, IPOB's agitation may have recently transformed from a tactic of nonviolence to one of violence, notably since 2020. In 2020, IPOB established the Eastern Security Network (ESN) to protect the Igbo people and the southeast from the threats and attacks from Fulani herders and armed militia groups, whose violent activities are fast spreading southward (away from their northern front). The creation of ESN was inspired by the establishment of a similar non–state security outfit, Amotekun, in the Yoruba southwest region. Faced with the threat of an expanding armed Fulani herder community, the perceived threat of Fulani domination of other ethnic groups in Nigeria, and, more important, the seeming complicity of a Fulani-led presidency (President Buhari's failure to strongly condemn his kith and kin was conspicuous), the Yoruba leaders in the southwest established Amotekun.[24] While Amotekun enjoys the state's patronage, ESN is seen as the armed wing of IPOB. Since the creation of ESN, there has been an escalation in violent encounters with the security forces. IPOB has been accused of attacking police stations and orchestrating a string of assassinations in the region.

In the Niger Delta, several militant groups, including the Niger Delta People's Volunteer Force, Niger Delta Vigilante, and Movement for the Emancipation of Niger Delta (an umbrella organization for more than a hundred smaller militia groups), engaged the Nigerian state in armed struggle between 2003 and 2009. The Niger Delta militants' modus operandi includes sustained attacks on oil facilities, kidnapping of expatriate oil workers, oil pipeline vandalization, and oil theft and piracy. The Niger Delta fought for self-determination and secession in its struggle against underdevelopment of the region and despoliation of the environment by the multinational oil companies, such as Shell and Chevron.

In northern Nigeria, since 2009, the Nigerian state has been involved in a counterterrorism operation against Boko Haram, with its many splinter groups such as Jamāʻatu Anṣāril Musliminafi Bilādis-Sūdān (popularly called Ansaru; 2012) and ISWAP (2015). Boko Haram is a

Salafi jihadist group that is seeking to overthrow the Nigerian secular state and create a Sharia state. Boko Haram has caused the death of more than thirty thousand people and led to the displacement of three million people.[25]

The Middle Belt region of Nigeria has remained a source of ethno-religious conflicts in the past two decades. Middle Belt states such as Kaduna, Benue, and Plateau State are notable for recurrent clashes between nomadic pastoralists (predominantly Muslim Fulani) and farmers (mostly Christian non-Hausa-Fulani indigenes of northern Nigeria). Between 2001 and 2018, about sixty thousand people were killed and three hundred thousand displaced across four Nigerian states.[26] The conflicts have often been described as religious conflicts, but they are primarily over scarce economic resources, including farmlands, grazing areas, and water. This long-standing conflict between the farmers and herders, involving damage to farmers' crops and rustling of herders' cattle, is adversely affected by climate change. Nigeria has witnessed a sharp increase in sea level and flooding, increasing temperature, drought and desertification, and freshwater shortages and this has been particularly felt in northern Nigeria.

The growing climate change in the North has forced the herders to move southward in search of fresh water and pasture for their cattle. But this has created huge tension and conflict between the migrating herder community and the southern host communities. Southerners, who are predominantly Christians, fear an encroaching Islamist threat as they associate Fulani herders with a broader Islamization and Fulanization agenda. This is based on a historical distrust between the predominantly Christian South and the Muslim North caused by British colonial policy of indirect rule which created a two-tier system that favored the Fulani Caliphate aristocrat and gave them unfair advantage in the control of the federal government and the precolonial Islamic conquest project of Uthman Dan Fodio, which reached the Yoruba state of Kwara.[27] The Fulani herders' spread southward has therefore been interpreted as a pretext for establishing a Fulani hegemonic regime. The Fulani herders have also become militarized as they deploy sophisticated weapons such as AK-47s to defend themselves and their cattle against local vigilantes. But the southerners have accused them of grievous crimes, including destruction of their farmland and rape of their women. It is in response to these threats of Fulanization and Islamization that the southwest region established the state-sponsored Amotekun, and IPOB created ESN. Nonetheless, "these fears of Islamisation have helped fuel cycles of vitriolic rhetoric and ethno-religious violence in Nigeria, undermining the country's stability."[28]

In recent times, several militia criminal networks, locally known as bandits and sometimes believed to consist of Fulani people, have been terrorizing northwest Nigeria by conducting mass hostage-for-ransom sting operations. Although the Fulani ethnic group constitutes most of the bandits, criminals from other ethnic groups across Nigeria also engage in the banditry.[29] These militias have over the years become more lethal in their attacks and engage in criminal and terrorist activities, earning them a place in the top five most lethal terrorist groups in 2015, according to the Global Terrorism Index. These militia or bandits consist of a loose network of several hundred armed groups whose motive is largely economic and whose modus operandi include kidnap-for-ransom. These militia are different from traditional Fulani herder communities, which frequently clash with host communities in northern and southern Nigeria in their search for new areas of pasture and freshwater. The herder-farmer conflict in Nigeria, although often couched as an ethno-religious conflict rooted in Nigeria's colonial legacy, should be seen more as a result of climate change.[30] The herder-farmer conflict can be viewed through the lens of glocalization, as it shows the intersection between a global phenomenon such as climate change and a local conflict. The response to climate change has become concerted in the past decade or so. Yet there remains a strong tendency toward the securitization of climate change in local conflicts induced by environmental factors.

Uganda

Like many countries in Africa, Uganda is a product of European imperialism. It therefore demonstrates the characteristics of postcolonial African countries' including a collage of multitude of ethnic identities. About fifty different tribes in Uganda can be broadly categorized under four ethnic groups—Bantu (the largest group situated in central Uganda, including the Baganda), Nilotics (largely groups from northern Uganda), Nilo Hamites, and the Hamites (Nilo Hamites and Hamites are also known as Central-Sudanic).

The various ethnic groups have a predilection toward interethnic tensions and conflicts.[31] Interethnic conflicts have remained pervasive since Uganda gained independence in 1962.[32] The interethnic conflicts are spurred by the often-violent jostling for power and control of the government by each region in north, south, and central Uganda and several ethnic groups embedded in these regions. Uganda's exclusionary power politics, which favor the ruling leader's region and ethnic group to the detriment of other groups and regions, have produced a great incentive for conflict.[33] For example, the governments of President Milton Obote (1966–71, 1980–85) and Idi Amin (1971–79) largely favored the northern group of Nubian-Kakwa and the Langi and Acholi, respectively. The uneven access to and distribution of power led to the emergence of several ideological and ethnic-based rebel movements that have often launched attacks from neighboring countries such as Tanzania, Rwanda, Sudan, and the Democratic Republic of the Congo (the DRC), where they are exiled and operate from. Therefore, Uganda's political history is intricately tied to the civil wars within the Horn and Great Lake region of eastern Africa. Current President Yoweri Museveni's National Resistance Movement, although credited with reducing civil war in Uganda through its broad-based inclusive policy, started off with a strong ethnic bias toward its core western Ankole group and the Bagandas from central Uganda, the latter enjoying the benefit of their cooperation in the struggle against President Obote.[34] Unsurprisingly, northern Uganda, including Acholi, Teso, and Karamojong, became the new frontier for insurgency following Museveni's emergence as the president.

Chief among the insurgent groups is the Acholi-dominated Lord Resistance Army (LRA), founded by Joseph Kony in 1987, and the Allied Democratic Forces (ADF), which operates mainly in southwestern Uganda and the border of the DRC.[35] Cattle raiders from the northeastern region of Karamojong also contribute to the insecurity in Uganda, as they produce a devastating consequence to the economy of the Acholis.[36] The proliferation of small arms and light weapons since the late 1990s has exacerbated the pastoral conflict in the northeastern region, on the border of Uganda and Kenya.[37] Since the late 1990s and early 2000s, and following 9/11, eastern Africa has gained notoriety as a center of insecurity, particularly terrorism, which has been couched within the framework of the GWOT. Al-Qaeda and the Islamic State (known as

ISIS, IS) have gained a foothold in the region. Prominent groups include Al-Shabaab and ISIS in Somalia and the ISIS Central African Province in the DRC, where the ADF is central to the emergence of ISIS Central African Province.[38] Interestingly, the ADF and other rebel movements such as the LRA have enjoyed the support of external governments, the DRC and the Sudanese government respectively. The ADF and LRA are provided with a safe haven and other military support and logistics in exchange for helping the weak governments in Khartoum and Kinshasa maintain their political control. Uganda has therefore been forced to conduct counterterrorism operations in these countries as well as supply troops in restoring and maintaining peace in the region's persistent civil wars. This reflects the complex interaction between the global and local and, in this case, national and regional. The externalization of the LRA and ADF through the GWOT and regional geopolitics in eastern Africa expands not only the geography of terror and insecurity but more so the globalized response to it.

THE GWOT AND THE MILITARIZED RESPONSE TO DOMESTIC (IN)SECURITY

Contemporary post–Cold War conflicts are transnational in nature, despite their strong local roots. Not only do they produce devastating consequences that transcend the borders of the conflict state, but the actors also often forge connections with a loose network of similar groups outside the state. This is clear in the relationship between Nigeria's Boko Haram and the global al-Qaeda and ISIS networks, as well as the cross-border activities of armed rebel movements in Uganda and bordering countries of Congo, Kenya, and Sudan. Boko Haram also operates outside Nigeria, including in bordering countries of Cameroon, Niger, and Chad around the Lake Chad Basin. The cross-border nature of these conflicts and the impact they have on regional and international security have motivated concerted responses established under bilateral and multilateral agreements. Notably, the 9/11-induced GWOT provides the singular most significant drive toward an internationalized (global collaboration) response to the threat of terrorism in the twenty-first century, notwithstanding the domestic angles to the conflicts. It is, however, important that the global and local dimensions be perfectly blended and that the domestic angles of the conflicts are given proper attention. Essentially a truly glocalized response is considered more useful.[39]

Nigeria

Nigeria joined the US-led global alliance against terrorism and has particularly benefited from the global support and regional cooperation against terrorism in its fight against Boko Haram and its splinter groups. For instance, in July 2013, the United Kingdom proscribed Boko Haram as a foreign terrorist organization, at the request of the Nigerian government. Several other foreign governments, including the United States (November 2013) and the European Union (June 2014) joined the UK in proscribing Boko Haram. Boko Haram had carried out suicide attack on Nigeria's police headquarters and the United Nations building in the capital city of Abuja in 2011, the first of its kind in Nigeria, but one that would soon become the group's preferred mode of attack as it escalated its terrorist agenda against the Nigerian state.[40] However, it was not until April 2014 that Boko Haram gained international notoriety, when it kidnapped nearly three hundred boarding-school girls in the Chibok area of Borno state in northeast Nigeria. Nigeria received counterterrorism support from several countries. For example, Israel, France, China, the US, and the UK offered Nigeria support in the form of aerial surveillance, hostage negotiation experts, development assistance, and special troops, among others, particularly in support of the search for the kidnapped schoolgirls.[41]

Nigeria benefits from several US counterterrorism partnerships and support, including the African Coastal and Border Security Program and the Trans-Sahara Counter-Terrorism Partnership, which provide military training and border and maritime security in Africa. These programs and similar military assistances are designed by the US Department of Defense within the broader framework of the US Africa Command, established by President George W. Bush in the aftermath of 9/11. Parallel to the military assistance is a development approach that is overseen by the Department of State (DoS) through its development agency United States Agency for International Development. For example, the DoS established in 2010 the US-Nigeria Bi-national Commission, which is aimed at improving good governance and transparency and promoting regional cooperation and development, energy reform and investment, and food security and agricultural investment. Nigeria benefits from a DoS Anti-terrorism Assistance (ATA) program that provides funding, equipment, and training to countries fighting terrorism.

In terms of direct assistance (largely military) toward the Boko Haram war, through the ATA program the United States trains the Nigeria Police Force in the detection and handling of improvised explosive devices. Also, through the Global Security Contingency Fund Counter–Boko Haram Program, the Nigeria Police Force and other relevant security agencies and personnel, such as immigration officers and custom officials, are given interagency border patrol training aimed at addressing rural border security challenges.[42] The Nigerian government also enjoys the benefits of the DoS Counterterrorist Finance Project, which helps to fight terrorist financing and curtails the flow of funds to terrorist groups. The United States and other Western countries support regional and other multilateral efforts, such as the Multinational Joint Task Force, comprising countries in the Lake Chad Basin (Niger, Nigeria, Cameroon, and Chad) that are fighting Boko Haram.

The external counterterrorism support against Boko Haram is partly due to the belief that Boko Haram is part of a global jihadist network. While this may be true, what is little known is that the Nigerian state, with its external partners, especially the United States, through their invasive surveillance and counterterrorism operations, may have radicalized jihadists in northern Nigeria in the 1990s who are suspected of having connections to the global jihadist network.[43] Boko Haram, most notably the Islamic State in West Africa Province (ISWAP), shares ideological and operational connections with transnational terrorist organizations such as ISIS. Yet, drawing from Kilcullen's observation, not every Islamist group should be put under such broad characterization.[44] A glocalized framework allows us to draw a useful distinction between the global and local perspectives and drivers of violence. It is fascinating that terrorism did not exist in Nigeria's penal code until 2011, which makes an examination of Nigeria's counterterrorism operations during this period necessary.[45] Boko Haram is believed to have officially started in 2002, although it did not become a full-blown insurgency until 2009. The Global War on Terror therefore seems to pre-date 9/11. In reality, 9/11 only escalated a process that was already underway. In the 1990s, during the dark days of General Sani Abacha's military regime, the concept of terrorism had already been applied, although an antiterrorism legislation was conspicuously absent.[46]

Interestingly, not everyone supports the idea that Boko Haram is a transnational terrorist organization. Rather, Boko Haram's concern is seen to be overwhelmingly localized.[47] On the contrary, scholars such as Ely Karmon and Jacob Zenn describe Boko Haram as a transnational organization.[48] Nonetheless, "Boko Haram is at once a local and transnational terrorist group," making the fight against it a quintessential case of glocalized security.[49] Boko Haram is, on the one hand, a consequence of northern Nigeria's long history of religious tensions and contestations between minority Christians and the majority Muslims and, more importantly, between different extremist and conservative Islamic groups.[50] On the other hand, Boko Haram is also part of a global Islamic renaissance—a contest between a traditional Muslim sensibility and modernity dominated by Western ideals, and ultimately a drive to reinstate the lost Muslim hegemony.[51] This modern contest started with the successful Iranian Revolution of 1979. Since then, several Islamist groups, including al-Qaeda and ISIS, have emerged in the Middle East and Africa to challenge the global dominance of Western standards. These groups have networks across the globe, and their acts of terror transcend national borders. Boko Haram's splinter groups, Jamā'atu Anṣāril Muslimīnafi Bilādis-Sūdān (popularly called Ansaru) and ISWAP are proxies of al-Qaeda and ISIS respectively.[52]

The Nigerian state's response to Boko Haram and other conflict groups, although uneven, remains primarily forceful and violent. Nigeria has favored a militarized response to real and perceived threats. Working within the GWOT frame and empowered by a newly and hastily constituted antiterrorism legislation, the Nigerian state, through its military (which was given the sole counterterrorism power), committed grave violations of human rights against the northeast population. For example, between May 2013 and November 2014, when the three northeastern states of Borno, Adamawa, and Yobe were placed under emergency rule, the Nigerian military routinely arrested young boys and men, arbitrarily detained some, and summarily killed others. It is therefore likely that the Nigerian military has killed as many civilians as the insurgents have killed.[53]

The Nigerian state also abuses its antiterrorism legislation. Since its promulgation in 2011, the Nigerian state has outlawed Boko Haram (2013) and two other groups, IPOB (2017) and the Islamic Movement of Nigeria (IMN, 2018). Notably, the proscription of IPOB and IMN by President Buhari has been viewed as unjustifiable and has been rightly condemned at home and abroad. The Buhari administration has deliberately misrecognized IPOB and IMN to justify its use of overwhelming force. This can have adverse outcomes, including provocation of the outlawed groups into using violence and transforming them into armed organizations, as exemplified by IPOB. The proscription of IPOB "delegitimises the group, including its legitimate claims of political and economic marginalisation and exclusion of the Igbos. The action also legalises the excessive use of force."[54] Since the proscription of IPOB, the Nigerian military has occupied several Igbo-dominated southeastern states, through the operational code name Operation Python. The relatively peaceful southeastern region has become militarized and a hotspot for conflict. The region is characterized by near-daily violent encounters between the Nigerian military, IPOB (with its armed wing, Eastern Security Network, ESN), and a third force that is described as simply "unknown gunmen." On April 5, 2021, "unknown gunmen" attacked the police headquarters in Owerri, the capital city of Imo state. In the same year, a prison was attacked, and 1,800 inmates were released. These were part of an organized attack on security and government targets in the southeast. IPOB, with its armed wing, ESN, has been blamed for most of the attacks.

However, it is likely that government agents are behind most of the killings, creating a pretext to justify the military clampdown on IPOB. As retired Nigerian military general Commodore Olawunmi asserted in our interview, "I think the federal government started sending fighters to go and start bombing police stations, saying that it is IPOB that did this. They just try to paint them black and they fell into the trap."[55] This view is not far-fetched, considering that the government has been careful not to directly accuse IPOB of most of these killings, instead ascribing them to "unknown gunmen." More so, the "illegal" proscription of IPOB presents a dilemma to the Nigerian government as it struggles to categorically describe the violence in the southeastern region as the handiwork of terrorist, rather choosing the vague name "unknown gunmen." The government has shown to have extraterritorial reach as it colluded with the Kenyan government in the extralegal rendition of Nnamdi Kanu in June 2021. Kanu, the leader of IPOB, has been in the custody of the Nigerian government, facing several charges including terrorism and treason. Interestingly, when Buhari was a military head of state (1983–84), he sparked a diplomatic row between Nigeria and the UK when he attempted to kidnap Umaru Dikko from the UK. Dikko was a minister of transport in the civilian government of Shehu Shagari (1979–83) and an outspoken critic of the Buhari military regime. Since the arrest of Kanu in June 2021, IPOB's activities have scaled down, but the "unknown gunmen" saga continues.

The proscription of IMN and IPOB and the ensuing violent response show a pattern of state response to perceived and real threats. For instance, in the Igbo southeast, the administrations of President Olusegun Obasanjo (1999–2003, 2003–7) and President Goodluck Jonathan (2010–11, 2011–15) engaged in multiple violent encounters with MASSOB. These led to the detention and murder of several members of MASSOB and numerous arrests of its founder, Ralph Uwazuruike, who was accused of treason in 2011. Since 2015, IPOB has become the new face of agitation in the southeast. IPOB and other groups in the southeast (and by extension other sociopolitical groups in Nigeria) express legitimate grievances that demand addressing the root cause of political violence. Governments fighting armed groups can deny such groups popular support by winning hearts and minds through addressing root causes of conflicts.[56] In one of the interviews, Miliki, a human rights activist and former Kogi state coordinator for Partnership against Violent Extremism in Nigeria, asserted that "the basis for conflict in Nigeria and lack of cohesiveness and peace is about lack of justice in the system."[57] Addressing the injustices of the Nigerian-Biafran civil war and the continual marginalization of the Igbo people are critical to lasting peace. Miliki is therefore right that "there can't be peace when there is no basic justice."

The Niger Delta insurgency, which is unsurprisingly described as Nigeria's only "serious secessionist rebellion," has attracted mixed response from the Nigerian state.[58] The mixed response to the Niger Delta struggle includes dialogue and negotiated settlement as well as a military approach. The Nigerian state was forced to negotiate with Niger Delta militants as the insurgent activities adversely affected Nigeria's largely oil-dependent economy. For example, within three years (2006–9), more than four thousand oil workers were kidnapped, twelve thousand oil pipelines were vandalized, and three thousand oil spills were recorded.[59] The Nigerian state offered presidential amnesty to approximately thirty thousand ex-militants in 2009 in exchange for their weapons. Since 2009, relative peace has returned to the Niger Delta, although incidents of crime, oil theft, and piracy go largely underreported. In 2016, following President Buhari's threat not to extend the amnesty beyond the initial 2015 deadline, there was a brief resurgence of insurgency in the region, mostly attributable to new militia groups such as the Niger Delta Avengers.

In terms of political economy, the Niger Delta presents higher stakes than most of the conflicts in Nigeria. Nigeria is one of the world's top producers of oil. At the height of the Niger Delta insurgency, 2003–9, it led to massive depletion of Nigeria's oil production output, down to 700,000 barrels per day from a daily average of 2.4/2.6 million barrels per day. This coincided with the war in Iraq and a consequent reduction in the global production of oil. The United States and other Western nations relied on a stable supply of oil from Nigeria to plug the shortage. Therefore, Nigeria received significant external military and development support in its fight against the Niger Delta insurgency. Essentially, the economic and security threat from the Niger Delta insurgency was externalized. The external counterinsurgency support that Nigeria received, however, failed to defeat the insurgency as it neglected the glocalized nature of the conflict. As such, the Nigerian state's initial militarized approach toward the Niger Delta conflict was counterproductive.

A militarized approach heightens the risk of escalating violent conflict. The form of government response to the threat and actual act of terror has a major impact on the potential escalation and protraction of violent conflict.[60] For instance, despite massive response, mostly military, from the Nigerian state and the Multinational Joint Task Force, a regional army (comprising armies from Chad, Niger, Nigeria, and Cameroon) constituted in 2015, as well as significant support from the international community, Boko Haram has remained dangerously active for more than a decade. Although the use of force is acceptable in some instances, as is the case with Boko Haram, its utility is short and limited. For instance, the heavy-handed approach adopted by the Nigerian state may have transformed a little-known social movement into one of the world's deadliest insurgencies. According to Baba Ahmed, a permanent secretary of the federal government of Nigeria and an executive member of the high-profile committee that was constituted by President

Jonathan in 2013 to engage with Boko Haram in search of a political solution, "It was actually the Nigerian state that was responsible for radicalizing the Boko Haram people, in the manner they misunderstood them, in the manner they were attacking, in the manner they fought them, in the manner they killed Mohammed Yusuf, and in the manner they subsequently handled the post–Mohammed Yusuf."[61]

The Nigerian state's heavy-handed response to the secessionist demands of MASSOB only escalated the crisis. Indeed, the detention and murder of several members of MASSOB and the repeated arrests of its founder, Ralph Uwazuruike, drastically reduced the impact of MASSOB in the southeast. However, the hard power approach failed to end the agitations and secessionist drives permanently. IPOB emerged in 2015 as the face of agitation for secession of the Igbo people from the Nigerian state. So far, the Nigerian state has failed to learn the right lessons about the war. The proscription of IPOB and militarized occupation of the southeast have only escalated the conflict with near-daily attacks in what was a relatively peaceful region. Nearly every region in Nigeria is seeking secession and self-determination, and the Nigerian military is spread thin as it is intervening in virtually all the internal conflicts across the geopolitical regions.[62] Unfortunately, the Nigerian military has usurped the traditional role of the Nigeria Police Force, a clear indication of the militarized state of the country.

Similarly, the proscription of IMN has pit the government against the Shiite group. The heavy-handed approach to the perceived threat that IMN presents and the ill-treatment of its leader El-Zakzaky can potentially create a serious problem for Nigeria. The Shiite government of Iran can capitalize on this and use IMN to engage in a proxy war. Ironically, the Nigerian government, particularly the Buhari administration (a Fulani presidency), has failed to respond militarily to the rather serious security threat that the Fulani militia groups present to Nigeria's stability.[63]

Uganda

The Horn and Great Lakes regions have long been hotbeds of insecurity, but terrorist attacks on US embassies in Tanzania and Kenya in 1998, the 9/11 attacks, and the 2002 al-Qaeda attack against an Israeli airliner and a hotel popular with Israeli tourists in Mombasa, Kenya, raised the security threats in the region to an unprecedented level.[64] In the aftermath of 9/11, the responses to the insecurities in Uganda and the region became heavily militarized. The major factor in the escalation of violence and insecurity is exogenous to the region.[65] The international community, working within the framework of the GWOT, abandoned negotiated settlement and political solution to the LRA, ADF, and other conflicts in the region. The United States declared the LRA and ADF terrorist organizations in 2001. Encouraged by the US action, the Museveni government in 2002 enacted its Anti-terrorism Act, which has since been amended multiple times as the Anti-terrorism (Amendment) Bill of 2015 and the Anti-terrorism (Amendment) Bill of 2017. The 9/11-induced GWOT adversely affected the nature of glocalized security in Uganda, as it undermined the relevance of the local factors and the need for a political solution rather than militarized solutions. Like many newly constituted counterterrorist legislations in Africa, the Ugandan antiterrorism law "threatened human rights and widened religious fissures."[66] For instance, Uganda proscribed the LRA and ADF under its new Anti-terrorism Act and carried out a large-scale military crackdown against the LRA (code-named Operation Iron Fist), further persuaded by the Sudanese government's withdrawal of support for the LRA (itself a reaction to the US-declared War on Terror on the LRA).[67] Evidently, the Ugandan government, just as in Nigeria, instrumentalized terrorism and the GWOT framework for its own political ends.

Uganda is a useful US ally and plays an important role in maintaining regional security.[68] Uganda is part of the US counterterrorism program for eastern Africa, including the East Africa Counterterrorism Initiative and the Combined Joint Task Force–Horn of Africa. It is part of the regional peacekeeping force in Somalia, the UN-backed African Mission in Somalia, which the United States supports.[69] Uganda has also been involved in stabilization and peacekeeping missions in the DRC, Sudan, and the Central African Republic. As such, Uganda has received significant counterterrorism support in the form of military training, military equipment, technology, weapons, and funding.[70] Although in recent years Western donors have taken more stringent measures to uphold liberal values in Uganda, the impact of their previous lax response to President Museveni's authoritarian rule remains evident. President Museveni enjoyed a warm relationship with Western governments and financial institutions as a result of his embrace of neoliberal economic policies.

The special relationship between Museveni-led Uganda and the Western governments has left the West blindsided to the growing militarization and authoritarianism in Uganda.[71] This has resulted in a dent in Western credibility as it shows hypocrisy in Western human rights aid conditionality where allies such as Uganda are spared scrutiny that other countries are subject to.[72] For instance, as "Uganda militarised and engaged in military adventures in Democratic Republic of Congo (DRC), it enjoyed an influx of foreign aid amounting to half its official budget and 80 percent of its development expenditures."[73] Although Uganda's Western partners have stopped providing budgetary support to Uganda in a bid to shore up their credibility, Uganda continues to receive substantial military support and funding.[74] Even the development and non-military assistance, including the humanitarian aid given to the Acholi people in government-built IDP (internally displaced people) camps, is facilitated by the military, yielding to militarization.[75]

The US proscription of the LRA and ADF and President Museveni's subsequent military crackdown on the rebels yielded only minor gains, notably a temporary halt to the activities of the ADF and forcing the ruling Sudanese National Islamic Front to withdraw its long-standing support for the LRA. However, insecurities continued as the LRA shifted its base to the war-torn DRC, whence it launched attacks on villages and government targets in northern Uganda.[76] The GWOT's influence in eastern Africa is therefore double-edged, stemming the tide of terrorism in some areas while increasing state violence and terrorist activity in others.[77] For instance, the ADF, which was temporarily defeated in 2004, transformed into an ISIS proxy in 2015.[78] Uganda also faced attack from an al-Qaeda–affiliated group in Somalia, Al-Shabaab. For example, Al-Shabaab carried out two suicide bombings in Kampala on July 11, 2010, leaving seventy-four people dead and seventy injured. Al-Shabaab attacked Uganda for Uganda's role in the UN stabilization and peacekeeping mission in Somalia, the UN-backed African Union Mission in Somalia. Since 2020, the ADF and the Islamic State have intensified attacks (include suicide bombings) in Uganda. Overall, the GWOT's overt focus on security has pushed the United States toward supporting the militarization of the region through its alliance with unscrupulous groups and authoritarian governments such as the one run by President Museveni of Uganda. Ironically, US counterterrorism policy in East Africa has involved partnerships with warlords in Somalia, an action that is most likely to escalate insecurity in Somalia and the region more broadly.[79]

Undeniably, 9/11 at the very least escalated the globalized response to security. The GWOT created an illusion of global insecurity where local conflicts and security threats have been improperly internationalized and the responses to such problems increasingly militarized under the GWOT frame. Unfortunately, the externalization of local conflicts runs the risk of undermining the local dynamics and increasing their militarization. Although local insurgencies that are driven by violent extremism do in fact produce global consequences and therefore require concerted efforts, globalized responses often suppress the local factors. A glocalized approach to security provides the chance of expressing the global dimensions without sacrificing the domestic angles to conflicts. Based on the experiences of Nigeria and Uganda, this chapter critically examined the influence of the GWOT on militarized responses to security issues and the impact of the militarized responses to domestic and regional security. In terms of the influence of the GWOT on counterterrorism and counterinsurgency strategies in Africa, Nigeria and Uganda show a lot of parallels. Nigeria and Uganda have a history of authoritarian governments and shared British colonial heritage that is marked by ethnic conflicts rooted in marginalization and struggles for power. There are also natural resource–related issues as most evident in pastoral conflicts.

As we see in both Nigeria and Uganda, counterterrorism can easily become regional in nature. Not surprisingly, both countries have embraced regional security strategies induced by the GWOT. Nigeria plays a central role in regional security and is part of several bilateral and multilateral agreements. Like Nigeria, Uganda also plays a crucial role in maintaining regional security in the Horn and Great Lakes regions. Both countries are also faced with domestic threats from multiple insurgencies that are fundamentally domestic but increasingly becoming connected to regional and global terrorist networks (e.g., the LRA and ADF in Uganda; Boko Haram, ISWAP, and IPOB in Nigeria).

Despite the legitimate domestic grievances, the responses of the Nigerian and Ugandan governments have been primarily military in nature. This militarized response dovetails with the 9/11-induced GWOT. In both countries, the GWOT and the antiterrorism legislations have been weaponized and deployed to silence dissents and discourage dialogue and political solutions, which essentially maintains the anti-democratic status quo. Proscribing groups such as the LRA, the ADF, IPOB, and IMN de-legitimizes any viable claims they may have and closes avenues for negotiated settlement. Unfortunately, the international community leads and supports militarization in some instances while turning a blind eye to other cases, creating moral and policy contradictions that further undermine security.

NOTES

1. Derek Lutterbeck, "Between Police and Military: The New Security Agenda and the Rise of Gendarmeries," *Cooperation and Conflict* 39.1 (2004): 45–68; Pádraig Carmody, "Transforming Globalization and Security: Africa and America Post-9/11," *African Today* 52.1 (2005): 97–120; Cyril I. Obi, "Terrorism in West Africa: Real, Emerging or Imagined Threats?," *African Security Studies* 15.3 (2006): 87–101; Abu B. Bah, *International Security and Peacebuilding: Africa, the Middle East, and Europe* (Bloomington: Indiana University Press, 2017).

2. Mary Kaldor, *New and Old Wars: Organized Violence in a Global Era* (Cambridge: Polity, 2012).

3. Mary Kaldor, "Old Wars, Cold Wars, New Wars, and the War on Terror," *International Politics* 42 (2005): 491–498; Martin Van Creveld, *The Transformation of War* (New York: Simon and Schuster, 1991); John Keegan, *A History of Warfare* (New York: Random House, 2011).

4. Meredith Reid Sarkees, "The COW Typology of War: Defining and Categorizing Wars (Version 4 of the Data)," https://correlatesofwar.org/wp-content/uploads/COW-Website-Typology-of-war.pdf; Stathis N. Kalyvas and Laia Balcells, "International System and Technologies of Rebellion: How the End of the Cold War Shaped Internal Conflict," *American Political Science Review* 104.3 (2010): 415–429.

5. Kalyvas and Balcells, "International System and Technologies of Rebellion," 9.

6. Stewart Patrick, "'Failed' States and Global Security: Empirical Questions and Policy Dilemmas," *International Studies Review* 9.4 (2007): 644–662.

7. Peter Hough, *Understanding Global Security* (London: Routledge, 2014).

8. Lutterbeck, "Between Police and Military."

9. Elke Krahmann, "Conceptualizing Security Governance," *Cooperation and Conflict* 38.1 (2003): 5–26; Rita Abrahamsen and Michael C. Williams, "Security beyond the State: Global Security Assemblages in International Politics," *International*

Political Sociology 3.1 (2009): 1–17; Abu Bakarr Bah, "Civil Non–state Actors in Peacekeeping and Peacebuilding in West Africa," *Journal of International Peacekeeping* 17.3–4 (2013): 313–336.

10. Roland Robertson, "Globalisation or Glocalisation?," *Journal of International Communication* 1.1 (1994): 33–52.

11. Robertson.

12. Peter Beyer, "Globalization and Glocalization," *The SAGE Handbook of the Sociology of Religion*, ed. James A. Beckford and Jay Demerath (Los Angeles: SAGE Publications, 2007), 98.

13. Roland Robertson and Kathleen E. White, "What Is Globalization?," in *The Blackwell Companion to Globalisation*, ed. George Ritzer (Oxford: Blackwell Publishing, 2007), 54–66; Norman Fairclough, *Language and Globalization* (London: Routledge, 2009).

14. Robertson and White, "What Is Globalization?," 54–66.

15. Stephen D. Reese, "Finding Frames in a Web of Culture: The Case of the War on Terror," in *Doing News Framing Analysis*, ed. Paul D'Angelo and Jim A. Kuypers (London: Routledge, 2010), 33–58; Alan Ingram, *Spaces of Security and Insecurity: Geographies of the War on Terror* (London: Routledge, 2016).

16. Fairclough, *Language and Globalization*.

17. Barry Buzan, "Will the 'Global War on Terrorism' Be the New Cold War?," *International affairs* 82.6 (2006): 1101–1118.

18. David J. Kilcullen, "Countering Global Insurgency," *Journal of Strategic Studies* 28.4 (2005): 597–617.

19. Kilcullen.

20. Michael Nwankpa, *Nigeria's Fourth Republic, 1999–2021: A Militarized Democracy* (London: Routledge, 2022).

21. Wale Adebanwi, "The Carpenter's Revolt: Youth, Violence and the Reinvention of Culture in Nigeria," *The Journal of Modern African Studies* 43.3 (2005): 339–365.

22. Michael Nwankpa, "Labelling Conflict Groups in Nigeria: A Comparative Study of Boko Haram, Niger Delta, IPOB and Fulani Militia," in *Armed Non–state Actors and the Politics of Recognition*, ed. Emmanuel Pierre Guittet and Peter Lawler (Manchester: Manchester University Press, 2021), 49–69.

23. Michael Nwankpa, "The Politics and Dynamics of Secession in Nigeria," *Journal of Central and Eastern European African Studies* 2.1 (2022): 31–47.

24. Michael Nwankpa, "The North–South Divide: Nigerian Discourses on Boko Haram, the Fulani, and Islamization," *Current Trends in Islamist Ideology* 29 (2021): 47–63.

25. Abdulbasit Kassim and Michael Nwankpa, *The Boko Haram Reader: From Nigerian Preachers to the Islamic State* (London: Hurst, 2018); James Forest, *Confronting the Terrorism of Boko Haram in Nigeria* (Tampa, FL: JSOU Press, 2012); David Cook, *Boko Haram: A Prognosis* (Houston: Baker Institute for Public Policy, 2011).

26. Aljazeera, "Horrors on the Plateau: Inside Nigeria's Farmer-Herder Conflict," November 28, 2021, https://www.aljazeera.com/features/2021/11/28/horrors-on-the-plateau-inside-nigerias-farmer-herder-conflict.

27. Larry Diamond, *Class, Ethnicity, and Democracy in Nigeria: The Failure of the First Republic* (Syracuse, NY: Syracuse University Press, 1998); Karl Maier, *This House Has Fallen: Nigeria in Crisis* (Boulder, CO: Westview Press, 2002).

28. Nwankpa, "The North–South Divide," 52.

29. Jimam T. Lar, "Violence and Insecurity in Northwest Nigeria: Exploring the Role and Resilience of Local Actors," *African Conflict & Peacebuilding Review* 9.2 (2019): 123–142; John Sunday Ojo, "Governing 'Ungoverned Spaces' in the Foliage of Conspiracy: Toward (Re)ordering Terrorism, from Boko Haram Insurgency, Fulani Militancy to Banditry in Northern Nigeria," *African Security* 13.1 (2020): 77–110.

30. Nwankpa, *Nigeria's Fourth Republic.*

31. Dominic Rohner, Matthias Thoenig, and Fabrizio Zilibotti, "Seeds of Distrust: Conflict in Uganda," *Journal of Economic Growth* 18 (2013): 217–252.

32. Rohner, Thoenig, and Zilibotti.

33. Stefan Lindemann, "LSE Research: Increased Territorial Power-Sharing in Museveni's Uganda Has Led to the Decline of Civil War," Africa at LSE, 2011.

34. Lindemann.

35. Rohner, Thoenig, and Zilibotti, "Seeds of Distrust."

36. Justine Nannyonjo, "Conflicts, Poverty and Human Development in Northern Uganda," *The Roundtable* 94.381 (2005): 473–488.

37. Mustafa Mirzeler and Crawford Young, "Pastoral Politics in the Northeast Periphery in Uganda: AK-47 as Change Agent," *The Journal of Modern African Studies* 38.3 (2000): 407–429; Kennedy Agade Mkutu, "Small Arms and Light Weapons among Pastoral Groups in the Kenya-Uganda Border Area," *African Affairs* 106.422 (2007): 47–70.

38. Jason Warner et al., *The Islamic State in Africa: The Emergence, Evolution, and Future of the Next Jihadist Battlefront* (London: Hurst, 2021).

39. Robertson, "Globalisation or Glocalisation?," 2.

40. Freedom C. Onuoha and Temilola A. George, "Boko Haram's Use of Female Suicide Bombing in Nigeria," *Al Jazeera Centre for Studies* 17 (March 2015): 1–9; Michael Nwankpa, *Boko Haram: Whose Islamic State?* (Houston: Baker Institute for Public Policy, 2015).

41. Michael Nwankpa, "The Political Economy of Securitization: The Case of Boko Haram, Nigeria," *The Economics of Peace and Security Journal* 10.1 (2015): 32–39.

42. See the DoS 2016 *Country Reports on Terrorism 2015.*

43. Andrea Brigaglia and Alessio Locchi, "Entangled Incidents: Nigeria in the Global War on Terror (1994–2009)," *African Conflict & Peacebuilding Review* 10.2 (2020): 10–42.

44. Kilcullen, "Countering Global Insurgency."

45. Jennifer Giroux and Michael Nwankpa, "A Vicious Cycle: The Growth of Terrorism and Counterterrorism in Nigeria, 1999–2016," in *Non-Western Responses to Terrorism*, ed. John Horgan (Manchester: Manchester University Press, 2019), 410–432.

46. Giroux and Nwankpa.

47. Marc-Antoine Pérouse de Montclos, "Boko Haram and Politics: From Insurgency to Terrorism," in *Islamism, Politics, Security and the State in Nigeria*, ed. Marc-Antoine Pérouse de Montclos (Leiden: African Studies Centre, 2014), 135–157; Cook, *Boko Haram*; Forest, *Confronting the Terrorism of Boko Haram*.

48. Ely Karmon, "Boko Haram's International Reach," *Perspectives on Terrorism* 8.1 (2014): 74–83; Jacob Zenn, *Unmasking Boko Haram: Exploring Global Jihad in Nigeria* (Boulder, CO: Lynne Rienner Publishers, 2020).

49. Michael Nwankpa, "Understanding the Local-Global Dichotomy and Drivers of the Boko Haram Insurgency," *African Conflict & Peacebuilding Review* 10.2 (2020): 49.

50. Nwankpa, "Boko Haram: Whose Islamic State?"; Abimbola O. Adesoji, "Between Maitatsine and Boko Haram: Islamic Fundamentalism and the Response of the Nigerian State," *Africa Today* 57.4 (2011): 99–119.

51. Paul Lubeck, "Nigeria: Mapping the Sharia Restorationist Movement," in *Shari'a Politics: Islamic Law and Society in the Modern World*, ed. Robert Hefner (Bloomington: Indiana University Press, 2011), 244–279.

52. Warner et al., *The Islamic State in Africa*; Nwankpa, "Understanding the Local-Global Dichotomy," 4.

53. Marc-Antoine Pérouse de Montclos, "The Nigerian Military's Response to Boko Haram," *African Conflict & Peacebuilding Review* 10.2 (2020): 65–82.

54. Nwankpa, "Understanding the Local-Global Dichotomy," 63.

55. Interview with Nigerian naval general, Commodore Olawunmi, 2021.

56. James D. Kiras, "Irregular Warfare: Terrorism and Insurgency," https://www.indianstrategicknowledgeonline.com/web/baylis3e_ch09.pdf.

57. Interview with Miliki, a human rights activist and Kogi state coordinator for the Partnership against Violent Extremism, 2016.

58. Paul Collier and Anke Hoeffler, *The Political Economy of Secession* (N.p.: Development Research Group, World Bank, 2002), 18.

59. Sofiri Joab-Peterside, Doug Porter, and Michael Watts, "Rethinking Conflict in the Niger Delta: Understanding Conflict Dynamics, Justice and Security," United States Institute of Peace (2012): 8.

60. Martha Crenshaw, "The Psychology of Terrorism: An Agenda for the 21st Century," *Political Psychology* 21.2 (2000): 405–420; Alex Schmid, "Terrorism as Psychological Warfare," *Democracy and Security* 1.2 (2005): 137–146; Kiras, "Irregular Warfare: Terrorism and Insurgency," https://www.indianstrategicknowledgeonline.com/web/baylis3e_ch09.pdf.

61. Interview with Baba Ahmed, 2014.

62. Nwankpa, *Nigeria's Fourth Republic*.

63. Nwankpa, "Labelling Conflict Groups in Nigeria"; Nwankpa, "The North–South Divide."

64. Peter Kagwanja, "Counter-terrorism in the Horn of Africa: New Security Frontiers, Old Strategies," *African Security Review* 15.3 (2006): 72–86; David H. Shinn, "Terrorism in East Africa and the Horn: An Overview," *Journal of Conflict Studies* 23.2 (2003): 79–91; Patrick Kimunguyi, "Terrorism and Counterterrorism in

East Africa," in *ARC Linkage Project on Radicalisaion: Conference 2010 Understanding Terrorism from an Australian Perspective; Radicalisation, De-radicalisation and Counter-radicalisation*, ed. G. Barton, P. Lentini, S. Moss, and J. Iiardi (Melbourne: Global Terrorism Research Centre and Monash European and EU Centre, Monash University, 2011), 1–23.

65. Rohner, Thoenig, and Zilibotti, "Seeds of Distrust," 2.

66. Kagwanja, "Counter-terrorism in the Horn of Africa," 73.

67. Rohner, Thoenig, and Zilibotti, "Seeds of Distrust."

68. Shinn, "Terrorism in East Africa and the Horn."

69. Lauren Ploch, *Countering Terrorism in East Africa: The US response*, vol. 3 (Washington, DC: Congressional Research Service, 2010).

70. David M. Anderson and Jonathan Fisher, "Authoritarianism and the Securitization of Development in Uganda," in *Aid and Authoritarianism in Africa: Development and Democracy*, ed. Tobias Hagmann and Filip Reyntjens (London: Zed Books, 2016), 67–90; Kimunguyi, "Terrorism and Counterterrorism in East Africa."

71. Larry Jay Diamond and Marc F. Plattner, *Democratization in Africa* (Baltimore: Johns Hopkins University Press, 1999); Ellen Hauser, "Ugandan Relations with Western Donors in the 1990s: What Impact on Democratisation?," *Journal of Modern African Studies* 37.4 (1999): 621–641; Adam Branch, "Humanitarianism, Violence, and the Camp in Northern Uganda," *Civil Wars* 11.4 (2009): 477–501; William Muhumuza, "From Fundamental Change to No Change: The NRM and Democratization in Uganda," *The East African Review* 41 (2009): 21–42.

72. Roger Tangri and Andrew M. Mwenda, "President Museveni and the Politics of Presidential Tenure in Uganda," *Journal of Contemporary African Studies* 28.1 (2010): 31–49.

73. Branch, "Humanitarianism, Violence, and the Camp in Northern Uganda," 481.

74. Anderson and Fisher, "Authoritarianism and the Securitization of Development in Uganda."

75. Branch, "Humanitarianism, Violence, and the Camp in Northern Uganda"; Jan Bachmann, "Militarization Going Places? US Forces, Aid Delivery and Memories of Military Coercion in Uganda and Kenya," *Critical Military Studies* 4.2 (2018): 102–120.

76. Rohner, Thoenig, and Zilibotti, "Seeds of Distrust."

77. Kagwanja, "Counter-terrorism in the Horn of Africa."

78. Warner et al., *The Islamic State in Africa*.

79. Kagwanja, "Counter-terrorism in the Horn of Africa."

BIBLIOGRAPHY

Abrahamsen, Rita, and Michael C. Williams. "Security Beyond the State: Global Security Assemblages in International Politics." *International Political Sociology* 3.1 (2009): 1–17.

Adebanwi, Wale. "The Carpenter's Revolt: Youth, Violence and the Reinvention of Culture in Nigeria." *The Journal of Modern African Studies* 43.3 (2005): 339–365.

Adesoji, Abimbola O. "Between Maitatsine and Boko Haram: Islamic Fundamentalism and the Response of the Nigerian State." *Africa Today* 57.4 (2011): 99–119.

Aljazeera. "Horrors on the Plateau: Inside Nigeria's Farmer-Herder Conflict." November 28, 2021. https://www.aljazeera.com/features/2021/11/28/horrors-on-the-plateau-inside-nigerias-farmer-herder-conflict.

Anderson, David M., and Jonathan Fisher. "Authoritarianism and the Securitization of Development in Africa." In *Aid and Authoritarianism in Africa: Development and Democracy*, edited by Tobias Hagmann and Filip Reyntjens, 67–90. London: Zed Books, 2016.

Bachmann, Jan. "Militarization Going Places? US Forces, Aid Delivery and Memories of Military Coercion in Uganda and Kenya." *Critical Military Studies* 4.2 (2018): 102–120.

Bah, Abu Bakarr. "Civil Non-state Actors in Peacekeeping and Peacebuilding in West Africa." *Journal of International Peacekeeping* 17.3–4 (2013): 313–336.

Bah, Abu Bakarr, ed. *International Security and Peacebuilding: Africa, the Middle East, and Europe.* Bloomington: Indiana University Press, 2017.

Beyer, Peter. "Globalization and Glocalization." In *The SAGE Handbook of the Sociology of Religion*, ed. James A. Beckford and Jay Demerath, 98–117. Los Angeles: SAGE Publications, 2007.

Branch, Adam. "Humanitarianism, Violence, and the Camp in Northern Uganda." *Civil Wars* 11.4 (2009): 477–501.

Brigaglia, Andrea, and Alessio Iocchi. "Entangled Incidents: Nigeria in the Global War on Terror (1994–2009)." *African Conflict & Peacebuilding Review* 10.2 (2020): 10–42.

Buzan, Barry. "Will the 'Global War on Terrorism' Be the New Cold War?" *International Affairs* 82.6 (2006): 1101–1118.

Carmody, Pádraig. "Transforming Globalization and Security: Africa and America Post-9/11." *Africa Today* 52.1 (2005): 97–120.

Collier, Paul, and Anke Hoeffler. *The Political Economy of Secession.* N.p.: Development Research Group, World Bank, 2002.

Cook, David. *Boko Haram: A Prognosis.* Houston: Baker Institute for Public Policy, 2011.

Crenshaw, Martha. "The Psychology of Terrorism: An Agenda for the 21st Century." *Political Psychology* 21.2 (2000): 405–420.

Creveld, Martin V. *The Transformation of War.* New York: Free Press, 1991.

de Montclos, Marc-Antoine Pérouse. "Boko Haram and Politics: From Insurgency to Terrorism." In *Islamism, Politics, Security and the State in Nigeria*, ed. Marc-Antoine Pérouse de Montclos, 135–157. Leiden: African Studies Centre, 2014.

———. "The Nigerian Military's Response to Boko Haram." *African Conflict & Peacebuilding Review* 10.2 (2021): 65–82.

Diamond, Larry. *Class, Ethnicity, and Democracy in Nigeria: The Failure of the First Republic.* Syracuse, NY: Syracuse University Press, 1988.

Diamond, Larry Jay, and Marc F. Plattner (eds.). *Democratization in Africa.* Baltimore: Johns Hopkins University Press, 1999.

Fairclough, Norman. *Language and Globalization.* London: Routledge, 2009.

Forest, James J. *Confronting the Terrorism of Boko Haram in Nigeria*. Tampa, FL: JSOU Press, 2012.

Giroux, Jennifer, and Michael Nwankpa. "A Vicious Cycle: The Growth of Terrorism and Counterterrorism in Nigeria, 1999–2016." In *Non-Western Responses to Terrorism*, ed. John Horgan, 410–432. Manchester: Manchester University Press, 2019.

Hauser, Ellen. "Ugandan Relations with Western Donors in the 1990s: What Impact on Democratisation?" *The Journal of Modern African Studies* 37.4 (1999): 621–641.

Hough, Peter. *Understanding Global Security*. London: Routledge, 2014.

Ingram, Alan. *Spaces of Security and Insecurity: Geographies of the War on Terror*. London: Routledge, 2016.

Joab-Peterside, Sofiri, Doug Porter, and Michael Watts. "Rethinking Conflict in the Niger Delta: Understanding Conflict Dynamics, Justice and Security." United States Institute of Peace (2012): 1–33.

Kagwanja, Peter. "Counter-terrorism in the Horn of Africa: New Security Frontiers, Old Strategies." *African Security Review* 15.3 (2006): 72–86.

Kaldor, Mary. *New and Old Wars: Organized Violence in a Global Era*. 3rd ed. Cambridge: Polity, 2012.

Kaldor, Mary. "Old Wars, Cold Wars, New Wars, and the War on Terror." *International Politics* 42 (2005): 491–498.

Kalyvas, Stathis N., and Laia Balcells. "International System and Technologies of Rebellion: How the End of the Cold War Shaped Internal Conflict." *American Political Science Review* 104.3 (2010): 415–429.

Karmon, Ely. "Boko Haram's International Reach." *Perspectives on Terrorism* 8.1 (2014): 74–83.

Kassim, Abdulbasit, and Nwankpa, Michael (eds.). *The Boko Haram Reader: From Nigerian Preachers to the Islamic State*. London: Hurst, 2018.

Keegan, John. *A History of Warfare*. New York: Random House, 2011.

Kilcullen, David J. "Countering Global Insurgency." *Journal of Strategic Studies* 28.4 (2005): 597–617.

Kimunguyi, Patrick. "Terrorism and Counterterrorism in East Africa." In *ARC Linkage Project on Radicalisation: Conference 2010 Understanding Terrorism from an Australian Perspective; Radicalisation, De-radicalisation and Counter-radicalisation*, ed. G. Barton, P. Lentini, S. Moss, and J. Iiardi, 1–23. Melbourne: Global Terrorism Research Centre and Monash European and EU Centre, Monash University, 2011.

Kiras, James. D. "Irregular Warfare: Terrorism and Insurgency in Understanding Modern Warfare." https://www.indianstrategicknowledgeonline.com/web/baylis3e _cho9.pdf.

Krahmann, Elke. "Conceptualizing Security Governance." *Cooperation and Conflict* 38.1 (2003): 5–26.

Lar, Jimam T. "Violence and Insecurity in Northwest Nigeria: Exploring the Role and Resilience of Local Actors." *African Conflict & Peacebuilding Review* 9.2 (2019): 123–142.

Lindemann, Stefan. "LSE Research: Increased Territorial Power-Sharing in Museveni's Uganda Has Led to the Decline of Civil War." Africa at LSE, 2011.

Lubeck, Paul M. "Nigeria: Mapping the Sharia Restorationist Movement." In *Shari'a Politics: Islamic Law and Society in the Modern World*, ed. Robert Hefner, 244–279. Bloomington: Indiana University Press, 2011.

Lutterbeck, Derek. "Between Police and Military: The New Security Agenda and the Rise of Gendarmeries." *Cooperation and Conflict* 39.1 (2004): 45–68.

Maier, Karl. *This House Has Fallen: Nigeria in Crisis*. Boulder, CO: Westview Press, 2002.

Mirzeler, Mustafa, and Crawford Young. "Pastoral Politics in the Northeast Periphery in Uganda: AK-47 as Change Agent." *The Journal of Modern African Studies* 38.3 (2000): 407–429.

Mkutu, Kennedy Agade. "Small Arms and Light Weapons among Pastoral Groups in the Kenya-Uganda Border Area." *African Affairs* 106.422 (2007): 47–70.

Muhumuza, William. "From Fundamental Change to No Change: The NRM and Democratization in Uganda." *The East African Review* 41 (2009): 21–42.

Nannyonjo, Justine. "Conflicts, Poverty and Human Development in Northern Uganda." *The Round Table* 94.381 (2005): 473–488.

Nwankpa, Michael. *Boko Haram: Whose Islamic State?* Houston: Baker Institute for Public Policy, 2015.

———. "Understanding the Local-Global Dichotomy and Drivers of the Boko Haram Insurgency." *African Conflict & Peacebuilding Review* 10.2 (2020): 43–64.

———. "Labelling Conflict Groups in Nigeria: A Comparative Study of Boko Haram, Niger Delta, IPOB and Fulani Militia." In *Armed Non–state Actors and the Politics of Recognition*, ed. Emmanuel Pierre Guittet and Peter Lawler, 49–69. Manchester: Manchester University Press, 2021.

———. "The North–South Divide: Nigerian Discourses on Boko Haram, the Fulani, and Islamization." *Current Trends in Islamist Ideology* 29 (2021): 47–63.

———. *Nigeria's Fourth Republic, 1999–2021: A Militarised Democracy*. London: Routledge, 2022.

———. "The Politics and Dynamics of Secession in Nigeria." *Journal of Central and Eastern European African Studies* 2.1 (2022): 31–47.

Nwankpa, Michael Okwuchi. "The Political Economy of Securitization: The Case of Boko Haram, Nigeria." *The Economics of Peace and Security Journal* 10.1 (2015): 32–39.

Obi, Cyril I. "Terrorism in West Africa: Real, Emerging or Imagined Threats?" *African Security Studies* 15.3 (2006): 87–101.

Ojo, John Sunday. "Governing 'Ungoverned Spaces' in the Foliage of Conspiracy: Toward (Re)ordering Terrorism, from Boko Haram Insurgency, Fulani Militancy to Banditry in Northern Nigeria." *African Security* 13.1 (2020): 77–110.

Onuoha, Freedom C., and Temilola A. George. "Boko Haram's Use of Female Suicide Bombing in Nigeria." *Al Jazeera Center for Studies* 17 (March 2015): 1–9.

Patrick, Stewart. "'Failed' States and Global Security: Empirical Questions and Policy Dilemmas." *International Studies Review* 9.4 (2007): 644–662.

Ploch, Lauren. *Countering Terrorism in East Africa: The US Response*. Vol. 3. Washington, DC: Congressional Research Service, 2010.

Reese, Stephen D. "Finding Frames in a Web of Culture: The Case of the War on Terror." In *Doing News Framing Analysis*, ed. Paul D'Angelo and Jim A. Kuypers, 33–58. London: Routledge, 2010.

Robertson, Roland. "Globalisation or Glocalisation?" *Journal of International Communication* 1.1 (1994): 33–52.

Robertson, Roland, and Kathleen E. White. "What Is Globalization?" In *The Blackwell Companion to Globalization*, ed. George Ritzer, 54–66. Oxford: Blackwell Publishing, 2007.

Rohner, Dominic, Mathias Thoenig, and Fabrizio Zilibotti. "Seeds of Distrust: Conflict in Uganda." *Journal of Economic Growth* 18 (2013): 217–252.

Sarkees, Meredith Reid. "The COW Typology of War: Defining and Categorizing Wars (Version 4 of the Data)." https://correlatesofwar.org/wp-content/uploads/COW-Website-Typology-of-war.pdf.

Schmid, Alex. "Terrorism as Psychological Warfare." *Democracy and Security* 1.2 (2005): 137–146.

Shinn, David H. "Terrorism in East Africa and the Horn: An Overview." *Journal of Conflict Studies* 23.2 (2003): 79–91.

Tangri, Roger, and Andrew M. Mwenda. "President Museveni and the Politics of Presidential Tenure in Uganda." *Journal of Contemporary African Studies* 28.1 (2010): 31–49.

Warner, Jason, Ryan O'Farrell, Héni Nsaibia, and Ryan Cummings. *The Islamic State in Africa: The Emergence, Evolution, and Future of the Next Jihadist Battlefront*. London: Hurst, 2021.

Zenn, Jacob. *Unmasking Boko Haram: Exploring Global Jihad in Nigeria*. Boulder, CO: Lynne Rienner Publishers, 2020.

Chapter 5

The Conundrums of International Military Interventions in Africa

The Cases of Côte d'Ivoire and Mali

ALFRED BABO

In his acclaimed book *The Wealth of the Nations*, Adam Smith stated that national security is the exclusive duty of a sovereign state.[1] Therefore, the state must raise an army to protect the territory and the population, which is the nation's workforce. After their independence, African countries undertook to build their own armies as a substantial entity for the construction of their nation-states and sovereignty.[2] However, while the armies were supposed to take over the security of these newly independent states, they instead found themselves at the center of internal political chaos. Through coups d'état, rebellions, and dictatorial powers, the armies became a source of national instability rather than one of security in many African countries. In Côte d'Ivoire, successive military crises since 1990 ended in a rebellion in 2002 and civil war in 2010 and 2011.[3] In Mali, the army has also played a central role in installing authoritarian regimes and later accelerating the democratization process.[4] Nevertheless, the governments failed to protect the territory against terrorists who invaded the North of the country and partnered with the long-standing Tuareg separatist groups to threaten the capital city of Bamako in 2012.[5] With the national armies plagued by ethnic division, lack of equipment, and corruption, the Ivorian and Malian governments called for foreign intervention, mainly by the French military, to help stop the rapid expansion of rebels (Côte d'Ivoire) and terrorist groups (Mali).[6]

Although requested and acclaimed by Africans, foreign security operations are criticized because of their anachronism, (neo)colonial-based approaches, extended installations, and the instrumental nature of a geopolitical battle between global powers. Diop and Traoré ascribed the foreign intervention in Mali to France's refusal to end (neo)colonialism and its hegemonic ideology because the military Operation Serval was just another avatar to maintain the controversial Françafrique ties in its—"pré-carré"—zone of influence.[7] In any case, the overt confrontation between some factions of Ivorians with UN and French troops in Côte d'Ivoire in 2011 and the street demonstrations in Mali against the French military operations necessitate a critical reflection on the meaning and limits of these military interventions. Notably, on October 29, 2021, a massive rally took place in Bamako demanding the withdrawal of French troops in response to France's political interference in the local political affairs of Mali.[8] On February 19, 2022, the Malian people, along with civil society leaders, celebrated the withdrawal of French troops from their country.[9]

The extant literature often leans upon the failed states theory to explain why African nations would call on foreign forces to take care of their security.[10] Other literature emphasizes the humanitarian principles underpinning the Responsibility to Protect (R2P) populations endangered by civil wars and terrorism.[11] International military interventions start with deployment of African troops under African Union or the Economic Community of West African States (ECOWAS) mandates but are often reinforced by Western troops.[12] Such interventions purport to offer global responses to local security problems and conflicts in countries such as Côte d'Ivoire and Mali. I discuss these two countries to demonstrate the common patterns of inconsistencies in policies and interests that plague foreign security intervention in Africa. More important, this chapter shows how common limitations and defects in these interventions tend to worsen local problems.

What explains the inconsistencies and limits of international military intervention in West Africa as global and local issues increasingly intertwine? How does the failure of the interventions in Côte d'Ivoire and Mali demonstrate the influence of geopolitics and the tensions between local and global security concerns? To what extent are these military interventions more instrumental to global liberal governance than to local peace? What makes the Ivorian and Malian cases insightful are the inconsistencies and partiality exhibited in the interventions, which morphed into hostility, that contradict the democracy and human rights promotion reason used to justify the interventions. While those kinds of flaws in international interventions are seldom discussed, this chapter aims to expose and analyze the paradoxes and limitations of foreign interventionism in line with their connection to conflicting global and local interests. In this chapter, I critically examine the shortcomings of foreign security interventions in West Africa. The chapter draws on the notions of failed states and glocalized security and uses a historical approach based on primary and secondary sources.

DILEMMAS AND ANACHRONISMS IN INTERNATIONAL MILITARY INTERVENTIONS

As in Côte d'Ivoire and Mali, weakened African authorities have often requested foreign military interventions to face internal and external threats. Though these interventions do gain initial victories and are acclaimed by local populations, they often end in failures, raising questions about intent and implementation. As such, debates regularly emerge about whether African countries should call foreign powers, especially their former colonizers, for help sixty years after independence while reiterating their sovereignty. When France engaged its soldiers in Mali on January 11, 2013, it was its forty-ninth military operation in Africa since 1960. In the past, French interventions in its former colonies were wrapped in the dominant anti-communist narrative of the Cold War aimed at eliminating Soviet influence in Africa. This was typically done by protecting regimes favorable to the West or supporting a coup to install a new government favorable to French political and economic interests.[13]

On February 18, 1964, for example, France launched a military operation in Gabon to reinstate the ousted President Leon Mba. Later, in 1967, as General Charles de Gaulle aimed to extend French influence beyond francophone Africa, he planned an operation in the Biafra secessionist region of Nigeria to stop hunger-related deaths caused by the embargo imposed by the Nigerian government. Besides, France has intervened in former Belgian colonies. The first French intervention, Operation Bonite, occurred in the Democratic Republic of the Congo (formerly Zaire) on May 17, 1978, to support President Mobutu Sesse Seko in dealing with internal protests. The second intervention occurred in 1994 in Rwanda under Operation Amarylis, which was connected to the UN-sponsored Operation Turquoise. France ended up being implicated in the Rwandan genocide.[14] Based on its colonial ties, most of the French military interventions (earlier and recent) have occurred in francophone countries. Notably, these include Operation Barracuda in the Central African Republic (CAR) on September 21, 1979, which supported a coup and installed the second regime of David Dako. Most recently, France conducted the military Operation Sangaris in CAR from December 5, 2013, to October 31, 2016, with the stated aim of halting the civil war and building a democratic order. Several other operations have taken place in Chad in the 1980s to keep Muammar Gaddafi's influence away from this central region of Africa and, most recently, in West Africa.

Failed States: Glocalized Security in the African Context

Several theories, including that of the failed states, have been advanced to justify foreign interventions in Africa. Even for the proponents of the humanitarian and new humanitarian approaches in civil wars, such as in Liberia, DRC, and Sierra Leone, the underlying idea of the state's failure is prevalent.[15] According to Rotberg, "Nation-states fail because they are convulsed by internal violence and can no longer deliver positive political goods to their inhabitants." As a result, "their governments lose legitimacy, and the very nature of the particular nation-state becomes illegitimate in the eyes and the hearts of a growing plurality of its citizens."[16] This situation is visible on the African continent via the violent disintegration and weakness of some states. In Côte d'Ivoire and Mali, the failure of the states to protect their territories and maintain the stability and functioning of institutions led to international intervention. The extant literature makes a distinction between state collapse and failure from state weakness. Some studies focus on the nature of state weakness and why some weak states succumb to failure or collapse while others remain weak but do not collapse.[17]

The concept of state failure is a matter of functional destruction—that is, when a state is unable to perform its fundamental functions, as noted by Hobbes and Locke.[18] This definition concurs with Rotberg, who distinguishes strong states from weak and collapsed ones based on the effective delivery of the most crucial political goods.[19] By political goods, Pennock means the intangible expectations and obligations that citizens make on states as a content to the social contract between the ruler and the ruled.[20] Rotberg further posits that political goods have a hierarchy and that "none is as critical as the supply of security, especially human security."[21] Overall, the state's prime function is to provide that security—to prevent cross-border invasions, infiltrations, loss of territory, and mass deaths. The state aims to avoid its own decay by eliminating domestic attacks upon the national order and social structure, preventing crime and any related domestic dangers to human security.[22] The failed state, therefore, is unable to provide the protection necessary for delivering a range of other desirable political provisions, such as the rule of law, essential freedoms, and fundamental civil and human rights that allow citizens to participate freely, openly, and entirely in politics and the political process. Finally, a failed state cannot supply its citizens with basic social needs, such as health care, education, and proper transportation infrastructure.[23]

These attributes of the state have been discussed to mirror the actual situation of a weakened state and to consider the external and international environment that affects the likelihood of states' going from one degree of weakness to failure or recovery into functional states.[24] Although the notion of failed states in Africa has been questioned, the debates rarely bring up the effects of flawed foreign interventions on states' failures.[25] In the western African region, the fragility of states is characterized by the disintegration of internal political and security institutions and the growing complexity of conflicts resulting from foreign involvement. The regionalization of armed conflicts in Africa can be analyzed in the light of the theory of "conflict systems" because of the intense circulation of populations, the porosity of borders, and global terrorism.[26] These multidimensional wars generate reactions that exceed humanitarianism as they become enmeshed in the glocalized security frame.

According to Marfo et al., glocalized peace and security architecture promotes a domestically relevant and internationally feasible approach because the classical peace paradigm turned deficient, resulting in impossible global peace.[27] The notion of glocalized security strongly relies on the idea that because the causes and conditions of conflicts and insecurity have increasingly become varied and multifaceted, the comprehensive solution for peace must combine local actions and interests with global norms.[28] Moreover, in this globalized world, it is almost impossible for domestic issues to remain exclusively out of international matters. In reality, intrastate problems often prompt external interventions. As such, I use a glocalized security approach that encompasses its aporias drawn from the limits and inconsistencies of external interventions in two western African countries: Côte d'Ivoire and Mali. As much as conflicts take the form of complex systems, the resolution prospects that include external interventions are made more difficult as a result of the diversity of actors whose opposing interests collide. While glocalized security sees peace as a critical step to the potential realization of the rule of law and democracy, the actions and roles of some external interveners impede the actualization of those values. The resolution of domestic problems becomes impossible when the competition for global dominance among mighty nations is added to the local security issues. In this sense, although glocalized security aims to resolve conflicts where external interests have deeply fused with internal interests, foreign military interventions mainly serve and tend to protect the interests of foreign powers.

Côte d'Ivoire's Failure and the Foreign Intervention

According to the 2010 Failed States Index, Côte d'Ivoire was twelfth on the list of failed states.[29] This failure was mainly due to factors such as de-legitimization of the state, factionalized elites, group grievance, and external intervention because of an internal political and ethnic conflict. The first sign of the failure was what Kieffer described as the army crisis when the political and ethnic divisions plagued the national army.[30] At the beginning of the 1990s, as the economic crisis worsened, political rivalries took a dangerous ethnic turn. Some political leaders used a narrow form of nationalism called *Ivoirité* to redefine Ivorian citizenship. This undermined the nascent and precarious democratic system, plunging the country into a civil war.[31] Some northern soldiers found refuge in Burkina Faso, where they organized the rebel Mouvement Patriotique de Côte d'Ivoire (MPCI) to combat xenophobia and discrimination against foreigners and nationals from the north of Côte d'Ivoire. When the MPCI rebels attacked in 2002, the weakness of the loyal army, Forces de Défense et de Sécurité (FDS), became apparent as it failed to defeat the insurgents. MPCI took over the north of the country and committed massacres against gendarmes and civilians in the west of the country that are yet to be tried.[32] Another visible sign of the military's weakness in protecting the population was the rise and promotion of self-defense groups and militias that populated the western regions and the capital city, Abidjan.[33] The armed community groups engaged in ethnic violence and violations of human rights.[34]

Internal efforts to resolve the conflict, such as the national reconciliation forum held in 2001, failed and further endangered the core principles of the Westphalian state, such as stability, democracy, the rule of law, predictability, and capitalism.[35] Côte d'Ivoire's crisis drew international attention, leading to a glocalized security approach as big powers were sucked into a vortex of anomic internal conflict and chaotic humanitarian relief through foreign interventions. Acting as an interposition force, the French army of the Forty-Third Infantry and naval battalion (BIMA), stationed in Côte d'Ivoire since 1961, intervened and enforced a ceasefire along with a diplomatic effort to resolve the crisis. Given the fact that Côte d'Ivoire has a high percentage of foreign population (more than 26 percent of the general population), including a large majority of West Africans, the countries in the region, especially Mali and Burkina Faso, expressed serious concerns. This was due to the fact that members of the Burkinabe community in Côte d'Ivoire were threatened and became victims of reprisal when Ivorians learned that the rebels had prepared in and attacked from Burkina Faso.[36]

ECOWAS quickly enacted diplomatic and military interventions to maintain the fragile peace agreement. However, the ECOWAS interposition troops showed financial, logistical, and agency limits. Although ECOWAS troops participated in the implementation of the peace agreement, it was French and UN forces that enforced the peace, with the African forces playing a secondary role as they gradually turned into a UN peacekeeping mission supported by four thousand French soldiers.[37] As the African initiatives through ECOWAS heavily leaned on the global powers, the international community, led by France, took over the peacebuilding process. At the same time, the inter-Ivorian peace talks that started in the wake of the attack in Lomé (Togo) failed as a result of the intrusive power of France, whose authorities summoned the government, significant political parties, and the rebels at the Marcoussis peace talks, which led to an agreement signed in 2003. In February 2004, UN resolution 1528 was passed, establishing the United Nations Mission in Côte d'Ivoire (UNOCI), which was deployed along with the French Licorne Operation. Licorne and UNOCI created the east-to-west dividing line that truncated Côte d'Ivoire into two halves—the Center-North-West zones, occupied by the rebellion (approximately 60 percent of the national territory); and the south, controlled by the government.

However, efforts to rebuild peace and security leaned primarily on the classic state-centric approach with the return of the state's monopoly on violence and the rule of law through elections. Consequently, eight years after the beginning of the international intervention, while the tasks of the foreign military operations encompassed the securitization of transparent and fair presidential elections, the signs of the failure of the Ivorian state did not fade. On the eve of the 2010 presidential election, several alarming patterns revealed that the country was heading toward a downfall. Despite peacebuilding meetings and agreements and reform measures,[38] the two belligerent armies never merged into the single republican national army prescribed by the peace agreements, notably the Marcoussis Accord of 2003 and the Accord Politique de Ouagadougou of 2007.[39] Instead, UNOCI, which reorganized to stand by candidate Alassane Ouattara, failed to disarm the rebels. An alarming report of the UN experts warned that both armies, the FAFN (the new name of the rebels) and the FDS (loyal to Laurent Gbagbo), violated UN resolution 1572 of November 2004 and purchased weapons in preparation for the post-election war.[40] Political violence that resulted in deaths broke out across the country between partisans of the two leading candidates, Laurent Gbagbo and Alassane Ouattara.

After the 2010 presidential election, the country ended up with "two" presidents, two armies, and two governments. There was no state that the citizens would trust, rely on, and work with. Instead, militias infiltrated the countryside and the capital city, Abidjan, where an armed group called "Commando Invisible" took over the town of Abobo, committing massacres and provoking a massive exodus of the population.[41]

This predicament aggravated ethnic violence and the civil war. In March 2011, reliable human rights organizations and the international media reported that FAFN massacred more than eight hundred people in Duekoue. Most of the victims are believed to have been supporters of Gbagbo.[42] On the other hand, the loyal army was accused of bombing residential neighborhoods and killing Ouattara's supporters in the capital city, Abidjan, including seven women in Abobo.[43] This latter event triggered a vigorous joint reaction by France and the UN in the form of a resolution to protect civilians and ultimately stop the war.

In March and April 2011, France led a coercive and intrusive operation to end the post-election war, even though French political and military authorities had refused to intervene in previous situations as they insisted on their principle of "neither interference nor indifference."[44] France's reluctance to intervene was also due to French parliamentarians' critiques of the French military operation in Côte d'Ivoire during the 2004 demonstrations, which fueled the internal crisis by the killing of several young Ivorians by the French army.[45] In any case, although he declared in South Africa on February 28, 2008, that he would no longer allow a "French soldier to shoot an African," French President Nicolas Sarkozy judged that France could not remain inactive as the Ivorian state was collapsing. On March 30, 2011, referring to the R2P principle, France, seconded by Nigeria, initiated and obtained the adoption of the UN Security Council resolution 1975, which authorized "UNOCI to use all means necessary to carry out its mandate to protect civilians, including to prevent the usage of heavy weapons."[46] Resolution 1975 allowed the violent intrusion of Western powers to end the war and establish peace.

Mali's Failure, Terrorism, and Foreign Intervention

In 2022, nine years after the international military intervention in Mali, the country still hosted thousands of foreign militaries from several African, European, and Asian countries. Since the NATO military intervention in Libya that killed President Muammar Gaddafi in 2011 and further destabilized the country, several terrorist groups have been established in the north of Mali. The international military intervention in Libya was based on the moral principle of protecting Libyan civilians against Gaddafi while backing up the rebellion born in Benghazi in the wake of the Arab Spring. It concurs with the R2P doctrine that "where the state fails or is unwilling to protect its citizenry, the international community has the normative obligation to intervene and rescue victims of armed conflict."[47] However, the paradox of this principle is revealed by the way Mali has been further destabilized by international military intervention in Libya and NATO's failure to protect Mali. The supposedly altruistic endeavor designed to save Libyan civilians endangered Malians because of the spread of weapons and terrorist groups into Mali after the destruction of Libya. The foreign intervention ultimately undermined R2P and showed its narrow application.

The failure of the international intervention amplified long-standing local security and political issues that began with the Tuareg rebellion in northern Mali. In 2012, terrorists associated with local Tuareg separatists tried to seize the Malian capital, Bamako, and take over power. Malian political and military institutions failed to protect the territory and the populations in the north primarily because of the increasing political divide and instability. The situation provoked a military coup in March 2012, increasing the national disorder. Moreover, problems of governance combined with corruption further weakened the Malian state's capacity to face the terrorists. The general breakdown of the Forces Armées Maliennes (FAMA) and the mismanagement of the army resulted in the lack of the primary military equipment and the motivation to combat the terrorist groups. As a result, for a few months, the terrorists took over major urban centers like Gao and Timbuktu, ousted the state's representatives, and imposed terror through Sharia law. As these groups advanced near the capital city, the weakened Malian state nearly collapsed.

The decay of the Malian state and the possible establishment of an Islamic state in the country posed perceived dangers beyond Mali. Notably, the application of Sharia law, which is a local issue, was considered a threat to the global liberal governance values such as religious freedom, human rights, rule of law, and democracy. Moreover, Sharia law became a serious concern for the safety of Europeans as a result of the expansion of the Islamic State (Daesh) and its ideology against Westerners. On the one hand, the EU feared the risk of terrorist attacks on its soil as illegal immigrants of all kinds tried to enter Europe in the wake of the collapse of Libya and the disorder caused by terrorists in the Sahel. Also, many Europeans had already been kidnapped for ransom in Mali and even killed. Thus, under the leadership of France, the United Nations

Security Council unanimously passed resolution 2085 on December 20, 2012, authorizing the deployment of the African-led International Support Mission to Mali.[48] As in Côte d'Ivoire, the African response lacked strength and rapid military reactivity. The situation in central and eastern Mali has worsened as a result of the spread of violence, endangering neighboring countries such as Burkina Faso and Niger. Consequently, it has become necessary for African agencies to intervene. In November 2015, five African countries (Mauritania, Mali, Niger, Burkina Faso, and Chad) created the G5 Sahel Force as a possible model for African states to take control of their security and fight jihadist groups in the region.[49] However, African initiatives are commonly marred by financial, organizational, and military capacity limitations. In Mali, limitations of African-led solutions necessitated a broader international force to take over a largely local security problem.

In early 2013, the president of the transitional government of Mali, Diacounda Traoré, called on France to help stop the progression of the terrorist groups that controlled large portions of Mali.[50] French President François Hollande responded positively to the desperate Malian request.[51] But by agreeing to intervene, France once again violated its principle of "neither interference nor indifference," which was supposed to keep it away from a neocolonial presence in Africa. According to Notin, the French military intervention entailed complexities and intricacies because France was responding not only to the Malians and Africans but also to the Americans and Europeans, who considered this area as the "French zone."[52]

On January 11, 2013, France launched Operation Serval with 1,700 soldiers to stop the advance of the terrorists toward Bamako as efforts to create the United Nations Multidimensional Integrated Stabilization Mission in Mali (MINUSMA) continued. MINUSMA was deployed on July 1, 2013, to take over from the International Support Mission in Mali formed by ECOWAS. MINUSMA, with a staff of 15,000 (including 12,169 soldiers and 1,741 police officers), became one of the most important UN missions. In August 2013, Operation Serval morphed into Operation Barkhane, which extended to the vast Sahelo–Saharan strip with approximately 4,500 French soldiers deployed.[53] While the UN renewed the mandate of the French mission for one year in June 2014, it strongly recommended that the Malian parties and, more broadly, the African subregional institutions make rapid peace progress.

However, the international intervention did not contribute to solving the local political and security problems of Mali. Malian internal tensions increased based on the deterioration of economic and democratic governance under the rule of President Ibrahim Boubacar Keita. For months protesters from civil society organizations and political coalitions such as the "mouvement M5" took to the streets of Bamako, demanding the departure of Keita's weak and corrupt government, which could not combat terrorism.[54] On the war front, a significant number of FAMA soldiers and civilians were being killed by terrorists. On the other hand, French troops prevented the Malian army from taking over the Azawad region in 2013, which allowed the terrorists to reorganize in the sanctuaries of the north—a decision that shows the contradictions of military interventions. Overall, Malian frustration against French troops mounted as internal tensions worsened and led to another coup in 2020.[55]

The politico-military disorder added to the instability of the Malian government and the growing insecurity caused by the terrorists. Despite criticisms of French actions that enabled the old Tuareg rebellion in Mali, France took the lead in trying to resolve the political disorder that erupted around the 2020 coup, which proved to be another failure. In collaboration with other European nations, France undertook to enhance the European Malian Army Training Mission, which was launched in February 2013. The mission was to bring together hundreds of (noncombat) soldiers from European countries to train the Malian army and G5 Sahel forces. On March 27, 2020, European governments issued a political statement expressing support for creating a task force named "Takuba" to tackle terrorist groups in the border regions of Mali, Burkina Faso, and Niger.[56]

CRITIQUES OF EXTERNAL MILITARY INTERVENTIONS IN AFRICA

Piccolino argued that recent foreign interventionism had raised both enthusiasm and criticism on the continent.[57] The proponents of intervention have used the theory of shared sovereignty in failing states to promote interventionism as a proper solution to conflicts.[58] Also, new humanitarianism and the R2P principle have been used to justify military interventions in Africa.[59] However, this enthusiasm has been met by criticisms of neocolonialism and doubts about global liberal governance in Africa. Although complaints about French intervention in postcolonial

Africa have long existed, what Piccolino does not point out is the clear and rigorous articulation of the limitations of interventions and their negative implications at the local level.[60] In an interview with *Le Magazine de l'Afrique* (October–November 2015) about NATO intervention in Libya, former US assistant secretary of state for African Affairs Herman J. Cohen confessed: "It was the Africans who were right, and we should have listened to them. But unfortunately, America and France made the wrong choice . . . with all the consequences we know today." Likewise, international interventions in western Africa have become unilateral, eventually exceeding the mandate of UN Security Council resolutions. According to Glaser, France surpassed its protector role in recent operations by ignoring Africans and displaying arrogance.[61]

Excesses in Military Operations and the Failure of Mandates

In Côte d'Ivoire, although the first intervention of the French Forty-Third BIMA at the beginning of the rebellion in September 2002 prevented an escalation into civil war, the intervention's neutrality was severely criticized by the belligerents. According to the Ivorian government, France ignored its approach to quickly solve the budding rebellion. Because it was planned and launched from Burkina Faso, the rebellion fell within the scope of the 1961 military agreement allowing France to side with the government.[62] But the refusal to implement the defense accord provided passive support to the rebels. More importantly, it contributed to grounding the rebellion and prolonging the local political and ethnic conflict. However, the rebels also found the French response problematic since the Forty-Third BIMA neutral intervention prevented the insurgents from progressing toward the capital city and taking power. As the leader of the rebellion stated, "The former colonial power chose unilaterally and without respect for international law to intervene decisively."[63] From its inception, the French military intervention in its former colony was already a controversial enterprise worsened by contradictions and inconsistencies in French policies during the conflict. Not only did France violate its neutrality principle of "neither interference nor indifference," but the intervention was marred by unilateral diplomacy, coercion, intrusion, and the use of discretionary military force.[64] Notably, when the 2010 elections turned sour and led to a second civil war, French Licorne forces and UNOCI took the side of Alassane Ouattara, effectively ending their neutrality. It was difficult to justify that the international military missions would side with former rebels, including some commandants accused of massacres by major human rights organizations.[65]

A notable feature of international military interventions in Africa is that foreign powers often stretch and exceed the provisions of the UN resolutions authorizing the missions. Humanitarian-based military interventions often morph into regime change. In Côte d'Ivoire, the Licorne and UNOCI military operations exceeded the original mandate of the UN resolution. Indeed, point 6 of UN Security Council resolution 1975 states: "Recalls its authorization and stresses its full support given to the UNOCI, while impartially implementing its mandate, to use all necessary means to carry out its mandate to protect civilians under imminent threat of physical violence, within its capabilities and its areas of deployment, including to prevent the use of heavy weapons against the civilian population . . ." However, international troops spared the heavy weapons of the rebels and targeted only the loyal army, even though all parties committed crimes against civilians. French and UN forces bombed President Gbagbo's palace on the pretext of destroying heavy weapons hidden in the presidential palace. In the process, the international mission exceeded the UN mandate by removing Gbagbo, thereby paving the way for the former rebels to install Ouattara as president.[66]

As in Côte d'Ivoire, France adopted a conceited unilateral approach in Mali that transformed its original operation. Notably, the mission was expanded to include other European troops. For Malian political leaders, France exceeded the actual Malian request for external help. According to the Malian prime minister, not only did the legal ground of the expansion remain unclear, but it was also inconsistent with the request stated in the initial letter requesting help. Even though the Malian president asked only for French airstrike and intelligence support, French soldiers were deployed on Malian soil, and France established military bases that morphed into Operation Serval—a limited urgent military assistance to combat terrorists—at the beginning of 2013, changing into Operation Barkhane in August 2013. The latter seemed henceforth to include a mission of interposition between the Malian army and the Azawad Tuareg rebels.[67]

Mali's security went out of the control of the national authority in the midst of the anarchy and confusion resulting from successive coups and transitional regimes. France virtually took control and tried to shape the country's security as it saw fit. For instance, the Europeanization of the intervention was done by France, acting as a "nation-cadre" on behalf of the international community to fight terrorism in the Sahara.[68] However, the multiplication of the operations from an array of entities, including the UN (MINUSMA), EU (Takouba), and G5 Sahel, resulted in tensions with the local authorities and populations, who raised concerns about the huge and unprecedented number of foreign soldiers on their territory.[69] Local actors rightly questioned whether the foreign troops were serving Malian interests or the ones of France and other Europeans.[70] It seemed that Mali and its international partners were pursuing different goals. When France collaborated with the Tuareg rebels of the Mouvement National pour la Liberation de l'Azawad and shifted its security mission in the Azawad region, it aimed to fight terrorists on the ground and contain terrorism far away from Europe. However, Malian authorities at the time wanted to end the conflict through dialogue as recommended during the inclusive national dialogue of 2019.[71]

Inconsistencies and Partialities in Military Interventions

Actual ground operations of the international military in Africa are often inconsistent with the humanitarian and democracy-promotion ideals waived to Africans. As Woods and Reese state, the interveners encounter difficulties related to their organizations and to unique local political circumstances.[72] It is a constant that foreign military interventions in Africa pretended to serve three pillars: fight terrorism, impose multiparty elections, and promote the rule of law. However, once mission operations start, political circumstances often evolve at the local and international levels, generating criticisms and questions about mission inconsistencies and partialities.

In Côte d'Ivoire, for example, while in 2002 France refused to use the 1960 military agreement to stop the rebellion, in 2011 France intervened when the presumed president-elect, Alassane Ouattara, called for international military intervention during the post-electoral war. The reversal of its neutrality principle was largely due to France and the UN's commitment to the peace enforcement process in which they have heavily invested and Gbagbo's contentious relations with international partners.[73] The international community led by France sponsored and endorsed most of the peace agreements signed after Gbagbo agreed to the UN's involvement in the peace process.[74] The classic paradigm of the power sharing and the instrumental presidential election were enacted as conflict-resolution mechanisms. However, Gbagbo and his government denounced the involvement of global powers, especially France, in the disputed outcome of the 2010 presidential election. Even though all parties agreed on the UN's role in certifying the election result, Gbagbo later played the ultranationalism and pan-Africanism cards to reject the UN's and France's capacity to declare or confirm the winner of the election.[75] Thus, the refusal of Gbagbo to leave power after the UN affirmed that he lost the election was perceived as defiance of the global liberal order.[76]

Indeed, the international military intervention in Côte d'Ivoire had incongruities with regard to the promotion of global liberal values of democracy and human rights. From the start, UNOCI and French Licorne troops sided with the rebels and used airstrikes to defeat Gbagbo, despite the attendant civilian casualties. Moreover, even though they were responsible for protecting all civilians based on the R2P principle and UN resolution 1975, they did not properly carry out their responsibility of protecting Gbagbo's supporters living in the west of the country. According to victims and media reports, the UN troops did not act to protect civilians when retaliatory violence perpetrated by partisans and soldiers of Ouattara occurred on July 20, 2012, in the UNHCR refugee camp of Nahibly.[77] During that attack, seven people were killed, forty were injured, and several others went missing.[78]

The election itself became a problem in the international intervention model. According to Bekoe, by prioritizing the holding of elections without ensuring sufficient levels of peace, security, and inclusivity in Côte d'Ivoire, the international intervention essentially enabled an environment inconducive to credible elections.[79] The precarious security situation before the 2010 election reignited the war.[80] In addition, the international community rejected other potential peaceful resolutions to the election crisis before resorting to a violent solution.[81] During the sixteenth African Union (AU) meeting on January 30, 2011, for example, the UN secretary-general refused to support a vote recount and instead backed the military solution. The UN secretary-general justified this option by stating that Gbagbo's refusal to leave power was a "direct and unacceptable challenge to the legitimacy of the United Nations."[82] Even though Gbagbo was allegedly trying to fool the international community by suggesting vote counting, one could question the UN's choice of a violent solution to a post-electoral dispute while claiming to be implementing a humanitarian operation. Ironically, while the international community was taking a hardline posture in the Ivoirian election dispute, the Organization of American States and UN Security Council resolution 10218 of April 6, 2011, endorsed vote recounting in Haiti's post-electoral disputes.[83] Ultimately, the military solution in Côte d'Ivoire resulted in more than three thousand deaths. One of the limitations of such intervention was that while it was acclaimed for saving lives, the casualties resulting from Licorne and UNOCI airstrikes during the Ivorian war have never been investigated.

Similar inconsistencies are evident in Mali, where the French army prematurely stopped the Malian military advances against the terrorists. According to Prime Minister Choguel Maiga, a Malian victory was hampered by the French troops, which prevented the FAMA from taking control of the Azawad region from the Tuareg rebels.[84] While the French authorities praised their troops' exceptional reactivity, professionalism, and determination in 2013, Malian leaders accused France of contentious actions that exacerbated the internal crisis. Even more, France collaborated with the Tuareg rebels, who had linked up with terrorists accused of atrocities in the north and center of Mali. In acknowledging the collaboration with the Mouvement National pour la Liberation de l'Azawad, on January 22, 2013, French defense minister Jean-Yves Le Drian declared, "I say it for today, but I also say it for tomorrow. The Tuaregs, except those who let themselves be recruited by terrorist groups that we totally condemn, ... are our friends."[85] French collaboration with Tuareg rebels had no mechanism to sort out the "good" rebels from the "bad" ones, despite this French authority's effort to distance his country from the atrocities committed by the Tuareg rebels. In 2018, French troops of the Barkhane Operation again worked hand-in-hand with the rebels of the Mouvement pour le Salut de l'Azawad and hosted in Paris its controversial leader accused of massive human rights violations.[86] In the end, while France intervened to protect the Malian state, it simultaneously affirmed friendship with the groups that threatened and undermined the Malian state.

As in Côte d'Ivoire, the international community led by France and ECOWAS prioritized organizing presidential elections in war-torn Mali, largely occupied by terrorist groups. In January 2022, ECOWAS and the West African Monetary and Economic Union imposed tough sanctions and an illegally questionable financial embargo on Mali over delayed elections.[87] The controversial agenda of the Malian junta prompted the restrictive measures pushed by France and the EU.[88] In this case, ECOWAS simply gave in to Western injunctions. Here again, the conundrum is that the international community was imposing an election without security through political and economic sanctions in violation of the 1965 UN Convention on Transit Trade of Land-Locked States.[89] As former South African president Thabo Mbeki noted in relation to Côte d'Ivoire, the international community pressured countries into holding elections despite the lack of security, even "though they knew that this proposition was fundamentally wrong" and that failed states could not withstand the international pressure to hold the elections.[90] In both Mali and Côte d'Ivoire, the rigidity of international normative views on democracy and their difficult adaptation to the local environment show the conundrums of glocalized security in Africa.

LOCAL VERSUS GLOBAL GOALS IN FOREIGN INTERVENTIONS

While there is usually a general apathy or acclaim for France and international interventions in African failed states to save them from collapse, one might wonder about the actual outcomes of those military operations. McGovern provided a critical view by framing them as largely cosmetic ethical efforts than real improvements to the situation.[91] According to him, international efforts at solving conflicts are often more a matter of being seen to be doing something than doing very much at all.[92] This observation concurs with the criticisms and limited results of UN peacekeeping missions in Africa. For instance, the United Nations Operation in Congo, one of the most significant military capabilities in scale and size established in 1960, did not prevent the country from falling deeper into endless wars. Successive missions in DRC, including the 1999 United Nations Organization Mission in the Democratic Republic of the Congo and the 2010 MONUSCO never stopped the massacres and war-crime rapes in the northeastern DRC.[93] Similar outcomes could be observed in the French Turkoise Operation in Rwanda and the Sangaris Operation in the Central African Republic.

In Côte d'Ivoire, French military presence and constant political involvement, along with several third parties (UN, AU, ECOWAS), for nine years did not prevent the country from sinking into the 2010 post-election war that resulted in three thousand deaths. Although the one-sided military intervention in April 2011 stopped the war and atrocities, it did not improve human rights and democracy, which had been the justifications for the intervention. Indeed, the postwar regime of Alassane Ouattara has formulated and implemented "ethnic *rattrapage*," which is an ethnic-based politics that is just as dangerous as the controversial *Ivoirité* that led to the initial war.[94] Through this new divisive politics, the regime has instilled horizontal inequalities. Since President Ouattara came to power in 2011, his opponents have been forced into exile or imprisoned. Three prominent opposition leaders were recently sentenced to twenty years based on trials rejected by the African Court on Human and People's Rights.[95] Even if the jail term is not implemented, the sentences prevent them from participating in future elections. In 2020, President Ouattara ran for a controversial third term against the 2016 constitution, which stipulated only two terms; his main opponents were disqualified from the race based on dubious legal technicalities.[96] This kind of pseudo-democracy observed in sub-Saharan Africa creates a favorable environment for electoral violence.[97] The 2020 election, in which Ouattara claimed to gain 94.27 percent of the vote, is blemished by the more than fifty deaths, the more than three thousand people forced to flee abroad, and the arrest of more than a dozen opposition leaders.[98] Clearly, international military intervention has not led to democracy in Côte d'Ivoire.

Likewise, foreign military intervention in Mali did not improve the security or the human rights conditions despite the presence of thousands of soldiers in the country. In spite of the Algiers peace deal signed in March 2015,[99] violence and terrorist attacks have persisted, spreading to the center and south and eventually into neighboring Burkina Faso and Niger. A cogent analysis of the recent interventions in Mali and, more broadly, in the Sahara region would suggest that success should have led to reduced foreign troops and even their withdrawal, as the Malian army would have gained more control over the territory. Surprisingly, nine years after the beginning of the massive foreign military interventions in Mali, not only have terrorist groups conquered more territories, but they have actually expanded into countries outside of the Sahel, such as Benin and Côte d'Ivoire.

Overall, the human rights situation deteriorated as a result of multiple forms of massacre carried out by all parties.[100] The north of the country became a hideout for terrorist groups who reorganized and returned to defeat the Malian army. Despite the training and support provided by France and the international intervention, the national army hierarchy was so plagued with extreme corruption that the soldiers on the front lines were missing weapons, ammunition, and medical assistance. As a result, civilians were massacred and villages destroyed by terrorists, as in Aklaz and Awkassa on April 26 and 27, 2018.[101] Unequipped Malian soldiers were also massively killed, provoking protests from the families of soldiers.[102] Moreover, the distortion in the chain of command within the national army led to massacres allegedly committed by Malian soldiers against civilians of a specific ethnicity.[103] Mali's precarious situation led to a junta government that is seeking peace talks with the terrorists and embracing non-Western military support from countries such as Russia. The junta's new orientation and policies poisoned relations with France, which opposed Russian participation in the Malian war against terrorism.[104] As in Côte d'Ivoire, the reluctance of external partners to properly consider and exhaust local approaches to peacebuilding has led Mali into deeper political and security predicaments.

Intervention in Africa for the Sake of Global Liberal Governance?

There is no Western intervention in Africa without deep geostrategic interests. Security interventions in francophone West African countries must be viewed through the lens of global liberal governance despite the claims to address global and domestic issues through a glocalized security approach.[105] In francophone Africa, global liberal governance is embodied in the neocolonial Françafrique relation constructed by French presidents and African political elites. According to Glaser, there was a time when they all claimed, "What is good for France is good for Africa."[106] While recent French presidents have proclaimed the end of the controversial relations, their actions have contradicted their discourses and instead perpetuated what Koulibaly called the "colonial pact" primarily serving French interests and role as guardian of francophone countries.[107] In both Côte d'Ivoire and Mali, French intervention created a territorial divide that reignited old internal conflicts. The strategy aimed to position France as an international leader in peacebuilding in the region. As one top French military officer acknowledged, "The security mission highlighted the return of France to its traditional area of interest."[108] With the military operations in Côte d'Ivoire, the CAR, and Mali, France is fulfilling a role that had been somewhat overshadowed by its engagement in Afghanistan (2008–12). Therefore, recent French interventions in Africa simply reaffirm France's notorious reputation as the "*gendarme* of Africa."[109]

Even though the Malian government has denied any relationship with private Russian security operations, French authorities have used this problematic political rhetoric of the Russian militia involvement to deny Mali's sovereign right to develop international partnerships to help it stop the killing of vulnerable populations. The French authorities' reaction to the Russian involvement in Mali has made the Malian government and populations think that foreign military operations in Mali and, more broadly, in the Sahel (Niger, Chad, and Burkina Faso) are merely aimed at serving French global geostrategic interests. Several reports by top French political leaders have recently raised concerns that France is losing footing in Africa.[110] Indeed, the French grip on Africa is being contested as the United States, China, and Russia are increasingly organizing high-profile forums on Africa and engaging in African security.[111] At the same time, the so-called anti-French feeling is growing in countries such as Mali, Burkina Faso, and Niger.[112]

In a way, the battle against terrorism in the Sahel has morphed into a geopolitical contest for Africa among great powers: the West, Russia, and China. Not surprisingly, the French defense ministry warned Malian authorities that the presence of Russians on Malian territory was unacceptable.[113] Even though Malian authorities point to the long-standing military cooperation between Mali and Russia and that their aim is primarily to protect their population, France threatened to stop its security mission; and in June 2021, France ended Operation Barkhane.[114] Malian authorities rejected French efforts to dictate the scope of Mali's international partnerships.[115] In May 2022, Mali ended military cooperation with France in line with Article 26 of the 2014 cooperation treaty between France and Mali.[116] Despite objections by African governments, France and, more generally, other Western powers have traditionally

The Conundrums of International Military Interventions in Africa

undervalued or ignored African standpoints on African security issues.[117] Western powers' attitude toward African solutions to African problems reinforces the view that foreign interventions in Africa serve primarily the Western vision of global liberal governance instead of the humanitarian and democratic principles they profess.

Overall, the fight against international terrorism in the Sahel has been instrumentalized for Western interests, as evident in the US Congressional Act HR 7311 of April 28, 2022 (Countering Malign Russian Activities in Africa Act).[118] The law requires the Department of State to report to Congress a strategy and implementation plan outlining US efforts to counter Russia's damaging influence and activities in Africa. Indeed, Russian military deployments in Africa, whether with a private organization or official military trainers, have become a source of tension between national and global security interests. Western powers are using their military operations in Africa to counterbalance Russia's growing influence in Africa, while Malians are more concerned with ending the terrorist violence in their country.

THE CONUNDRUM OF GLOCALIZED SECURITY IN CÔTE D'IVOIRE AND MALI

The core analysis of this chapter revolves around the inconsistencies of Western military interventions in Africa and whether these interventions comply with the broad humanitarian and democratic ideals of a globalized world. Are the interests of African countries properly addressed under glocalized security implemented through international military interventions? The military interventions of Western powers, especially former colonizers, in African countries, whether in Sierra Leone with the British Royal Army or more recently in Côte d'Ivoire, the Central African Republic, and Mali with the French army, have traditionally been perceived by Africans as normative. This is because these interventions are expected to end the turmoil, save civilians, and promote democracy. Indeed, for the international community that supports and regulates those interventions through UN resolutions, military interventions are part of the general efforts by external actors to bring stability to failed states and, more broadly, to enhance global security. Very often, such interventions begin with a request by African political leaders or the masses.

However, the Ivorian and Malian cases analyzed in this chapter show patterns of inconsistencies, limitations, and flaws in military interventions. The embeddedness of domestic problems into global issues has often been presented as a threat to global liberal governance. But the implementation of glocalized security solutions is often skewed toward the strategic interests of foreign powers. This inherent bias toward Western interests has made military interventions incoherent, often worsening domestic problems and undermining proper solutions to African problems. Such failures are often rooted in dubious geopolitical interests of major powers and repeated mistakes of the international peacebuilding model, which supports rebels, bifurcates countries, and prioritizes elections over security along the lines of the Western visions of global liberal governance and global security.

NOTES

1. Adam Smith, *The Wealth of the Nations* (London: W. Strahan and T. Cadell, 1776), 393–97.

2. Crawford Young, *The Postcolonial State in Africa: Fifty Years of Independence* (Madison: University of Wisconsin Press, 2012); Jean-François Bayart, *L'etat en Afrique: La politique du ventre* (Paris: Fayard, 2006).

3. Arthur Banga, "La reconstruction de la défense ivoirienne depuis avril 2011: Un enjeu de paix, de stabilité nationale et sous-régionale," in *Gouvernance et sécurité en Afrique subsaharienne francophone: Entre corruption politique et défis sécuritaires*, ed. Ibrahim Mouiche and Samuel Kale Ewusi, 305–326 (Addis Ababa: Université des Nations Unies pour la Paix, 2015); Guy André Kieffer, "Armée ivoirienne: Le refus du déclassement," *Politique Africaine* 2.78 (2000): 26–44; Mike McGovern, *Making War in Côte d'Ivoire* (Chicago: University of Chicago Press, 2012).

4. Alex Thurston, "Mali: The Disintegration of a 'Model African Democracy,'" *Stability* 2.1 (2013): 1–7; Andrew F. Clark, "From Military Dictatorship to Democracy: The Democratization Process in Mali," in *Democracy and Development in Mali*, ed. James R. Bingen, David Robinson, and John M. Staatz, 251–264 (East Lansing: Michigan State University Press, 2000).

5. Julia Dufour, "Mouvement national de libération de l'Azawad," Fiche documentaire du GRIP, May 22, 2012, https://archive.grip.org/fr/siteweb/dev_bc271d59 .asp.html; Alain Antil, *Rébellion Touareg et crise de l'État* (Paris: Ramses, 2009); Gérard-François Dumont, "La géopolitique des populations du Sahel," *La revue politique*, April 7, 2010, http://www.diploweb.com/La-geopolitique-des -populations-du.html; Mouiche and Ewusi, *Gouvernance et sécurité en Afrique subsaharienne francophone*; Abdoul Karim Saidou, "Conflits armés et sécurité au Sahel: Analyse comparée des politiques sécuritaires du Niger et du Mali face aux rébellions touarègues," in Mouiche and Ewusi, *Gouvernance et sécurité en Afrique subsaharienne francophone*.

6. Guillaume Soro, *Pourquoi je suis devenu rebelle* (Paris: Hachette, 2005); Jean-Christian Notin, *La guerre de la France au Mali* (Paris: Tallandier, 2014); Isabelle

Lassere and Thierry Oberle, *Notre guerre secrète au Mali: Les nouvelles menaces contre la France* (Paris: Fayard, 2013).

7. Boubacar Boris Diop and Aminata Dramane Traoré, *La gloire des imposteurs: Lettres sur le Mali et l'Afrique* (Paris: Philippe Rey, 2014); Abundant literature exists about this shadow African politics of France directly by a presidential cell of African affairs instead of the minister of foreign affairs.

8. AFP, "Mali: Manifestation contre la présence française dans les rues de Bamako," YouTube video, 1:27, October 31, 2021 https://www.youtube.com/watch?v=F5354feYujk.

9. Le Figaro, "Mali: Manifestation célébrant le départ des soldats français," Le Figaro, February 19, 2022, https://www.lefigaro.fr/flash-actu/mali-manifestation-celebrant-le-depart-des-soldats-francais-20220219.

10. Noam Chomsky, *Failed States: The Abuse of Power and the Assault on Democracy* (New York: Metropolitan Books, 2006); Robert I. Rotberg (ed.), "Failed States, Collapsed States, Weak States: Causes and Indicators," in *State Failure and State Weakness in a Time of Terror*, ed. Robert Rotberg (Washington, DC: Brookings Institution Press, 2003); Alfred Babo, "Faillite de l'Etat et administration de l'espace public politique par les 'jeunes patriotes' en Côte d'Ivoire," *Afrique en Développement* 34.3–4 (2009): 27–45; Abu Bakarr Bah, "State Decay: A Conceptual Frame for Failing and Failed States in West Africa," *International Journal of Politics, Culture, and Society* 25. 1–3 (2012): 71–89.

11. Abu Bakarr Bah, "The Contours of New Humanitarianism: War and Peacebuilding in Sierra Leone," *Africa Today* 60.1 (2013): 3–26; Larry J. Woods and Timothy R. Reese, *Military Interventions in Sierra Leone: Lessons from a Failed State* (Morrisville, NC: Lulu Press, 2011); Ella Abatan and Yolanda Spies, "African Solutions to African Problems? The AU, R2P and Côte d'Ivoire," *South African Journal of International Affairs* 23.1 (2016): 21–38; Foluke Ipinyomi, "Is Côte d'Ivoire a Test Case for R2P? Democratization as Fulfilment of the International Community's Responsibility to Prevent," *Journal of African Law* 56.2 (2012) 151–174.

12. Abu Bakarr Bah, "African Agency in New Humanitarianism and Responsible Governance," in *International Security and Peacebuilding: Africa, the Middle East, and Europe*, ed. Abu Bakarr Bah (Bloomington: Indiana University Press, 2017).

13. Olivier Jouvray, *Bob Denard, le dernier mercenaire* (Paris: Glenart, 2021); Antoine Glaser and Thomas Hofnung, *Nos chers espions en Afrique* (Paris: Fayard, 2018); Francois-Xavier Verschave, *L'horreur qui nous prend au visage: L'État français et le génocide; Rapport de la Commission d'enquête citoyenne sur le rôle de la France dans le génocide des Tutsi au Rwanda* (Paris: Karthala, 2005); Thomas Borrel et al., *L'Empire qui ne veut pas mourir: Une histoire de la Françafrique* (Paris: Seuil, 2021).

14. Francois-Xavier Verschave, *Complicité de genocide? La politique de la France au Rwanda* (Paris: La decouverte, 2013); Raphaël Doridant and François Graner, *L'État français et le génocide des Tutsis au Rwanda* (Marseille: Agone, 2020).

15. Bah, "The Contours of New Humanitarianism."

16. Rotberg, *Failed States, Collapsed States, Weak States*, 1.
17. Roland J. Pennock, "Political Development, Political Systems, and Political Goods," *World Politics* 38.433 (1966): 420–426; William I. Zartman, "Introduction: Posing the Problem of State Collapse," in *Collapsed States: The Disintegration and Restoration of Legitimate Authority*, ed. William I. Zartman (Boulder, CO: Lynne Rienner, 1995); Rotberg, *Failed States, Collapsed States, Weak States*; Bah, "State Decay."
18. Zartman, "Introduction: Posing the Problem of State Collapse"; Chandra Lekha Sriram and Karin Wermester, *From Promise to Practice: Strengthening UN Capacities for the Prevention of Violent Conflict* (New York: International Peace Academy, 2003).
19. Rotberg, *Failed States, Collapsed States, Weak States*.
20. Pennock, "Political Development, Political Systems, and Political Goods."
21. Rotberg, *Failed States, Collapsed States, Weak States*, 3.
22. Bah, "State Decay."
23. Rotberg, *Failed States, Collapsed States, Weak States*.
24. René Lemarchand, "The Democratic Republic of the Congo: From Failure to Potential Reconstruction," in *State Failure and State Weakness in a Time of Terror*, ed. Robert Rotberg (Washington, DC: Brookings Institution Press, 2003); Gérard Prunier and Rachel Gisselquist, "The Sudan: A Successfully Failed State," in *When States Fail: Causes and Consequences*, ed. Robert I. Rotberg (Washington, DC: Brookings Institution Press, 2003); Jennifer A. Widner, "State and Statelessness in Late Twentieth-Century Africa," in Rotberg, *When States Fail*, 222–237.
25. Turkan Firinci Orman, "An Analysis of the Notion of a 'Failed State,'" *International Journal of Social Science Studies* 4.1 (2016): 77–85; Hussein Solomon and Cornelia Cone, "The State and Conflict in the Democratic Republic of Congo," *South African Journal of Military Studies* 32.1 (2004): 51–75; Bah, "State Decay."
26. Michel Luntumbue, "Groupes armés, conflits et gouvernance en Afrique de l'Ouest: Une grille de lecture," *Note d'Analyse du GRIP*, January 27, 2012, 327–346; Roland Marchal, "Tchad/Darfour: Vers un système de conflits," *Politique africaine* 2.102 (2006): 135–154; Marc Memier, *Systèmes de conflits et enjeux sécuritaires en Afrique de l'Ouest* (Dakar: Gorée Institute, 2012); Mouiche and Ewusi, *Gouvernance et sécurité en Afriquesubsaharienne francophone*.
27. Samuel Marfo, Halidu Musah, and Arthur Dominic DeGraft, "Beyond Classical Peace Paradigm: A Theoretical Argument for a 'Glocalized Peace and Security,'" *African Journal of Political Science and International Relations* 10.4 (2016): 47–55.
28. Peace Medie, *Global Norms and Local Action: The Campaigns to End Violence against Women in Africa* (Oxford: Oxford University Press, 2020).
29. Failed States Index 2010, https://foreignpolicy.com/2010/06/16/2010-failed-states-index-interactive-map-and-rankings/.
30. Kieffer, "Armée ivoirienne."
31. Abu Bakarr Bah, "Democracy and Civil War: Citizenship and Peacemaking in Côte d'Ivoire," *African affairs* 109.437 (2010): 597–615; McGovern, *Making War*

in Côte d'Ivoire; Alfred Babo, *L'étranger en Côte d'Ivoire: Crises et controverses autour d'une catégorie sociale* (Paris: L'Harmattan, 2013).

32. Human Rights Watch, "Attaques contre les civils et autres non-combattants perpétrées par les groupes rebelles ivoiriens," Human Rights Watch, August 2003, https://www.hrw.org/legacy/french/reports/2003/cotedivoire0803/9.htm.

33. Alfred Babo, "Les enjeux de la violence politique chez les milices des 'jeunes patriotes' d'Abidjan en Côte d'Ivoire," *Annales de l'Université de Lomé* 31.1 (2011): 247–260.

34. Human Rights Watch, "Côte d'Ivoire: West African Immigrants Massacred," Human Rights Watch, March 31, 2011, https://www.hrw.org/news/2011/03/31/cote-divoire-west-african-immigrants-massacred; AI Report, "Côte d'Ivoire: A Succession of Unpunished Crimes," Amnesty International, February 27, 2003, https://www.amnesty.org/en/wp-content/uploads/2021/06/afr310072003en .pdf.

35. N'guessan Kouamé, "Le Forum pour la réconciliation nationale: 9 octobre–18 décembre 2001," in *Côte d'Ivoire: L'année terrible 1999–2000*, ed. Marc Le Pape (Paris: Karthala, 2003), https://www.cairn.info/--9782845863170-page-325 .htm.

36. Elio Comarin, "Côte d'Ivoire: Gbagbo dénonce la 'complicité' du Burkina," Radio France Internationale, October 25, 2002, http://www1.rfi.fr/actufr/articles/034 /article_17719.asp; Babo, *L'étranger en Côte d'Ivoire*; Pierre Janin, "Peut-on encore être étranger à Abidjan?," *Monde diplomatique* 559 (2000): 22.

37. Mathieu Adjagbe, "Les Dessous de l'opération Licorne En Côte d'Ivoire: Pour une lecture géopolitique nouvelle des interventions françaises en Afrique," *Afrique et Développement* 34.2 (2009): 159–175.

38. Especially peace agreements called Accra I, II, and III.

39. Côte d'Ivoire, "Linas Marcoussis Agreement," S/2003/99, January 27, 2003, https://peacemaker.un.org/sites/peacemaker.un.org/files/CI_030123 _LinasMarcousisAgreement.pdf; Côte d'Ivoire, "Accord Politique de Ouagadougou," United Nations Peacemaker, March 2007, https://peacemaker.un .org/sites/peacemaker.un.org/files/CI_070304_Accord%20Politique%20de %20Ouagadougou%20%28French%29.pdf.

40. UN General Assembly and Security Council, "Rapport du Groupe d'experts sur la Côte d'Ivoire," S/2009/521, October 9, 2009, 62–82, http://www.un.org /french/documents/view_doc.asp?symbol=S/2009/521; UN Security Council Resolution 1572 du C.S.N.U. S/RES/1572, November 15, 2004, https://www.un .org/securitycouncil/s/res/1572-%282004%29.

41. Leslie Varenne, *Abobo la guerre: Côte d'Ivoire; Terrain de jeu de la France et de l'ONU* (Paris: Edition Mille et une nuit, 2011); Babo, *L'étranger en Côte d'Ivoire*.

42. AI Report, "Côte d'Ivoire: A Succession of Unpunished Crimes"; *Le Monde*, "Des affrontements ont fait au moins 800 morts à Duékoué, selon le CICR," *Le Monde*, April 2, 2011, https://www.lemonde.fr/afrique/article/2011/04/02/des -affrontements-ont-fait-au-moins-800-morts-a-duekoue-selon-le-cicr_1502042 _3212.html.

43. Varenne, *Abobo la guerre.*

44. Stephen Smith, "La France dans la crise ivoirienne: Ni ingérence, ni indifférence, mais indolence post-coloniale," in Le Pape, *Côte d'Ivoire.*

45. Mamadou Koulibaly, Garry K. Busch, and Antoine Ahua, *La guerre de la France contre la Côte d'Ivoire* (Paris: L'Harmattan, 2003).

46. United Nations, "Security Council Demands End to Violence in Cote d'Ivoire, Imposing Sanctions against Former President and Urging Him to 'Step Aside,' in Resolution 1975," United Nations, Meetings Coverage and Press Releases, March 30, 2011, https://www.un.org/press/en/2011/sc10215.doc.htm.

47. Bah, "African Agency in New Humanitarianism and Responsible Governance," 49.

48. United Nations, "Security Council Authorizes Deployment of African-Led International Support Mission in Mali for Initial Year-Long Period," United Nations, Meetings Coverage and Press Releases, December 20, 2012, https://press.un.org/en/2012/sc10870.doc.htm.

49. G5 Sahel, "La force conjointe du G5 Sahel a atteint la maturité déclare son commandant," G5 Sahel, March 12, 2021, https://www.g5sahel.org/la-force-conjointe-a-atteint-la-maturite-declare-son-commandant.

50. L'Express, "Le Mali appelle la France au secours," L'Express, January 11, 2011, https://www.lexpress.fr/actualite/monde/afrique/le-mali-appelle-la-france-au-secours_1208549.html.

51. Natalie Nougayrède, "La lettre du président malien, base légale de l'intervention française," *Le Monde,* January 25, 2013, https://www.lemonde.fr/afrique/article/2013/01/25/la-base-legale-de-l-action-francaise-une-lettre-de-m-traore_1822493_3212.html.

52. Notin, *La guerre de la France au Mali.*

53. Vox of America, "Les opérations militaires au Mali depuis 2013," Vox of America, July 27, 2018, https://www.voaafrique.com/a/les-op%C3%A9rations-militaires-au-mali-depuis-2013/4502522.html.

54. Radio France Internationale, "Mali, la manifestion du M5 contre IBK dégénère à Bamako," Radio France Internationale, July 10, 2020, https://www.rfi.fr/fr/afrique/20200710-mali-le-m5-nouveau-la-rue-r%C3%A9clamer-la-d%C3%A9mission-pr%C3%A9sident-ibk.

55. Paul Lorgerie and Jean-Philippe Rémy "Coup d'état au Mali: Le président Ibrahim Boubacar Keita démissionne," *Le Monde,* August 18, 2020, https://www.lemonde.fr/afrique/article/2020/08/18/coup-d-etat-au-mali-le-president-ibrahim-boubacar-keita-et-son-premier-ministre-aux-mains-des-putschistes_6049272_3212.html.

56. G5 Sahel, "Formation de la force Takuba," G5 Sahel, March 28, 2020, https://www.g5sahel.org/formation-de-la-task-force-takuba/.

57. Giulia Piccolino, "Ultranationalism, Democracy and the Law: Insights from Côte d'Ivoire," *The Journal of Modern African Studies* 52.1 (2014): 45–68.

58. Stephen D. Krasner, "Sharing Sovereignty: New Institutions for Collapsed and Failing States," *International Security* 29.2 (2004): 85–120.

The Conundrums of International Military Interventions in Africa 169

59. Bah, "African Agency in New Humanitarianism and Responsible Governance."
60. Piccolino, "Ultranationalism, Democracy and the Law."
61. Antoine Glaser, *Arrogant comme un Français en Afrique* (Paris: Fayard, 2016).
62. Mamadou Koulibaly, *Les servitudes du pacte colonial* (Abidjan: CEDA et NEI, 2005); Richard Banégas and Ruth Marshall-Fratani, "Côte d'Ivoire, un conflit régional?," *Politique africaine* 1.89 (2003): 5–11.
63. Soro, *Pourquoi je suis devenu rebelle*, 125.
64. Radio France Internationale, "Le Nigeria demande à l'ONU d'autoriser l'usage éventuel de la force," Radio France Internationale, January 25, 2011, https://www.rfi.fr/fr/mfi/20110125-le-nigeria-demande-onu-autoriser-usage-eventuel-force.
65. Human Rights Watch, "Côte d'Ivoire: Les forces de Ouattara ont tué et violé des civils pendant leur offensive," Human Rights Watch, April 9, 2011, https://www.hrw.org/fr/news/2011/04/09/cote-divoire-les-forces-de-ouattara-ont-tue-et-viole-des-civils-pendant-leur.
66. Afrik.com, "Nicolas Sarkozy: 'On a sorti Gbagbo et installé Ouattara, sans aucune polémique,'" Afrik.com, December 19, 2014, https://www.afrik.com/nicolas-sarkozy-on-a-sorti-gbagbo-et-installe-ouattara-sans-aucune-polemique.
67. Vox of America, "Les opérations militaires."
68. The concept of "nation-cadre" presented by Germany within NATO in 2013 and adopted by the Alliance at the Newport Summit in 2014 aims at multilateral defense cooperation. The idea is to add the few capacities that remain in the small armies to those of a large nation-cadre, which would constitute the organizing keystone.
69. According to Africa News, more than twenty-five thousand foreign soldiers were in Mali in February 2022. Lauriane Noelle Vofo Kana, "France and European Allies to Withdraw Troops from Mali but Remain in Region," Africa News, January 7, 2022, https://www.africanews.com/2022/02/17/france-and-european-allies-to-withdraw-troops-from-mali-but-remain-in-region.
70. The Conversation, "Pourquoi l'opinion publique malienne a une vision négative de l'opération Barkhane," The Conversation, February 10, 2020, https://theconversation.com/pourquoi-lopinion-publique-malienne-a-une-vision-negative-de-loperation-barkhane-130640.
71. TV5 Monde, "Djihadisme au Mali: Des négociations sont-elles possibles?," TV5 Monde, December 24, 2021, https://information.tv5monde.com/afrique/djihadisme-au-mali-des-negociations-sont-elles-possibles-429909; Marc-Antoine Pérouse de Montclos, "Faut-il négocier avec les djihadistes au Sahel?," *Politique étrangère* 1 (2020): 175–187.
72. Woods and Reese, *Military Interventions in Sierra Leone*.
73. Christian Henderson, "International Measures for the Protection of Civilians in Libya and Côte d'Ivoire," *International and Comparative Law Quarterly* 60.3 (2011): 767–778.
74. UN Peacekeeping, "Côte d'Ivoire, MINUCI Background," UN Peacekeeping, accessed November 11, 2023, https://peacekeeping.un.org/en/mission/past/minuci/background.html.

75. Piccolino, "Ultranationalism, Democracy and the Law."

76. Giulia Piccolino, "David against Goliath in Côte d'Ivoire? Laurent Gbagbo's War against Global Governance," *African Affairs* 111.442 (2011): 1–23.

77. Amnesty International, "Côte d'Ivoire: Revenge and Repression under the Pretense of Ensuring Security," Amnesty International, February 26, 2013, https://www.amnesty.org/en/latest/news/2013/02/c-te-d-ivoire-revenge-and-repression-under-pretence-ensuring-security.

78. About this incident, see also this report by Al Jazeera: Al Jazeera English, "Cote d'Ivoire Partial Justice: People and Power," YouTube video, 2:08, January 26, 2017, https://www.youtube.com/watch?v=9ErFmPye-xY. See also Amnesty International, "Revenge and Repression in Cote d'Ivoire," YouTube video, 3:39, February 25, 2013, https://www.youtube.com/watch?v=UDI22b9hevk.

79. Dorina A. Bekoe, "The United Nations Operation in Côte d'Ivoire: How a Certified Election Still Turned Violent," *International Peacekeeping* 25.1 (2018): 128–153.

80. Abidjan.net, "Le patron de l'ONU Ban-ki Moon rejette le recomptage des voix," Abidjan.net, February 3, 2011, https://news.abidjan.net/videos/5738/crise-ivoirienne-le-patron-de-lonu-ban-ki-moon-rejette-le-recomptage-des-voix.

81. Bérangère Rouppert, "La Côte d'Ivoire un an après: Rétrospective sur cinq mois de crise électorale, ses impacts et ses questionnements," Rapport du GRIP, 2012, 8, https://www.grip.org/product/cote-divoire-un-an-apres-retrospective-sur-cinq-mois-de-crise-electorale-ses-impacts-et-ses-questionnements/.

82. Philippe Leymarie, "L'ONU en Côte d'Ivoire, combien de divisions?," *Le Monde diplomatique* (blog), December 23, 2010, https://blog.mondediplo.net/2010-12-23-L-ONU-en-Cote-d-Ivoire-combien-de-divisions.

83. United Nations, "Recognizing Interconnected Nature of Haiti's Long-term Development Challenges, Security Council Reiterates Need for Sustained International Support," United Nations, Meetings Coverage and Press Releases, April 6, 2011, https://www.un.org/press/en/2011/sc10218.doc.htm; Institute for Justice and Democracy in Haiti, "Report on the of the Role International Community in Ensuring Fair Elections in Haiti," July 5, 2010, archived at the Wayback Machine, https://web.archive.org/web/20110813083218/http://ijdh.org/archives/13186; Centre for Economic and Policy Research, "The Organization of American States in Haiti: Election Monitoring or Political Intervention?," Centre for Economic and Policy Research, August 2011, https://cepr.net/documents/publications/haiti-oas-2011-10.pdf.

84. Interview on Radio France International, "Mali—Choguel K. Maïga: 'Pourquoi je parle de trahison . . . ,'" YouTube video, 16:58, February 22, 2022, https://www.youtube.com/watch?v=5Fq-ANyUASg&t=22s.

85. Ségolène Allemandou, "Mali: Le MNLA, un nouvel allié pour l'armée française?," France 24, January 23, 2013, https://www.france24.com/fr/20130123-mnla-armee-francaise-mali-negociations-bamako-rebelles-touaregs-islamistes-ansar-dine; Francis Simonis, "Au Mali, l'étrange alliance de la France avec les Touaregs du MNLA," *L'Obs*, January 24, 2017, https://www.nouvelobs.com/rue89/rue89

-afrique/20130211.RUE3171/au-mali-l-etrange-alliance-de-la-france-avec-les
-touaregs-du-mnla.html.

86. Radio France Internationale, "Moussa Ag Acharatoumane: Au Mali, 'nous comb-attons une organisation criminelle,'" Radio France Internationale, April 23, 2018, https://www.rfi.fr/fr/emission/20180423-moussa-ag-acharatoumane-porte -parole-msa-mouvement-le-salut-azawad.

87. OCHA, "Final Communique: 4th Extraordinary Summit of the ECOWAS Authority of Heads of State and Government on the Political Situation in Mali," ReliefWeb, January 9, 2022, https://reliefweb.int/report/mali/final -communique-4th-extraordinary-summit-ecowas-authority-heads-state-and -government. The sanctions were lifted after six months in July 2022.

88. Agence Ecofin, "Mali: La France menace les dirigeants de sanctions, alors que la Russie les soutient," Agence Ecofin, November 22, 2021, https://www .agenceecofin.com/actualites/2211-93334-mali-la-france-menace-les-dirigeants -de-sanctions-alors-que-la-russie-les-soutient.

89. United Nations, "Convention on Transit Trade of Land-Locked States," United Nations Treaty Collection, July 8, 1965, https://treaties.un.org/Pages/ ViewDetails.aspx?src=IND&mtdsg_no=X-3&chapter=10&clang=_en.

90. Mbeki Thabo, "What the World Got Wrong in Côte D'Ivoire," Foreign Policy, April 29, 2011, https://foreignpolicy.com/2011/04/29/what-the-world-got -wrong-in-cote-divoire.

91. McGovern, *Making War in Côte d'Ivoire.*

92. Piccolino, "David against Goliath in Côte d'Ivoire?," 4.

93. In June 2008 the situation in the DRC led to the UN Resolution 1820 identify-ing "rape as a war crime."

94. Alfred Babo, "Postwar Governance: Human Rights and Peacebuilding in Côte d'Ivoire," *African Conflict & Peacebuilding Review* 9.1 (2019): 24–53.

95. Former president Laurent Gbagbo, former leader of Young Patriots Charles Ble Goude, and former leader of the rebellion and former speaker of the National Assembly Soro Guillaume; see also ACtHPR, case/0442019, https://www .african-court.org/cpmt/fr/details-case/0442019.

96. HRW, "Côte d'Ivoire: Post-election Violence, Repression." https://www.hrw.org /news/2020/12/02/cote-divoire-post-election-violence-repression.

97. Abu Bakarr Bah, "Changing World Order and the Future of Democracy in Sub-Saharan Africa," *Proteus-Shippensburg* 21.1 (2004): 3–12.

98. Corentin Bainier and Alexandre Capron, "Côte d'Ivoire: À Daoukro, une mani-festation de l'opposition dégénère dans l'horreur," France 24, November 11, 2020, https://observers.france24.com/fr/20201111-cote-ivoire-daoukro-manifestation -opposition-horreur-homme-decapite; United Nations, "Côte D'ivoire: UN Reports 3,000 Flee Abroad amid Electoral Violence," UN News, November 3, 2020, https://news.un.org/en/story/2020/11/1076762.

99. Mali, "Accord Pour la Paix et la Reconciliation au Mali—Issu du Processus d'Al-ger," United Nations Peacemaker, March 1, 2015, https://peacemaker.un.org/ node/2681.

100. See list of killings in Mali since 2012. "Liste de massacres de la guerre du Mali," Wikipedia, last updated November 2, 2023, https://fr.wikipedia.org/wiki/Liste_de_massacres_de_la_guerre_du_Mali.

101. "Massacres d'Aklaz et Awkassa," Wikipedia, last updated October 1, 2022, https://fr.wikipedia.org/wiki/Massacres_d%27Aklaz_et_Awkassa; L'Aube, "Sobane Da: Le bilan fait état de 101 morts!," Maliweb.net, July 15, 2019, https://www.maliweb.net/nouvelles-breves/sobane-da-le-bilan-fait-etat-de-101-morts-2828485.html.

102. Vox of America, "Manifestations de femmes et d'enfants de militaires tués dans le centre du Mali," Vox of America, March 22, 2019, https://www.voaafrique.com/a/manifestations-de-femmes-et-d-enfants-de-militaires-tu%C3%A9s-dans-le-centre-du-mali/4842896.html.

103. Radio France Internationale, "Mali: Possibles découvertes de charniers vers Nantaka et Kobaka, dans le centre," Radio France Internationale, June 18, 2018, https://www.rfi.fr/fr/afrique/20180618-mali-possibles-decouvertes-charniers-peuls-nantaka-kobaka-armee-fama.

104. TV5 Monde, "Paris menace de retirer ses troupes si le Mali s'allie avec le groupe russe Wagner," TV5 Monde, September 14, 2021, https://information.tv5monde.com/afrique/paris-menace-de-retirer-ses-troupes-si-le-mali-s-allie-avec-le-groupe-russe-wagner-424414. In a statement, the French minister of foreign affairs, Jean-Yves Le Drian, warned that cooperation between the junta in power in Mali and the private Russian company Wagner would be "incompatible" with the maintenance of a French force in this country.

105. Mark Duffield, *Global Governance and the New Wars: The Merging of Development and Security* (London: Zed Books, 2001).

106. Glaser, *Arrogant comme un Français en Afrique*, 18.

107. Koulibaly, *Les servitudes du pacte colonial*; Francois-Xavier Verschave, *La Francafrique: Le plus long scandale de la République* (Paris: Stock, 1998).

108. Olivier Tramond and Philippe Seigneur, "French Army Operation Serval Another Beau Geste of France in Sub-Saharan Africa?," *Military Review* 94.6 (2014): 85.

109. Marco Wyss, "The Gendarme Stays in Africa: France's Military Role in Côte d'Ivoire," *African Conflict and Peacebuilding Review* 3.1 (2013): 81–111.

110. Glaser, *Arrogant comme un Français en Afrique*.

111. "Second Summit, Russia-Africa Economic and Humanitarian Forum, Declaration of the First Russia-Africa Summit," accessed November 14, 2023, https://summitafrica.ru/en/.

112. Africa 24, "Mali, manifestations Anti-politique française," YouTube video, 1:46, January 13, 2020, https://www.youtube.com/watch?v=AF3MpmtAsOA; France 24, "Burkina: Un convoi militaire français toujours bloqué par des manifestants," YouTube video, 4:28, November 23, 2021, https://www.youtube.com/watch?v=wB1AvJfAR4g; France 24, "Le convoi militaire de l'opération Barkhane attaqué au Niger est arrivé à Gao," YouTube video, 7:37, November 29, 2021, https://www.youtube.com/watch?v=6ZhzMUlrYZo.

113. Interview on France 24 and RFI, "Florence Parly: La présence du groupe Wagner au Mali serait 'inacceptable,'" YouTube video, 14:13, December 6, 2021, https://www.youtube.com/watch?v=DU2VfPxYxO4.

114. France completed its total removal of troops and military equipment on August 16, 2022. Radio France Internationale, "Mali: Fin du retrait de la force française Barkhane," YouTube video, 2:06, August 16, 2022, https://www.youtube.com/watch?v=M7ug5PCwXdg.

115. Malian minister of foreign affairs address to the UN Security Council on June 13, 2022. ORTM, "Discours M. Abdoulaye DIOP devant le conseil de sécurité de l'ONU," YouTube video, 27:26, June 13, 2022, https://www.youtube.com/watch?v=ZXxuFsR_kE4.

116. Geneviève Sagno, "Accords de défense militaire: Pourquoi le Mali rompt avec la France et l'Europe et quels sont ces accords?," BBC News, May 3, 2022, https://www.bbc.com/afrique/region-61313497.

117. Abatan and Spies, "African Solutions to African Problems?," 21–38.

118. Congress.gov, H.R.7311—Countering Malign Russian Activities in Africa Act, Congress.gov, April 28, 2022, https://www.congress.gov/bill/117th-congress/house-bill/7311/text.

BIBLIOGRAPHY

Abatan, Ella, and Yolanda Spies. "African Solutions to African Problems? The AU, R2P and Côte d'Ivoire." *South African Journal of International Affairs* 23.1 (2016): 21–38.

Abidjan.net. "Le patron de l'ONU Ban-ki Moon rejette le recomptage des voix." Abidjan .net, February 3, 2011. https://news.abidjan.net/videos/5738/crise-ivoirienne-le -patron-de-lonu-ban-ki-moon-rejette-le-recomptage-des-voix.

Adjagbe, Mathieu. "Les Dessous de l'opération Licorne En Côte d'Ivoire: Pour une lecture géopolitique nouvelle des interventions françaises en Afrique." *Africa Development* 34.2 (2009): 159–75. http://www.jstor.org/stable/24484024.

Afrik.com. "Nicolas Sarkozy: 'On a sorti Gbagbo et installé Ouattara, sans aucune polémique.'" Afrik.com, December 19, 2014. https://www.afrik.com/nicolas -sarkozy-on-a-sorti-gbagbo-et-installe-ouattara-sans-aucune-polemique.

Agence Ecofin. "Mali: La France menace les dirigeants de sanctions, alors que la Russie les soutient." Agence Ecofin, November 22, 2021. https://www.agenceecofin.com /actualites/2211-93334-mali-la-france-menace-les-dirigeants-de-sanctions-alors -que-la-russie-les-soutient.

Allemandou, Ségolène. "Mali: Le MNLA, un nouvel allié pour l'armée française?" France24, January 23, 2013. https://www.france24.com/fr/20130123-mnla-armee -francaise-mali-negociations-bamako-rebelles-touaregs-islamistes-ansar-dine.

Amnesty International. "Côte d'Ivoire: A Succession of Unpunished Crimes." Amnesty International, February 27, 2003. https://www.amnesty.org/en/wp-content/ uploads/2021/06/afr310072003en.pdf.

———. "Côte d'Ivoire: Revenge and Repression under the Pretence of Ensuring Security." Amnesty International, February 26, 2013. https://www.amnesty.org/

en/latest/news/2013/02/c-te-d-ivoire-revenge-and-repression-under-pretence
-ensuring-security.

Antil, Alain. *Rébellion Touareg et crise de l'État*. Paris: Ramses, 2009. www.ifri.org/
downloads/ramses2009parties_1.pdf.

Babo, Alfred. "Faillite de l'Etat et administration de l'espace public politique par les
'jeunes patriotes' en Côte d'Ivoire." *Afrique en Développement* 34.3–4 (2009):
27–45.

———. "Les enjeux de la violence politique chez les milices des 'jeunes patriotes' d'Abidjan en Côte d'Ivoire." *Annales de l'Université de Lomé* 31.1 (2011): 247–260.

———. *L'étranger en Côte d'Ivoire: Crises et controverses autour d'une catégorie sociale*.
Paris: L'Harmattan, 2013.

———. "Postwar Governance: Human Rights and Peacebuilding in Côte d'Ivoire." *African Conflict & Peacebuilding Review* 9.1 (2019): 24–53.

Bah, Abu Bakarr. "Changing World Order and the Future of Democracy in Sub-
Saharan Africa." *Proteus-Shippensburg* 21.1 (2004): 3–12.

———. "Democracy and Civil War: Citizenship and Peacemaking in Côte d'Ivoire."
African Affairs 109.437 (2010): 597–615.

———. "State Decay: A Conceptual Frame for Failing and Failed States in West Africa." *International Journal of Politics, Culture, and Society* 25.1–3 (2012): 71–89.

———. "The Contours of New Humanitarianism: War and Peacebuilding in Sierra
Leone." *Africa Today* 60.1 (2013): 3–26.

———. "African Agency in New Humanitarianism and Responsible Governance." In
International Security and Peacebuilding: Africa, the Middle East, and Europe, ed.
Abu Bakarr Bah, 148–169. Bloomington: Indiana University Press, 2017.

Bainier, Corentin, and Alexandre Capron. "Côte d'Ivoire: À Daoukro, une manifestation de l'opposition dégénère dans l'horreur." France24, November 11, 2020.
https://observers.france24.com/fr/20201111-cote-ivoire-daoukro-manifestation
-opposition-horreur-homme-decapite.

Banégas, Richard, and Ruth Marshall-Fratani. "Côte d'Ivoire, un conflit régional?" *Politique africaine* 1.89 (2003): 5–11.

Banga, Arthur. "La reconstruction de la défense ivoirienne depuis avril 2011: Un enjeu
de paix, de stabilité nationale et sous-régionale." In *Gouvernance et sécurité en
Afrique subsaharienne francophone: Entre corruption politique et défis sécuritaires*,
ed. Ibrahim Mouiche et Samuel Kale Ewusi, 305–326. Addis Ababa: Université
des Nations Unies pour la Paix, 2015.

Bayart, Jean-François. *L'état en Afrique: La politique du ventre*. Paris: Fayard, 2006.

Bekoe, A. Dorina. "The United Nations Operation in Côte d'Ivoire: How a Certified
Election Still Turned Violent." *International Peacekeeping* 25.1 (2018): 128–153.

Borrel, Thomas, Amzat B. Yabara, Benoit Collombat, and Thomas Deltombe. *L'Empire
qui ne veut pas mourir: Une histoire de la Françafrique*. Paris: Seuil, 2021.

Centre for Economic and Policy Research. "The Organization of American States in
Haiti: Election Monitoring or Political Intervention?" Centre for Economic and
Policy Research, August 2011. https://cepr.net/documents/publications/haiti
-oas-2011-10.pdf.

Chomsky, Noam. *Failed States: The Abuse of Power and the Assault on Democracy*. New York: Metropolitan Books, 2006.

Clark, F. Andrew. "From Military Dictatorship to Democracy: The Democratization Process in Mali." In *Democracy and Development in Mali*, ed. James R. Bingen, David Robinson, and John M. Staatz, 251–264. East Lansing: Michigan State University Press, 2000.

Comarin, Elio. "Côte d'Ivoire: Gbagbo dénonce la 'complicité' du Burkina." Radio France Internationale, October 25, 2002. http://www.rfi.fr/actufr/articles/034/article17719.asp.

Congress.gov. "H.R.7311—Countering Malign Russian Activities in Africa Act." Congress.gov, April 28, 2022. https://www.congress.gov/bill/117th-congress/house-bill/7311/text.

Côte d'Ivoire. "Accord Politique de Ouagadougou." United Nations Peacemaker, March 2007. https://peacemaker.un.org/sites/peacemaker.un.org/files/CI_070304_Accord%20Politique%20de%20Ouagadougou%20%28French%29.pdf.

———. "Linas Marcoussis Agreement." S/2003/99, January 27, 2003. https://peacemaker.un.org/sites/peacemaker.un.org/files/CI_030123_LinasMarcousisAgreement.pdf.

Diop, Boubacar Boris, and Aminata Dramane Traoré. *La gloire des imposteurs: Lettres sur le Mali et l'Afrique*. Paris: Philippe Rey, 2014.

Doridant, Raphaël, and François Graner. *L'État français et le génocide des Tutsis au Rwand*. Marseille: Agone, 2020.

Duffield, Mark. *Global Governance and the New Wars: The Merging of Development and Security*. London: Zed Books, 2001.

Dufour, Julia. "Mouvement national de libération de l'Azawad." May 22, 2012, Fiche documentaire du GRIP. https://archive.grip.org/fr/siteweb/dev_bc271d59.asp.html.

Dumont, Gérard-François. "La géopolitique des populations du Sahel." *La revue politique*, April 7, 2010. http://www.diploweb.com/La-geopolitique-des-populations-du.html.

Eboulé, Christian. "Djihadisme au Mali: Des négociations sont-elles possibles?" TV5 Monde, December 24, 2021. https://information.tv5monde.com/afrique/djihadisme-au-mali-des-negociations-sont-elles-possibles-429909.

G5 Sahel. "La force conjointe du G5 Sahel a atteint la maturité déclare son commandant." G5 Sahel, March 12, 2021. https://www.g5sahel.org/la-force-conjointe-a-atteint-la-maturite-declare-son-commandant.

———. "Formation de la force Takuba." G5 Sahel, March 28, 2020. https://www.g5sahel.org/formation-de-la-task-force-takuba.

Glaser, Antoine. *Arrogant comme un Français en Afrique*. Paris: Fayard, 2016.

Glaser, Antoine, and Thomas Hofnung. *Nos chers espions en Afrique*. Paris: Fayard, 2018.

Henderson, Christian. "International Measures for the Protection of Civilians in Libya and Côte d'Ivoire." *International and Comparative Law Quarterly* 60.3 (2011): 767–778.

Human Rights Watch. "Attaques contre les civils et autres non-combattants perpétrées par les groupes rebelles ivoiriens." Human Rights Watch, August 2003. https://www.hrw.org/legacy/french/reports/2003/cotedivoire0803/9.htm.

———. "Côte d'Ivoire: West African Immigrants Massacred." Human Rights Watch, March 31, 2011. https://www.hrw.org/news/2011/03/31/cote-divoire-west-african-immigrants-massacred.

———. "Côte d'Ivoire: Les forces de Ouattara ont tué et violé des civils pendant leur offensive." Human Rights Watch, April 9, 2011. https://www.hrw.org/news/2011/04/09/cote-divoire-ouattara-forces-kill-rape-civilians-during-offensive.

———. "Côte d'Ivoire: Post-election Violence, Repression." Human Rights Watch, December 2, 2020. https://www.hrw.org/news/2020/12/02/cote-divoire-post-election-violence-repression.

Institute for Justice and Democracy in Haiti. "Report on the Role of the International Community in Ensuring Fair Elections in Haiti." July 5, 2010. Archived at the Wayback Machine. https://web.archive.org/web/20110813083218/http://ijdh.org/archives/13186.

Ipinyomi, Foluke. "Is Côte d'Ivoire a Test Case for R2P? Democratization as Fulfilment of the International Community's Responsibility to Prevent." Journal of African Law 56.2 (2012): 151–174.

Janin, Pierre. "Peut-on encore être étranger à Abidjan?" Monde diplomatique 559 (2000): 22.

Jouvray, Olivier. Bob Denard, le dernier mercenaire. Paris: Glenart, 2021.

Kieffer, Guy André. "Armée ivoirienne: Le refus du déclassement." Politique Africaine 2.78 (2000): 26–44.

Kouamé, N'guessan. "Le Forum pour la réconciliation nationale: 9 octobre–18 décembre 2001." In Côte d'Ivoire: L'année terrible 1999–2000, ed. Marc Le Pape, 325–35. Paris: Karthala, 2003.

Koulibaly, Mamadou. Les servitudes du pacte colonial. Abidjan: CEDA et NEI, 2005.

Koulibaly, Mamadou, Garry. K Busch, and Antoine Ahua. La guerre de la France contre la Côte d'Ivoire. Paris: L'Harmattan, 2003.

Krasner, D. Stephen. "Sharing Sovereignty: New Institutions for Collapsed and Failing States." International Security 29.2 (2004): 85–120.

Lassere, Isabelle, and Thierry Oberle. Notre guerre secrète au Mali: Les nouvelles menaces contre la France. Paris: Fayard, 2013.

Le Figaro. "Mali: Manifestation célébrant le départ des soldats français." Le Figaro, February 19, 2022. https://www.lefigaro.fr/flash-actu/mali-manifestation-celebrant-le-depart-des-soldats-francais-20220219.

Lemarchand, René. "The Democratic Republic of the Congo: From Failure to Potential Reconstruction," In State Failure and State Weakness in a Time of Terror, ed. Robert Rotberg, 29–70. Washington, DC: Brookings Institution Press, 2003.

Le Monde. "Des affrontements ont fait au moins 800 morts à Duékoué, selon le CICR." Le Monde, April 2, 2011. https://www.lemonde.fr/afrique/article/2011/04/02/des-affrontements-ont-fait-au-moins-800-morts-a-duekoue-selon-le-cicr_1502042_3212.html.

Leymarie, Philippe. "L'ONU en Côte d'Ivoire, combien de divisions?" *Le Monde diplo-matique* (blog), December 23, 2010. https://blog.mondediplo.net/2010-12-23-L -ONU-en-Cote-d-Ivoire-combien-de-divisions.

L'Express. "Le Mali appelle la France au secours." L'Express, January 11, 2011. https:// www.lexpress.fr/actualite/monde/afrique/le-mali-appelle-la-france-au-secours _1208549.html.

Lorgerie, Paul, and Jean-Philippe Rémy. "Coup d'état au Mali: Le président Ibra-him Boubacar Keita démissionne." *Le Monde*, August 18, 2020. https://www .lemonde.fr/afrique/article/2020/08/18/coup-d-etat-au-mali-le-president -ibrahim-boubacar-keita-et-son-premier-ministre-aux-mains-des-putschistes _6049272_3212.html.

Luntumbue, Michel. "Groupes armés, conflits et gouvernance en Afrique de l'Ouest: Une grille de lecture." *Note d'Analyse du GRIP*, January 27, 2012, 327–346.

Mali. "Accord Pour la Paix et la Reconciliation au Mali—Issu du Processus d'Alger." United Nations Peacemaker, March 1, 2015. https://peacemaker.un.org/node/ 2681.

Marchal, Roland. "Tchad/Darfour: Vers un système de conflits." *Politique africaine* 2.102 (2006): 135–154.

Marfo, Samuel, Musah Halidu, and Arthur Dominic DeGraft. "Beyond Classical Peace Paradigm: A Theoretical Argument for a 'Glocalized Peace and Secu-rity.'" *African Journal of Political Science and International Relations* 10.4 (2016): 47–55.

McGovern, Mike. *Making War in Côte d'Ivoire*. Chicago: University of Chicago Press, 2012.

Medie, Peace. *Global Norms and Local Action: The Campaigns to End Violence against Women in Africa*. Oxford: Oxford University Press, 2020.

Memier, Marc. *Systèmes de conflits et enjeux sécuritaires en Afrique de l'Ouest*. Dakar: Gorée Institute, 2012.

Mouiche, Ibrahim, and Samuel Kale Ewusi (eds.). *Gouvernance et sécurité en Afrique-subsaharienne francophone: Entre corruption politique et défis sécuritaires*. Addis Ababa: Université des Nations Unies pour la Paix, 2015.

Notin, Jean-Christian. *La guerre de la France au Mali*. Paris: Tallandier, 2014.

Nougayrède, Natalie. "La lettre du président malien, base légale de l'intervention française." *Le Monde*, January 25, 2013. https://www.lemonde.fr/afrique/article /2013/01/25/la-base-legale-de-l-action-francaise-une-lettre-de-m-traore _1822493_3212.html.

OCHA. "Final Communique: 4th Extraordinary Summit of the ECOWAS Authority of Heads of State and Government on the Political Situation in Mali." Relief-Web, January 9, 2022. https://reliefweb.int/report/mali/final-communique-4th -extraordinary-summit-ecowas-authority-heads-state-and-government.

Orman, Turkan Firinci. "An Analysis of the Notion of a 'Failed State.'" *International Journal of Social Science Studies* 4.1 (2016): 77–85.

Pennock, J. Roland. "Political Development, Political Systems, and Political Goods." *World Politics* 38.433 (1966): 420–426.

Pérouse de Montclos, Marc-Antoine. "Faut-il négocier avec les djihadistes au Sahel?" *Politique étrangère* 1 (2020): 175–187.

Piccolino, Giulia. "David against Goliath in Côte d'Ivoire? Laurent Gbagbo's War against Global Governance." *African Affairs* 111.442 (2011): 1–23.

———. "Ultranationalism, Democracy and the Law: Insights from Côte d'Ivoire." *The Journal of Modern African Studies* 52.1 (2014): 45–68.

Prunier, Gérard, and Rachel Gisselquist. "The Sudan: A Successfully Failed State." In *State Failure and State Weakness in a Time of Terror*, ed. Robert Rotberg, 101–127. Washington, DC: Brookings Institution Press, 2003.

Radio France Internationale. "Le Nigeria demande à l'ONU d'autoriser l'usage éventuel de la force." Radio France Internationale, January 25, 2011. https://www.rfi.fr/fr/mfi/20110125-le-nigeria-demande-onu-autoriser-usage-eventuel-force.

———. "Moussa Ag Acharatoumane: Au Mali, 'nous combattons une organisation criminelle.'" Radio France Internationale, April 23, 2018. https://www.rfi.fr/fr/emission/20180423-moussa-ag-acharatoumane-porte-parole-msa-mouvement-le-salut-azawad.

———. "Mali: Possibles découvertes de charniers vers Nantaka et Kobaka, dans le centre." Radio France Internationale, June 18, 2018. https://www.rfi.fr/fr/afrique/20180618-mali-possibles-decouvertes-charniers-peuls-nantaka-kobaka-armee-fama.

———. "Mali, la manifestation du M5 contre IBK dégénère à Bamako." Radio France Internationale, July 10, 2020. https://www.rfi.fr/fr/afrique/20200710-mali-le-m5-nouveau-la-rue-r%C3%A9clamer-la-d%C3%A9mission-pr%C3%A9sident-ibk.

Rotberg, Robert I. "Failed States, Collapsed States, Weak States: Causes and Indicators." In *State Failure and State Weakness in a Time of Terror*, ed. Robert Rotberg, 1–28. Washington, DC: Brookings Institution Press, 2003.

Rouppert, Bérangère. "La Côte d'Ivoire un an après: Rétrospective sur cinq mois de crise électorale, ses impacts et ses questionnements." Rapport du GRIP, 2012. https://www.grip.org/product/cote-divoire-un-an-apres-retrospective-sur-cinq-mois-de-crise-electorale-ses-impacts-et-ses-questionnements/.

Sagno, Geneviève. "Accords de défense militaire: Pourquoi le Mali rompt avec la France et l'Europe et quels sont ces accords?" BBC News, May 3, 2022. https://www.bbc.com/afrique/region-61313497.

Saidou, Abdoul Karim. "Conflits armés et sécurité au Sahel: Analyse comparée des politiques sécuritaires du Niger et du Mali face aux rébellions touarègues." In *Gouvernance et sécurité en Afrique subsaharienne francophone: Entre corruption politique et défis sécuritaires*, ed. Mouiche Ibrahim et Samuel Kale Ewusi, 327–347. Addis Ababa: Université des Nations Unies pour la Paix, 2015.

Simonis, Francis. "Au Mali, l'étrange alliance de la France avec les Touaregs du MNLA." *L'Obs*, January 24, 2017. https://www.nouvelobs.com/rue89/rue89-afrique/20130211.RUE3171/au-mali-l-etrange-alliance-de-la-france-avec-les-touaregs-du-mnla.html.

Smith, Adam. *Inquiry into the Nature and Causes of the Wealth of Nations*. London: W. Strahan and T. Cadell, 1776.

Smith, Stephen. "La France dans la crise ivoirienne: Ni ingérence, ni indifférence, mais indolence post-coloniale." In *Côte d'Ivoire: L'année terrible 1999–2000*, ed. Marc Le Pape, 311–324. Paris: Karthala, 2003.

Solomon, Hussein, and Cornelia Cone. "The State and Conflict in the Democratic Republic of Congo." *South African Journal of Military Studies* 32.1 (2004): 51–75. http://scientiamilitaria.journals.ac.za.

Soro, Guillaume. *Pourquoi je suis devenu rebelle*. Paris: Hachette, 2005.

Sriram, Chandra Lekha, and Karin Wermester. *From Promise to Practice: Strengthening UN Capacities for the Prevention of Violent Conflict*. New York: International Peace Academy Report, 2003.

Thabo, Mbeki. "What the World Got Wrong in Côte D'Ivoire." Foreign Policy, April 29, 2011. https://foreignpolicy.com/2011/04/29/what-the-world-got-wrong-in-cote-divoire.

The Conversation. "Pourquoi l'opinion publique malienne a une vision négative de l'opération Barkhane." The Conversation, February 10, 2020. https://theconversation.com/pourquoi-lopinion-publique-malienne-a-une-vision-negative-de-loperation-barkhane-130640.

Thurston, Alex. "Mali: The Disintegration of a 'Model African Democracy.'" *Stability* 2.1 (2013): 1–7.

Tramond, Olivier, and Philippe Seigneur. "French Army Operation Serval: Another Beau Geste of France in Sub-Saharan Africa?" *Military Review* 94.6 (2014): 76–86.

TV5 Monde. "Paris menace de retirer ses troupes si le Mali s'allie avec le groupe russe Wagner." TV5 Monde, September 14, 2021. https://information.tv5monde.com /afrique/paris-menace-de-retirer-ses-troupes-si-le-mali-s-allie-avec-le-groupe -russe-wagner-424414.

UN Peacekeeping. "Côte d'Ivoire, MINUCI Background." UN Peacekeeping, accessed November 11, 2023. https://peacekeeping.un.org/en/mission/past/minuci/ background.html.

United Nations General Assembly and Security Council. "Rapport du Groupe d'experts sur la Côte d'Ivoire." S/2009/521, October 9, 2009, 62–82. http://www.un .org/french/documents/view_doc.asp?symbol=S/2009/521.

United Nations Security Council Resolution. 1572 du C.S.N.U. S/RES/1572, November 15, 2004. https://www.un.org/securitycouncil/s/res/1572-%282004%29.

United Nations. "Convention on Transit Trade of Land-Locked States." United Nations Treaty Collection, July 8, 1965. https://treaties.un.org/Pages/ViewDetails .aspx?src=IND&mtdsg_no=X-3&chapter=10&clang=_en.

———. "Security Council Demands End to Violence in Cote d'Ivoire, Imposing Sanctions against Former President and Urging Him to 'Step Aside,' in Resolution 1975." United Nations, Meetings Coverage and Press Releases, March 30, 2011. https://www.un.org/press/en/2011/sc10215.doc.htm.

———. "Recognizing Interconnected Nature of Haiti's Long-term Development Challenges, Security Council Reiterates Need for Sustained International Support." United Nations, Meetings Coverage and Press Releases, April 6, 2011. https:// www.un.org/press/en/2011/sc10218.doc.htm.

———. "Security Council Authorizes Deployment of African-Led International Support Mission in Mali for Initial Year-Long Period." United Nations, Meetings Coverage and Press Releases, December 20, 2012. https://press.un.org/en/2012/sc10870.doc.htm.

Varenne, Leslie. *Abobo la guerre: Côte d'Ivoire: Terrain de jeu de la France et de l'ONU.* Paris: Edition Mille et une nuit, 2011.

Verschave, Francois-Xavier. *La Francafrique: Le plus long scandale de la République.* Paris: Stock, 1998.

———. *L'horreur qui nous prend au visage: L'État français et le génocide; Rapport de la Commission d'enquête citoyenne sur le rôle de la France dans le génocide des Tutsi au Rwanda.* Paris: Karthala, 2005.

———. *Complicité de genocide? La politique de la France au Rwanda.* Paris: La decouverte, 2013.

Vox of America. "Les opérations militaires au Mali depuis 2013." Vox of America, July 27, 2018. https://www.voaafrique.com/a/les-op%C3%A9rations-militaires-au-mali-depuis-2013/4502522.html.

———. "Manifestations de femmes et d'enfants de militaires tués dans le centre du Mali." Vox of America, March 22, 2019. https://www.voaafrique.com/a/manifestations-de-femmes-et-d-enfants-de-militaires-tu%C3%A9s-dans-le-centre-du-mali/4842896.html.

Widner, A. Jennifer. "State and Statelessness in Late Twentieth-Century Africa." In *When States Fail: Causes and Consequences,* ed. Robert I. Rotberg, 222–237. Princeton, NJ: Princeton University Press, 2003.

Woods, Larry J., and Timothy R. Reese. *Military Interventions in Sierra Leone: Lessons from a Failed State.* Morrisville, NC: Lulu Press, 2011.

Wyss, Marco. "The Gendarme Stays in Africa: France's Military Role in Côte d'Ivoire." *African Conflict and Peacebuilding Review* 3.1 (2013): 81–111.

Young, Crawford. *The Postcolonial State in Africa: Fifty Years of Independence.* Madison: University of Wisconsin Press, 2012.

Zartman, William I. "Introduction: Posing the Problem of State Collapse." In *Collapsed States: The Disintegration and Restoration of Legitimate Authority,* ed. William I. Zartman, 1–11. Boulder, CO: Lynne Rienner, 1995.

Chapter 6

African Agency in Securitization

Assimilating International Capacities

TENLEY K. ERICKSON

In the wake of the end of the Cold War, a major force driving collective action in Africa has been the need to respond to regional insecurity that is due to the wars of the 1990s and early 2000s.[1] Today, the threat of increasing instability stemming from extremist groups, global economic exigencies, virulent diseases, and climate change creates a sense of urgency such that cooperative measures are necessary to enhance regional defense against continual disaster. This trajectory for integrated security cooperation occurs within the process of glocalization, where global norms are assimilated amid existing local spheres of interests and institutions. The resulting adaptation of global norms and practices produced hybridized approaches based on interaction with the African security environment.[2]

Different definitions of globalization imply international diffusion of norms and practices. Some theoretical concepts perceive interaction to be a contestation between dominant and oppressive global processes that are imposed upon weaker countries where the local-level agents may not be effective in protecting the interests of the community.

Another commonly held perspective is that globalization is essentially a Western construct to provide solutions to conflict through the "Wilsonian Triad"—that is, peace, democracy, and free markets.[3] This view of globalization is, in essence, a "Peace-Building Consensus that involves methods of conflict resolution via a variety of means (e.g., arbitration, development programs, security enforcement)."[4] Glocalization involves the internalization of globalized perspectives in regional and national frameworks. The glocalization process entails a shift in how individual states assimilate and express processes of institutional/regulatory arrangements (e.g., UN peacekeeping missions).

This chapter examines the regionalism of glocalized security cooperation using Regional Security Complex Theory (RSCT) augmented by Social Evolution Theory (SET).[5] RSCT provides a framework for understanding processes of norm diffusion that help explain the African expression of regionalization in security cooperation. SET augments RSCT by providing greater explanatory power for agency within the African national and subnational levels. RSCT and SET offer insights into the expanding regional cooperation in the African Great Lakes region as influenced by the international community, contextualized within local security concerns, and actualized by motivated elite actors. These constructs reveal growing agency and capacity, in particular, on the part of East African countries.

While economic regionalism is well researched, security cooperation as an important area of normative diffusion in sub-Saharan Africa has received minimal attention.[6] Most studies of African peacekeeping operations focus on deficiencies in comparison with Western standards and ignore one of the most noteworthy aspects, that of the processes of normative change within African securitization efforts.[7] In fact, "a normative bias in the existing peacekeeping training literature emphasizes Western ethnocentric ideas of progress over socially embedded agency and obscures appreciation of relative advances of capacity building. Some recent research, however, notes that peacekeeping as a professional socialization process is a particularly powerful mechanism in internalizing norms and institutionalizing universal values."[8]

The emerging emphasis on African stabilization efforts in conjunction with greater regional interdependence in the past two decades is having a profound impact in shaping contemporary Africa. The transition from dependence on international peacekeepers two decades ago to providing military leadership and initiative, as well as the majority of troops in stabilization operations today, is evident in strengthened regional mechanisms and institutions. Growing African agency in security cooperation demonstrates the globalization of international norms aimed at providing stabilization measures in conflict areas. Much as in the western European experience, where regionalization demonstrated the possibility to "create regions of peace, prosperity, and cooperation, thereby eliminating the causes of tensions and conflicts between some states,"[9] likewise in Africa, mutually reinforcing mechanisms are motivating collective action in peacekeeping efforts. The western European experience of postconflict security cooperation and economic integration in the seven decades of peace and prosperity since the second world war created a positive model that is recognized as a major globalization force.

Glocalization can be seen in the African Union (AU) security and economic institutions at the subcontinental regional level based on ideas inherent in the European model. However, the African security framework exhibits unique characteristics in response to each subregion's historical and current influences. Because of normative influences within the African continent, African regionalism is fundamentally different from the western European model of a "Democratic Peace." Specifically, interstate relations in Africa are transforming from an offensive realist focus to defensive realism combined with cooperative integration.

Moreover, in the neo-patrimonial system prevalent in Africa, national transformation does not mirror the West European Westphalian model of state building. Unlike the historic transition from patrimonial governance systems to the development of functional governance structures in western Europe, a general lack of hierarchy and stakeholders (e.g., business elite power brokers) in Africa has inhibited requisite normative diffusion for the transformation of individual states to accept overarching authority in regional security cooperation as driven by burgeoning elite interests in economic development.[10] Because of the importance of substate motivational factors, RSCT provides greater explanatory power for regionalization in Africa than the historical western European model. In spite of a different state-building trajectory from that of western Europe, a confluence of global and local influences created forces for change that are promoting a greater willingness to seek opportunities for peaceful cooperation that have had some positive effects on state-capacity building—for example, agency in peacekeeping and peace enforcement. Moreover, this transformation indicates an evolution along the spectrum of intrastate relations as described by Keohane and Nye from an offensive realist focus to one of defensive realism and/or cooperative interdependence.[11] Exemplifying this transformation is the increasing African agency in securitization operations and willingness to supplant international peacekeeping operations with African-led forces.[12]

Burgeoning agency and deepening security cooperation highlight dynamics inherent in changing relations, especially in eastern Africa. Eastern Africa offers the most distinct evidence of the assimilation of global ideas and interests in regional security within a glocalized context of cooperation. The case study of the evolution of security cooperation between members of the eastern African community and the Democratic Republic of Congo (DRC) demonstrates the transformation from antagonistic relations to increased bilateral and multilateral cooperation.

This chapter first reviews the literature on security cooperation within an RSCT framework and employs a SET perspective to ground the study in changing local norms and capacities. The next section discusses transformative security cooperation and security agency within an African construct. The third section illustrates the evolving nature of African security cooperation through a case study concentrating on the Great Lakes regional conflict. It examines the nascent transformation of the East African Community from an economic-focused institution to a regional security organization. All of these are tied to a glocalized security perspective.

GLOCALIZATION OF SECURITY COOPERATION

Two theories of change provide useful propositions for explaining expanding security cooperation in eastern Africa. RSCT explores the global spread of regionalism in response to the breakup of the bipolar system after the end of the Cold War. SET explains the dynamics of individual levels of change in countries that assimilate and promulgate regionalism on the local level.

Regional Security Complex Theory

In the anarchic post–Cold War period, regional groups were established when states exhibited self-help characteristics by choosing regional integration in security and economic cooperation in an effort to benefit from group unity. RSCT offers an explanation for how interdependent security concerns drive regional securitization among a set of states that are in geographic proximity to one another.[13] This theoretical construct enables an understanding of the interplay of regional powers and the influence of the global system. Founded upon neorealism, RSCT adds a constructivist theoretical approach in that relations (enmity-amity patterns) are important variables affecting the distribution of power and the social construction of insecurity.[14] RSCT borrows from the English school, which highlights the transition of states from Westphalian to post-Westphalian international relations based on the "three traditions" of Hobbesian (realism), Grotian (rationalism), and Kantian (revolutionism) worlds.[15] While the original RSCT construct does not explain how societies are transformed, subsequent scholarship has attempted to address the processes through which identity is constructed as a result of the interaction of agents and security-building institutions.[16] The securitization process involves political leaders' perception of issues as security concerns that are affected by internal as well as external factors defined within a social environment (e.g., group identity formation, national historical events, global forces).[17] State actors, in turn, define regional security problems and interact to create regional consensus in addressing mutual concerns.

RSCT has three main typologies of regional relations: (1) regional security complexes, which are well-structured security groups; (2) unstructured groups, comprising weak and isolated states; and (3) overlayed (i.e., imposed) arrangements dominated by great power interests. Less well-defined typologies include (1) pre-complex formations where clear bilateral security relations are not strongly bound by regional security linkages and (2) proto-complex groupings that have developed security interdependence within a delineated region whose security dynamics are weaker than those of a formally structured regional security complex.[18] Additionally, RSCT highlights different levels of international relations: domestic, state to state, interregional-global, and state-global. For example, at the interregional level, the European Union (EU) has established linkages with Africa in support of European security interests, which include building peacekeeping and security cooperation mechanisms in order to enhance stability and reduce negative spillover.

These linkages reflect European perceptions that the two regions are interconnected and that the security of one can have repercussions for the other. The origins of regional security complexes represent the fear and aspirations of separate states in relation to one another. The experience of western Europe after the Second World War, where enmity between France and Germany evolved into amity, serves as a valuable example of how distrust between states can be transformed through regional security complexes.[19]

Social Evolution Theory

While acknowledging that security is a social construct and may change over time through a multitude of processes and actors' perceptions, agency in RSCT is not fully specified nor does it say how societies and institutions evolve. Walsh emphasizes the importance of understanding African leadership in order to acquire a broader perspective of the various influences on power.[20] While, in general, African states do not share the same institutional development as those of the West and many scholars have highlighted the lack of modern state-building development as fundamental to the persistent neo-patrimonialism in Africa,[21] there is evidence of a growing state capacity. A growing body of research indicates that a transformation in national capacities, leadership, and problem solving has influenced increasing regional cooperation in the past two decades, exemplifying developing state-building mechanisms through the importation of global constructs such as regionalism. SET can identify specific processes crucial to building, strengthening, and sustaining important institutions critical for establishing peace and stability.

Institutions, the embodiment of ideas, norms, and interests, facilitate formal socialization processes to transfer norms through institutions such as regional integration mechanisms.[22] A major trend driving the rise in regionalism during the post–Cold War period is the spreading acceptance of the potential benefits of economic cooperation. The EU, for example, has had a huge influence on the growth of regional organizations in Africa.[23]

Risse highlights four main conditions that tend to facilitate norm diffusion. For one, domestic interests and incentives motivate assimilation when domestic actors demand change and policies that meet their objectives. Second, the degree of statehood affects the ability of states to adopt, implement, and enforce decisions. Third, a regime's democratic quality influences the willingness of leaders to promote change in response to internal and external influences. Finally, the global exchange of ideas and tangible products stimulates national transformative connections within the international community.[24]

Tang's theory of social evolution borrows from Jervis's concepts of selection and evolutionary forces in effecting systematic processes and change.[25] The mechanism of variation-selection-inheritance generates phases of institutional change. The process of institutional change is difficult but facilitated when stabilizing tendencies no longer hold. Four destabilizing factors can act as catalysts for revolutionary forces: (1) new ideas, (2) new power, (3) systemic incompatibilities, and (4) external shocks that can result in dynamic change under certain conditions.

In addition to norms transfer processes, significant institutional change needs "an effective anti-ideology and political entrepreneurship that can overcome the problems of collective action and create a social movement."[26] Motivated leaders who are energized with vision inculcate others to enact social change. This combination of visionary leadership enables agency to generate glocalized action that is the driving mechanism behind security cooperation in Africa's growing regionalism. The emergence of agency in changing norms of protection and collective security in Africa is traceable to the 1990s, when the violent conflicts in Liberia and Sierra Leone instigated the West African regional organization, the Economic Community of West African States, to deploy security forces in the first unilateral action by an African regional security organization.[27] Since then, East African militaries have likewise demonstrated regional security cooperation and agency in Somalia, Mozambique, and the DRC.[28]

AFRICAN REGIONAL SECURITY AND THE GLOCALIZATION OF NORMS

Since the end of the Cold War, African militaries have increased engagement in international peacekeeping, counterterrorism, and humanitarian assistance missions.[29] Regional security became institutionalized on a continental level when the AU established the Peace and Security Architecture in 2003. African countries took on a new, proactive security approach within the Regional Economic Communities as well as through individual state contributions to UN and AU securitization operations.[30] This transformation reflects the importance of ideas and interests with regard to processes of legitimation and institutional reproduction. An emphasis on ideas and their evolution is useful for exploring how relations and institutions change over time, as can be seen in the transfer of certain aspects of the western European integration model to the African Union regional organizational structure.[31] The EU has been a critical actor in promoting regionalism as a means to transform conflict in Africa.[32] In response to the violent upheaval in Africa at the end of the Cold War, Western powers advocated for cooperation as security was seen as a precondition for economic progress.[33]

The most successful international institution, the EU, is viewed as a model for regional integration, peace, and prosperity despite the current political disunity (e.g., "Brexit") and its failure to eradicate all ambitions of territorial expansionism (e.g., Russia's invasion of Ukraine). The EU has nonetheless influenced many similar replications, including that of the AU.[34] The EU emerged as the result of the hegemonic peace imposed by the Allied powers at the end of the Second World War. As a result of this successful paradigm, a new form of international relations based on the benefits of regional integration began to spread globally.[35] In Africa, the EU has actively acted to promote capacity building in integration. For example, it supported the establishment of the International Conference on the Great Lakes Region, the most active regional institution in the area.[36] Furthermore, EU involvement in supporting peacekeeping operations and good governance in Africa since the early 2000s began to increase when security concerns resulting from expanding extremism in Africa intensified Western interest in deepening relations with Africa. Recognizing that addressing these mutual concerns requires regional cooperation, African leaders have made gradual but increasingly perceptible progress in integration. Determined to become a key partner of the UN and the AU, the EU greatly expanded its cooperation with the AU in securitization in the early 2000s and became a major promoter of regional integration and security cooperation in Africa.[37] Because of this symbiotic relationship, the EU has been one of the most important supporters of Africa's emerging security architecture. As of 2022, the EU has dedicated €40.5 million to this commitment.[38]

Major forces for change in sub-Saharan Africa include growing interest in creating conditions conducive to enhancing security and stability. Evidence of expanding interest in cooperation can be seen in the evolution of security operations from unitary self-help missions to bilateral and multilateral operations.[39] This demonstrates glocalization in mutually supportive domains of securitization and economic development. A transformation in intra-regional relations is most evident through integrated regional organizations committed to both security operations and economic development.

As a result of twenty years of partnering with international organizations (e.g., the World Bank, the International Monetary Fund, the EU), the AU and sub-Saharan Africa have undergone significant changes, creating programs and institutions designed to respond to and ameliorate security concerns, although progress has been slow, and many challenges remain. Nevertheless, when the present is compared with the late twentieth century, it is evident that the continent is gradually transitioning from conflict-prone relations to greater cooperation within an evolutionary process influenced by the effects of global norm diffusion.

These dynamics have become more prevalent as a result of concerted international efforts to enhance regional stability through sustained security assistance. Advances in African institutions and capacity in peacekeeping and peace enforcement operations provide evidence of evolving perceptions of the potential benefits of interdependence and future well-being through cooperation. Transformation in integration efforts, not only in terms of the number of peacekeeping force contributions but also in terms of the quality of those forces, demonstrates positive outcomes. As the world has experienced a transition to complex relationships since the end of the Cold War era, so too is Africa. This is not to say that cooperation and integration are synonymous with harmonious, conflict-free relations. Rather, despite ongoing competition, regional actors are creating processes and institutions to regulate and mediate areas of tension, thereby facilitating conflict resolution.

Africa's history of extreme violence since the end of colonial rule is a defining characteristic of its security context. The relationship between state fragility, conflict, and inadequate state capacity has received considerable attention from scholars of the historical process of state building. A lack of state capacity to govern, which is essentially the definition of an absence of authority (i.e., what structural realists define as anarchy), results in distrustful relations and self-help mechanisms, for example, forming security alliances to overcome uncertainty.[40] State capacity-building is intrinsically linked with a greater ability to provide an environment of security and social services.

Today African countries are the main force contributors to UN peacekeeping operations, totaling more than sixty-five thousand troops, and have been the region providing the greatest number for more than a decade.[41] Moreover, they also demonstrate a growing commitment to securitization by initiating indigenous security operations in response to threats to regional stability. The recent trends to enter into security cooperation arrangements such as in Somalia, Mozambique, and the DRC to address the growing threat of violent armed groups exemplifies a concerted effort on the part of eastern African countries to create conditions conducive for peace and prosperity.[42] A notable transition from self-help security cooperation arrangements in which states took unilateral actions is evident in today's preference for joint military strategies. In the late 1990s and early 2000s, the numerous cross-border incursions included the Ethiopian operations in Somalia, Ugandan counter–Lord's Resistance Army and counter–Allied Defense Forces operations, and Rwandan counter–Democratic Liberation Rwanda Forces operations. African agency in combined operations in eastern Africa include the Ugandan-led African Union Mission in Somalia; the Southern African Development Community (SADC) Force Intervention Brigade in the DRC; the cooperative arrangement between Rwandan forces and SADC in Mozambique; and the deployment of Ugandan, Burundian, and Kenyan troops as the initial East African Community commitment of a regional force to the eastern DRC.

The first successful African intervention, the Economic Community of West African States (ECOWAS) mission in the Liberian crisis in the 1990s, transferred lessons learned in conflict management and mechanisms for peacebuilding to AU members that have been replicated, albeit not entirely successfully, in the Horn of Africa, Lake Chad region, and the African Great Lakes.[43] African agency in conflict management interventions since the 1990s includes the ECOWAS missions in Sierra Leone, Liberia, Côte d'Ivoire, and Gambia; the African Union Mission in Somalia; the SADC Force Intervention Brigade in the DRC; and AU member states' leadership of UN Missions in Sudan, South Sudan, Mali, the Central African Republic, and Mozambique.[44]

Military cooperation has been described by many African and US officials as "one of the most impressive and well-established aspects of the integration agenda" that could eventually move eastern Africa into some sort of a "security regime where norms and institutions restrain fear of aggression and conflict traps."[45] While no regional security cooperation arrangement has managed to eliminate instability completely, such arrangements have had some effectiveness in reducing conflict; and more important for this chapter, these actions demonstrate an evolution in cooperation to address instability and promote peace and security.[46] Increasing African agency in indigenous peace enforcement operations (e.g., in Somalia and Mozambique) also reflects the sustained interest of regional leaders to take responsibility for collective action in the face of armed violence and regional instability as reflected in the mantra "African solutions for African problems."[47]

In the past two decades, international peacekeeping has relied on closer cooperation with African regional actors to provide a quicker reaction to regional security threats, a clear indication of the growing agency and ability of certain African nations.[48] Perhaps not surprisingly, the majority of the UN and AU contributions come from eastern Africa. This is likely due to lengthy exposure to combat operations given that for almost three decades, eastern Africa has been home to the most protracted conflicts, such as the civil war that split Sudan in two, clan warfare that opened the door for Islamic extremism in Somalia, and regional spillover from anarchy in the eastern DRC.[49] The transition in relations since the 1990s from a regional war centered on the DRC to a regional security coalition in 2023 to stabilize the eastern DRC demonstrates a profound evolution in interests and norms, serious challenges notwithstanding.[50]

EAST AFRICAN COMMUNITY CASE STUDY

Eastern Africa is marked by some of Africa's longest-running violent conflicts, specifically in Somalia, South Sudan, and Sudan. Officials in the region identify the top African security priorities as terrorism, poverty, conflict over resources, and governance.[51] All states in eastern Africa have been affected by terrorism and armed groups that prey upon local communities. The region is seen as an easy target for militia attacks because of state fragility coupled with porous borders that provide cover for terrorists and militants in ungoverned spaces. Organized groups take advantage of widespread poverty and violence and by providing some modicum of security and services where state governance is lacking. The uptick in acts of terrorism in the region is a major impetus for an unprecedented concerted effort to form regional security organizations to address threats emanating from al-Qaeda–aligned Al-Shabaab in Somalia, the Islamic State–aligned Ansar al-Sunna Wa Jamma in Mozambique, and roughly one hundred armed groups, including the Islamic State–aligned Allied Democratic Forces, and the Rwandan Democratic Liberation Forces (FDLR), in the eastern DRC. In many ways, the DRC has become the most complicated and notorious case of insecurity in the region.

Conflict in the DRC erupted in the early 1990s in the aftermath of the 1994 Rwandan genocide. The intensity of this long-standing violence led to labels such as "Africa's World War,"[52] the "Recurring Great Lakes Crisis,"[53] and an "Unending Conflict."[54] The case study of the evolution of security cooperation between members of the East African Community (EAC) and the DRC demonstrates the transformation from antagonistic relations to bilateral and multilateral cooperation. This progress transpired in parallel with economic integration. In the mid-1990s, the region was consumed by the conflagration of "Africa's World War," centered on the fighting between the DRC-supported alliance and the contingent led by Rwanda and Uganda. The case study of the African Great Lakes conflict highlights transforming interests and institutions in this region that lead to greater interdependence and cooperation among EAC members. This case study focuses on the role played by state building, insecurity, and peace operations in the eastern DRC, primarily in North Kivu, following a series of agreements beginning in the late 1990s to make peace among regional factions and promote reconciliation in the immediate aftermath of the war. Specifically, it addresses periods of attempted securitization in the past twenty years.[55]

The DRC, which is located in the Great Lakes region of Africa, borders Uganda, Rwanda, and Burundi along the northeastern territories of North and South Kivu. Since mid-1990, the region has been the focus of two regional wars and residual cycles of violent conflict between various factions dominated by Rwandaphone (i.e., Kinyarwanda-speaking) groups (e.g., Congolese Tutsis and remnants of the predominantly Hutu group responsible for the 1994 Rwandan genocide, known as the FDLR). The ongoing conflict results from an absence of government authority, which allows some one hundred armed groups to act in the region with impunity.

In the past two decades, proxy forces supported by the DRC and neighboring countries such as Uganda, Rwanda, and Burundi have vied for territorial control in pursuit of economic and security interests. This period can be divided into three transitional phases of an evolutionary progression in intra-regional relations from overt war of the 1990s to tentative cooperation: (1) DRC military (FARDC) defeat under National Congress for the Defense of the People (CNDP) leader Laurent Nkunda, (2) CNDP integration into the FARDC, March 23 Movement (M23) revolt under Bosco Ntaganda, and defeat by the UN-aligned forces, and (3) M23 resurgence under President Tshisekedi and formation of an EAC regional security organization.[56] These three phases reflect a transformation in regional relations from hostile offensive realism to a greater willingness to institutionalize cooperative mechanisms. Security cooperation on a regional level demonstrates the diffusion of norms, ideas, and interests from the international community.

While there has been a clear progression from substantial support for various armed groups at the end of the Congo wars to sustained actions to eliminate violent conflict, complete peace remains elusive. Current tensions are due to a resurgence of the decade-long dormant March 23 Movement, known as M23, and have energized regional actors and international partners to intensify collaboration in pursuing avenues for lasting stability. The progression of these efforts reveals an evolution of interests and capacities that demonstrate a glocalization of norms related to integration. This does not mean that cooperation is always amicable or devoid of conflict and competition. What the case study shows, however, is a normative change from aggressive bilateral relations to a diffusion of a shared understanding that mutual benefits accrue from security cooperation in order to achieve national goals such as regional stability.[57]

In the past twenty years, the security dynamics between the DRC and Rwanda have undergone numerous cycles of armed conflict and cooperation.[58] After the two Congolese wars that started with the Hutu leaders of the Rwanda genocide fleeing to the DRC in 1994 and ended with the 2003 peace agreement, the eastern DRC remains immersed in violence. One of the most vicious of these militia groups is the FDLR. The leaders of the FDLR are former *genocidaires* involved in the 1994 Rwanda genocide, who remain committed to overthrowing the current Rwandan administration led by President Paul Kagame. Moreover, they receive support from elements in the DRC, which makes the FDLR a main source of the ongoing regional conflict.

Several agreements between Rwanda and the DRC between 2006 and 2021 had some positive effects, most notably periodic arrests and elimination and demobilization of FDLR members. However, despite having the largest and longest UN peacekeeping operation (the UN Stabilization Operation in the Congo, MONUSCO) along with various regional attempts to stabilize the eastern DRC, the region remains deeply insecure. Many factors are often cited for the insecurity, including the lack of government authority in the area, armed groups that seek to maintain territorial control over resources, and corrupt officials that benefit from collaborating with armed groups. What is not always appreciated are factors influencing national political dynamics and decision-making. Facing tremendous opposition in the eastern DRC in 2007, 2011, and 2016, President Joseph Kabila turned to Rwanda for help in stabilizing the region. In return, he agreed to support joint counter-FDLR operations, a long-standing security concern for Rwanda. Congolese Rwandaphone forces known as the National Congress for the Defence of the People (CNDP), which later became the M23, provided the main counter-FDLR capacity on the condition that they would be allowed to remain in North Kivu. Since the M23 defeat in 2013 combined with Tshisekedi's assuming the presidency in 2019, regional relations improved, despite the uptick in tensions in late 2021. Current agreements to establish an EAC regional security organization in the eastern DRC indicate a normative shift from bilateral attempts to eliminate armed groups to a more structured regional security complex.

What follows is a review of those dynamics at work during the three periods since DRC president Joseph Kabila assumed power after the Congo peace agreements (Arusha Accords). These periods are (1) CNDP dominance under Laurent Nkunda, (2) CNDP integration and revolt under Bosco Ntaganda, and (3) M23 resurgence and regional security cooperation under President Tshisekedi. Throughout each phase,

African Agency in Securitization　195

the FDLR is a major player in creating instability and tension between the DRC and Rwanda. In the first two phases, bilateral and international efforts to eliminate this source of friction failed. During the third phase, efforts are underway to create a formal regional security complex to better leverage regional agents and institutionalize regional security regimes and mechanisms in concert with global norms.

Phase I: CNDP Dominance under Nkunda

The first phase of attempts to resolve regional tensions in the immediate period following the Congo wars failed because of the lack of security in the eastern DRC, which allowed Ugandan, Burundian, and Rwandan rebels, most notably the FDLR, freedom of movement. The reasons for Joseph Kabila's resistance to eliminating the FDLR lie in the history of the way he came to power. The "Second Congo War" began in 1998 when the previous president (Joseph Kabila's father, Laurent Kabila) turned against his sponsors (the Rwandans), who helped him topple President Mobutu. Rwanda assisted Laurent Kabila mainly because of Mobutu's collusion with what is now the FDLR. After a protracted war, the various factions negotiated an end to hostilities in early 2003, while the Rwandan-supported Congolese Tutsis integrated into the DRC military. However, by the end of the year, the Congolese Tutsis broke away and formed a rebel group known as the National Congress for the Defense of the People (CNDP) under the leadership of General Laurent Nkunda.[59]

The next few years witnessed increasing violence and atrocities in the run-up to the 2006 presidential election. All three presidents (Mobutu and both Kabilas) were ineffectual in stabilizing the conflict in North and South Kivus in the eastern DRC and at times used proxy forces to maintain political and economic power.[60] Joseph Kabila sought help from Rwanda to pacify the east during the 2006 elections in return for giving the Tutsi community semi-autonomy after the elections, a tactic Joseph Kabila would use again in 2011. According to Stearns,[61] Joseph Kabila did not follow through on any of his pledges, but these negotiations gave him the temporary security he needed to win the election for president. In early 2006 Joseph Kabila sent his representatives to Kigali to ask for help in gaining control over the east. Kagame agreed, provided that the Congolese Tutsis were given positions in Joseph Kabila's government.[62]

The election results were overwhelmingly in favor of Joseph Kabila, who reneged on his promise. When the Congolese Tutsis lost power as a result of the 2006 election, the fear of persecution combined with the loss of most of their business and political interests fueled a new rebellion by the end of 2006 under Laurent Nkunda.[63]

Between 2006 and 2007, President Joseph Kabila faced a series of revolts in the western DRC, including the capital, Kinshasa, while Nkunda was becoming very powerful in the Kivus. For the next three years, Nkunda humiliated President Kabila and incited the animosity of the Congolese people by repeatedly and soundly defeating the poorly organized and led Congolese army (FARDC). Joseph Kabila's inability to pacify the east severely weakened his power.[64] The ignominious blow of Nkunda's troops taking the major city of Goma on the border with Rwanda in 2009 (reportedly with help from Rwandan supporters) threatened to destabilize Kabila's government. President Kabila, facing tremendous opposition in 2009, especially in the Kivus, turned to Rwanda for help in stabilizing the region. In return for allowing Rwanda to send troops into the DRC to hunt down the FDLR, Kagame agreed to arrest Nkunda.[65] Additionally, Kabila consented to integrate CNDP rebels into the Congolese army in return for election support in the Kivus. This stage in the conflict-trap relationship between the DRC and Rwanda exemplifies an offensive realist self-help situation wherein both countries' elites adopted tactics in order to survive the extremely volatile environment. The lack of sufficiently mature conditions (e.g., the degree of state capacity to implement decisions, regional support via norm entrepreneurs, domestic power brokers) inhibited norm diffusion and institutionalization of security mechanisms for peaceful coexistence.[66]

Phase II: CNDP/M23 Integration and Revolt under Ntaganda

The DRC–Rwandan agreement to conduct joint counter-FDLR operations in return for arresting Nkunda and mobilizing political support for Kabila's election was very successful in 2010 and 2011 in large part because of CNDP and Rwandan intelligence and operational prowess. However, operations were abruptly broken off after Kabila won the 2012 election.[67] The agreement unraveled as Kabila came under increasing political pressure from anti-Tutsi elements, causing him to transfer former CNDP members out of their Rwandaphone enclave in the Kivus.

Tensions mounted between the government and former CNDP soldiers when the Congolese government tried to break up the CNDP power structure. When Joseph Kabila announced plans to disperse former CNDP members out of the Kivus, a group led by Bosco Ntaganda launched a rebellion in November 2012, calling themselves the March 23 Movement, M23.[68] They claimed that the Congolese government did not adhere to the integration agreement in terms of proper salaries, repatriation of Congolese refugees, and Tutsi representation in government. The Congolese government claimed that the CNDP had become an army within the army, running its own power network in the eastern part of the DRC while smuggling minerals illegally.[69] This charge, while true, was essentially the agreement Kabila had made with the CNDP in return for helping him get re-elected. As a result, the Congolese Tutsi minority population became apprehensive that it would once again become a target for discrimination and repression by the other Congolese ethnic groups that considered the Rwandan-speaking community to be intruders.[70]

The crisis escalated to the point that many observers feared another Congo war after FDLR troops took advantage of the conflict to strengthen their positions along the border and conducted incursions into western Rwanda. According to UN reports, the FDLR collaborated with some Congolese military units; their doing so escalated Tutsi fears of ethnic cleansing operations and increasing M23 support and recruitment.[71] To block Rwandan support to M23, the international community imposed sanctions on Rwanda, causing serious economic repercussions for Rwanda. This international pressure likely instigated the breakup of M23 into factions, forcing Ntaganda to flee to Rwanda. Ntaganda was refused sanctuary in Rwanda. He eventually gave himself up to the US Embassy and was sent to the International Court in The Hague.

International pressure intensified when sanctions placed on Rwanda did not result in M23's ending its revolt. African and UN officials agreed to form a new offensive unit by SADC members that would be subordinate to MONUSCO, dubbed the Force Integration Brigade (FIB). The FIB succeeded in defeating M23, whose members eventually fled to Uganda and Rwanda. The defeat of M23 happened in conjunction with intense negotiations in which Rwanda was assured that the DRC and UN forces would eliminate all armed groups, including the FDLR. Although a peace agreement was signed, the Kabila government never implemented it and the FIB never conducted counter-FDLR operations.[72]

International sanctions and UN invocation of Chapter VII on the use of force powers increased the opportunity cost of continued regional conflict for the DRC, especially for Rwanda. Accordingly, diplomatic overtures between the two countries were reinitiated, leading to a meeting between the Rwandan and DRC defense ministers to discuss mutual security issues. In September 2015, Rwandan defense minister Kabarebe and Congolese defense minister Ngoi-Mukena met in the Rwandan capital, Kigali, the first such high-level meeting between the two countries in three years.[73] The talks focused on stabilizing the border between the two countries and addressing the FDLR militia. Kabarebe and Ngoi-Mukena declared the bilateral talks a "historic period" and announced a follow-up summit between the military chiefs in June in Kinshasa. They also released a joint statement committing both sides to eradicating the 3,500-strong FDLR in the eastern DRC, which posed threats to both Rwanda and the DRC.[74]

In May 2016, the Congolese army arrested the chief of staff of the FDLR, General Leopold Mujyambere, who was the highest-level FDLR member ever captured in the DRC. The operation was conducted with the assistance of Rwandan commandos and intelligence units, which have an extensive intelligence network in the eastern DRC. In August 2016, President Joseph Kabila met with President Paul Kagame in Gisenyi, along with several of their cabinet ministers. This historic meeting was the first time the two presidents had met after years of animosity and counter-accusations of harboring rebels.[75] Another significant high-level meeting took place in August 2016 as the two countries agreed to work together to improve security and economic ties. The DRC announced that it was initiating an operation to dislodge the FDLR from its base in North Kivu.[76] In October 2016, two top commanders of the FDLR were arrested, signaling a renewed relationship of security cooperation between Rwanda and the DRC.[77]

Phase III: M23 Resurgence and Regional Security Cooperation under Tshisekedi

A new opening in relations took place when newly elected DRC president Felix Tshisekedi went on a diplomatic offensive in 2019 establishing new security agreements with the DRC's neighbors—Uganda, Rwanda, and Burundi—in response to growing instability by armed groups in the eastern DRC. His first diplomatic efforts to increase security within the region began with Rwanda. The two countries reached agreements on economic cooperation and the elimination of the FDLR. Similar agreements were concluded with Uganda and Burundi. All three neighbors have experienced an increase in attacks from rebel groups based in the DRC disrupting their economic interests—for example, Ugandan oil production and Rwanda's grand foreign policy strategy of long-term development of regional economic partnerships.[78]

However, there was a resurgence in M23 activities in 2021 as it expanded territory along the Uganda-DRC border after failed DRC operations on M23 strongholds.[79] M23 has consistently complained that the DRC has not lived up to its agreement. Renewed M23 activities led to heightened political opposition against President Tshisekedi and anti-Rwandan riots. Facing an election in 2023, Tshisekedi accused Rwanda of supporting M23 and pledged to end the turmoil in the east.[80] As the newest member of the East African Community (EAC), DRC president Tshisekedi turned to the EAC for support to end the escalating violence.

In September 2022, the EAC signed an agreement with the DRC to deploy an EAC Joint Regional Force to fight negative forces in the eastern DRC. The goal was to eliminate destabilizing armed groups and help the DRC focus on economic and social growth that could be a catalyst for regional progress. This security force, which is the first for the EAC, was tasked to deploy for an initial six-month period under the command of a Kenyan major general. In return, the DRC agreed to address key issues to facilitate the DRC's full integration into the EAC.[81] While many details have not been made public and the deployment of the full complement of the joint EAC force was delayed, components from Burundi and Uganda entered the DRC in the summer of 2022 under EAC auspices. In September 2022, Kenyan forces started deploying nine hundred troops and matériel to the DRC, while South Sudan and Tanzania also planned to send contingents to support UN and Congolese forces. The EAC force would exclude Rwandan combat forces, similar to past agreements on border security, because of local sensibilities regarding Rwandan intervention in the DRC.[82] However, Rwanda would have a significant role as the head of the intelligence function for the EAC force.[83]

Many details of the new EAC force have yet to be fully laid out, and political disconnects will likely cause friction between members. Nevertheless, a new phase in African agency in security cooperation appears to be on the horizon. The EAC agreement to deploy a regional force to the DRC to ensure stability supports the DRC demobilization strategy to integrate former fighters by helping them build livelihoods within their civilian communities. Unlike past operations that lacked local buy-in and were plagued by graft and patronage, the new initiative is designed to stimulate economic alternatives to joining armed groups. This economic angle to the EAC security operation is an interesting element in the institutional security framework, which connects economic development to security.

Moreover, in mid-2023, a quadripartite community organized under the auspices of the AU and the UN facilitated a multi-subregional response to the protracted instability in the eastern DRC.[84] The group was composed of the EAC, the SADC, the International Conference on the Great Lakes Region, and the Economic Community of Central African States. Leaders committed additional funds and troops to support the EAC military force. This multiregional activity following the EAC's lead in attempting to stabilize the volatility in its most resource-rich member, the DRC, is a clear example of norm diffusion, coalescing interests, and institutionalization of driving forces.

The EU has been an important player in the institutionalization of security norms and processes. EU support for conflict prevention efforts has dramatically increased since 2004. Through its African Peace Facility, the EU has provided almost three-quarters of a billion euros for African-led peace support operations, capacity building, and conflict prevention initiatives.[85] New EU funding mechanisms allow for more robust support for conflict prevention and resolution.[86] As African military professionalism and capacity enabled a broader range of African-led securitization operations, the international community (e.g., the UN and EU) has increasingly provided direct training and equipment to national militaries in addition to the traditional means of channeling funds through AU structures. In 2022, the EU created the European Peace Facility, comprising two funds that will support military and defense operations and provide for development aid in order to address the dual-sided processes of stability, specifically security and social well-being.[87]

This revised program allows the EU flexibility in funding, training, and equipping the best-qualified recipients. EU assistance is to be complemented by appropriate European partners through bilateral support.

AFRICA'S EVOLVING REGIONAL SECURITY COMPLEX

The African experience in security cooperation provides a valuable window into how regional security complexes are diffused within an evolving social construct of global and regional security. The influence of Western involvement demonstrates how norm transfer resulted in new security regimes and institutions in eastern Africa. The leadership of elites has been crucial in the growing African agency in the region as an awareness of the importance of economic development to security became an overarching shared vision.

The latest security cooperation proposal by EAC in the DRC is increasingly viewed as a progression along a continuum of complex interdependence described by Keohane and Nye in regional willingness to take cooperative approaches to security issues. In the past two decades, a transformation in international relationships can be traced through a series of security arrangements from offensive realism and unilateral self-help mechanisms to defensive realism and multilateral cooperation.[88] These developments stand in contrast to the distrustful belligerence and horrific violence of the 1990s. The series of capacity-building efforts, including support to UN peacekeeping missions and AU-UN hybrid counterterrorism operations, shows international norm diffusion and more sophisticated professional capabilities. The resulting institutionalization of regional organizations demonstrates a progressive evolution from a pre–security complex situation marked by competitive and distrustful relations to a proto–security complex designed to advance mutual security benefits.

Early unilateral operations, such as Ugandan support to South Sudan, Ethiopian involvement in Somalia against Islamic militants, and Rwandan incursion into the DRC against the FDLR, are less preferred today compared with regional integrated security operations that align with international norms. Glocalization of security cooperation involves accepting the benefits of international expertise (e.g., enhanced training and tactics, greater interoperability) in return for accepting international rules and regulations. However, local political, economic, and security concerns determine the glocalization of regional security complexes. International support for competent management of eastern African securitization through mentorship and setting standards opened the way for Uganda to lead the effort in Somalia beginning in 2007. The glocalization of the ideas and interest in African agency is evident today in the Rwandan–southern African collaboration in Mozambique in 2021, the EAC force in the DRC in 2022, and a Rwandan security cooperation agreement with Benin in 2023. That said, future evolution to a mature regional security complex is not necessarily a guaranteed outcome. State fragility, low levels of human and economic development, and elite interests at the expense of good governance will continue to influence regional security cooperation.

Nonetheless, this evolution in security programs exemplifies changing security relationships as African states have become more capable partners. In particular, the eastern African relationship with various international actors has grown from a dependent, subordinate role to a more fulsome partnership wherein countries are taking a more leadership position supported by the international community. The transition to a formal regional security complex demonstrates norm transfer of security cooperation as a fundamental requisite for economic development. These norms and ideas are glocalized through the pursuit of national interests and institutionalization. In the case of the DRC, the countries in near-proximity to the eastern DRC have the most at stake in establishing regional security and have been the most active in advancing stabilization processes and mechanisms. With the inclusion of the DRC in the EAC, Kenyan and Tanzanian national interests in economic integration have raised their willingness to participate in regional stabilization efforts in the DRC. While each of the EAC members responds to their own inherent internal and external pressures, their overarching interest in regional stability and economic development is driving a greater willingness to cooperate. The formation of the first-ever EAC force, while at a very early stage, is a clear indication of both norm transfer from the global level and local interests to institutionalize those norms.

NOTES

1. Thomas Risse, "The Diffusion of Regionalism," in *The Oxford Handbook of Comparative Regionalism*, ed. Tanja A. Börzel and Thomas Risse (Oxford: Oxford University Press, 2016).

2. Roland Robertson, "Glocalization: Time-Space and Homogeneity-Heterogeneity," in *Global Modernities*, ed. M. Featherstone, S. Lash, and R. Robertson (Newbury Park, CA: SAGE, 1995); Victor C. Iwuoha et al., "Glocalization of COVID-19 Responses and Management of the Pandemic in Africa," *Local Environment* 25.8 (2020): 641–647.

3. Michael Mandelbaum, *The Ideas That Conquered the World* (New York: Public Affairs, 2004).

4. Oliver P. Richmond, "The Globalization of Responses to Conflict and the Peace-building Consensus," *Cooperation and Conflict* 39.2 (2004): 129–150.

5. Barry Buzan and Ole Wæver, *Regions and Powers: The Structure of International Security* (Cambridge: Cambridge University Press, 2003); Shiping Tang, *The Social Evolution of International Politics* (Oxford: Oxford University Press, 2013).

6. Thomas Diez and Nathalie Tocci (eds.), *The EU, Promoting Regional Integration, and Conflict Resolution* (Berlin: Springer International Publishing, 2017).

7. John Karlsrud, *Norm Change in International Relations: Linked Ecologies in UN Peacekeeping Operations* (Oxford: Routledge, 2015); Cedric de Coning, Linnéa Gelot, and John Karlsrud (eds.), *The Future of African Peace Operations: From the Janjaweed to Boko Haram* (London: Zed Books, 2016).

8. Georgina Holmes, "Norms and Practices of Peace Operations: Evolution and Contestation" (paper presented at the 4th European Workshop in International Studies, Cardiff, UK, June 7–9, 2017), 16.

9. Svitlana Radziyevska and Ivan Us, "Regionalization of the World as the Key to Sustainable Future," E3S Web of Conferences, 166 (2020): 13016. https://www.e3s-conferences.org/articles/e3sconf/abs/2020/26/e3sconf_icsf2020_13016/e3sconf_icsf2020_13016.html.

10. Barney Walsh, "Revisiting Regional Security Complex Theory in Africa: Museveni's Uganda and Regional Security in East Africa," *African Security* 13.4 (2020): 300–324.

11. Robert O. Keohane and Joseph S. Nye, *Power and Interdependence*, 4th ed. (Glenview, IL: Pearson, 2012).

12. In 1963, the Organization of African Unity (OAU) was founded by the independent states of Africa. The OAU aimed to promote cooperation between African states. In 2012, African heads of government agreed to establish a continental free trade area. In March 2018, at the Tenth Extraordinary Session of the African Union on AfCFTA, forty-four countries (of fifty-five) signed the African Continental Free Trade Agreement. The agreement went into force on May 30, 2019—thirty days after ratification by twenty-two of the signatory countries—and entered its operational phase following a summit on July 7, 2019. As of 2022, almost 82 percent of the continent (forty-four countries) has ratified the AfCFTA—a clear indication of interest in economic integration, despite the potential challenges and risks involved in economic competition.

13. Buzan and Wæver, *Regions and Powers*.

14. Walsh, "Revisiting Regional Security Complex Theory in Africa," 300–324.

15. Buzan and Wæver, *Regions and Powers*.

16. Walsh, "Revisiting Regional Security Complex Theory in Africa," 300–324.
17. Barry Buzan, *From International to World Society? English School Theory and the Social Structure of Globalisation*, Cambridge Studies in International Relations 95 (Cambridge: Cambridge University Press, 2004).
18. Walsh, "Revisiting Regional Security Complex Theory in Africa," 300–324.
19. Buzan and Wæver, *Regions and Powers*.
20. Walsh, "Revisiting Regional Security Complex Theory in Africa," 300–324.
21. Jeffrey Herbst, "States and War in Africa," in *The Nation-State in Question*, ed. Paul V. Thazha, John Ikenberry, and John A. Hall (Princeton, NJ: Princeton University Press, 2003), 166–180.
22. Risse, "The Diffusion of Regionalism."
23. Diez and Tocci, *The EU, Promoting Regional Integration, and Conflict Resolution*.
24. Thomas Risse, *Domestic Politics and Norm Diffusion in International Relations: Ideas Do Not Float Freely* (London: Routledge, 2017).
25. Shiping Tang, *A General Theory of Institutional Change* (London: Routledge, 2011); Robert Jervis, *System Effects: Complexity in Political and Social Life* (Princeton, NJ: Princeton University Press, 1997).
26. Tang, *A General Theory of Institutional Change*, 17.
27. See Abu Bakarr Bah, "The Contours of New Humanitarianism: War and Peacebuilding in Sierra Leone," *Africa Today* 60.1 (2013): 3–26.
28. Linda Darkwa and Philip Attuquayefio, "Analysis of Norm Diffusion in the African Union and the Economic Community of West African States," *African Conflict and Peacebuilding Review* 4.2 (2014): 11–37; Karlsrud, *Norm Change in International Relations*.
29. Maggie Dwyer, "The Military in African Politics," in *The Oxford Encyclopedia of African Politics*, ed. Nic Cheeseman et al. (Oxford: Oxford University Press, 2019), https://doi.org/10.1093/acrefore/9780190228637.013.710.
30. Peter Arthur, "Promoting Security in Africa through Regional Economic Communities (RECs) and the African Union's African Peace and Security Architecture (APSA)," *Insight on Africa* 9.1 (2017): 1–21; Paul D. Williams, *War and Conflict in Africa* (Hoboken, NJ: John Wiley & Sons, 2016); Paul D. Williams, *Fighting for Peace in Somalia: A History and Analysis of the African Union Mission (AMISOM), 2007–2017* (Oxford: Oxford University Press, 2018); for a discussion of the agency of Africa/AU, see Abu Bakarr Bah, "African Agency in New Humanitarianism and Responsible Governance," in *International Security and Peacebuilding: Africa, the Middle East, and Europe*, ed. Abu Bakarr Bah (Bloomington: Indiana University Press, 2017).
31. Dubi Kanengisser, "How Ideas Change and How They Change Institutions: A Memetic Theoretical Framework" (paper presented at the American Political Science Association Annual Meeting, 2014); Diez and Tocci, *The EU, Promoting Regional Integration, and Conflict Resolution*; Daniela Sicurelli, *The European Union's Africa Policies: Norms, Interests, and Impact* (Farnham, UK: Ashgate Publishing, 2013).
32. Risse, "The Diffusion of Regionalism"; Diez and Tocci, *The EU, Promoting Regional Integration, and Conflict Resolution*.

33. Benedikt F. Franke, "Competing Regionalisms in Africa and the Continent's Emerging Security Architecture," *Africa Studies Quarterly* 9.3 (2007): 34–64; Benedikt F. Franke, "Africa's Evolving Security Architecture and the Concept of Multilayered Security Communities," *Cooperation and Conflict* 43.3 (2008): 313–340.

34. Thomas Diez, Mathias Albert, and Stephan Stetter (eds.), *The European Union and Border Conflicts: The Power of Integration and Association* (Cambridge: Cambridge University Press, 2008); Soji Oyeranmi, "European Union and African Union: A Study of Regionalism for Global Integration and Development," *Journal for the Advancement of Developing Economies* 3.1 (2014): 1–16, https://digitalcommons.unl.edu/cgi/viewcontent.cgi?article=1007&context=jade.

35. Mario Telò (ed.), *European Union and New Regionalism: Competing Regionalism and Global Governance in a Post-hegemonic Era* (Farnham, UK: Ashgate Publishing, 2014).

36. Diez and Tocci, *The EU, Promoting Regional Integration, and Conflict Resolution.*

37. Franke, "Africa's Evolving Security Architecture," 313–340; Sicurelli, *The European Union's Africa Policies.*

38. ReliefWeb, "The African Union and the European Union Join Forces for Ensuring Peace in Africa: The European Union Renews Its Support to the African Peace and Security Architecture with a New Financial Agreement of 40.5 Million Euro," ReliefWeb press release, March 17, 2020, https://reliefweb.int/report/world/african-union-and-european-union-join-forces-ensuring-peace-africa.

39. Abu Bakarr Bah and Nikolas Emmanuel, "Migration Cooperation between Africa and Europe: Understanding the Role of Incentives," *Oxford Research Encyclopedia of International Studies*, September 15, 2022, https://doi.org/10.1093/acrefore/9780190846626.013.735.

40. See Bah, "State Decay: A Conceptual Frame of Failing and Failed States in West Africa," *International Journal of Politics, Culture, and Society* 25.1 (2012): 71–89; Bah, "State Decay and Civil War: A Discourse on Power in Sierra Leone," *Critical Sociology* 37.2 (2011): 199–216.

41. UN Peacekeeping Open Data Portal, https://peacekeeping.un.org/en/data-troop-and-police-contributions.

42. Oliver Liffan and Joan Tilouine, "East African Community Sets Out Battle Plan for Regional Force in Eastern DRC," *Africa Intelligence*, July 12, 2022, https://www.africaintelligence.com/central-africa/2022/07/12/east-african-community-sets-out-battle-plan-for-regional-force-in-eastern-drc,109798904-art.

43. Simon Mulongo, *Report of Conflict Assessment in the East African Community (EAC) Partner States*, EAC Short Term Consultancy Study (Arusha: EAC, 2010), 116.

44. Arthur, "Promoting Security in Africa," 1–21; Barnabas Olusegun Obasaju et al., "Regional Economic Integration and Economic Upgrading in Global Value Chains: Selected Cases in Africa," *Heliyon* 7.2 (2021): e06112.

45. Walsh, "Revisiting Regional Security Complex Theory in Africa," 311, 317.

46. Victor Adebola O. Adetula, Redie Bereketeab, and Cyril Obi, *Regional Economic Communities and Peacebuilding in Africa: Lessons from ECOWAS and IGAD,*

Routledge Studies in African Politics and International Relations (New York: Routledge, 2021); Williams, *Fighting for Peace in Somalia*.

47. Michael D. Rettig, "The Evolution of African Peacekeeping," Africa Center for Strategic Studies, May 26, 2016, https://africacenter.org/spotlight/evolution-african-peacekeeping/; de Coning, Gelot, and Karlsrud, *The Future of African Peace Operations*; James Dobbins et al., *Africa's Role in Nation-Building: An Examination of African-Led Peace Operations* (Santa Monica, CA: RAND Corporation, 2019).

48. De Coning, Gelot, and Karlsrud, *The Future of African Peace Operations*.

49. Cedric de Coning, "Africa and UN Peace Operations: Implications for the Future Role of Regional Organisations," in *United Nations Peace Operations in a Changing Global Order*, ed. Cedric de Coning and Mateja Peter (Cham: Palgrave Macmillan, 2019).

50. Ntirenganya, "EAC and AU Sign US\$2 Million Grant Agreement to Support Regional Force in DRC," *RegionWeek*, June 29, 2023, https://regionweek.com/eac-and-au-sign-us2-million-grant-agreement-to-support-regional-force-in-drc/.

51. Roselyn Anjalo, Pontian Okoth, and Sussy Kimokoti, "Threats to Regional Security and Integration within the Jurisdiction of the East African Community," *International Journal of Education and Research* 6.9 (2018): 83–94.

52. Gérard Prunier, *Africa's World War: Congo, the Rwandan Genocide, and the Making of a Continental Catastrophe* (Oxford: Oxford University Press, 2008).

53. Jean-Pierre Chrétien and Richard Banégas, *The Recurring Great Lakes Crisis: Identity, Violence and Power* (London: Hurst, 2008).

54. Jason Stearns, *The War That Doesn't Say Its Name: The Unending Conflict in the Congo* (Princeton, NJ: Princeton University Press, 2021).

55. Gatete Ruhumuliza Nyiringabo, "Security Crisis and Complex Banyarwanda Equation in DRC," *The EastAfrican*, May 8, 2022, https://www.theeastafrican.co.ke/tea/news/east-africa/security-crisis-and-complex-banyarwanda-equation-in-drc-3904854.

56. Gatete Ruhumuliza Nyiringabo, "The M23 Problem, Kigali's Headache and Some Truths Few Want to Hear," *The Africa Report*, December 7, 2022, https://www.theafricareport.com/224594/drc-rwanda-felix-tshisekedis-headache; Romain Gras, "DRC-Rwanda: Felix Tshisekedi's Headache," *The Africa Report*, July 20, 2022, https://www.theafricareport.com/224594/drc-rwanda-felix-tshisekedis-headache/.

57. Mohammed Yusuf, "East African Regional Bloc Begins Deployment of Troops to DRC," Voice of America, August 18, 2022, https://www.voanews.com/a/east-african-regional-bloc-begins-deployment-of-troops-to-drc/6706964.html.

58. Stearns, *The War That Doesn't Say Its Name*.

59. Jason Stearns, "Laurent Nkunda and the National Congress for the Defence of the People (CNDP)," *L'Afrique des Grands Lacs: Annuaire* (2008): 245–267.

60. Chrétien and Banégas, *The Recurring Great Lakes Crisis*.

61. Stearns, "Laurent Nkunda and the CNDP," 245–267.

62. Hugo de Vries, *Going Around in Circles: The Challenges of Peacekeeping and Stabilization in the Democratic Republic of Congo*, Conflict Research Unit (CRU) Report (The Hague: Clingendael Institute, 2015).

63. Stearns, "Laurent Nkunda and the CNDP," 245–267.

64. Clement Namangale, "Dynamics of Conflict Management in the Democratic Republic of the Congo," *Prism* 5.2 (2015): 72–83.

65. Jason Stearns, *From CNDP to M23—The Evolution of an Armed Movement in Eastern Congo* (London: Rift Valley Institute, 2012).

66. Diez and Tocci, *The EU, Promoting Regional Integration, and Conflict Resolution*; Risse, *The Diffusion of Regionalism*; Tang, *A General Theory of Institutional Change*.

67. Peter Mugabo, "The FDLR Preparing for Mass Surrender," News of Rwanda, November 4, 2016.

68. Jason Stearns, Judith Verweijen, and Maria Eriksson Baaz, *The National Army and Armed Groups in the Eastern Congo: Untangling the Gordian Knot of Insecurity* (London: Rift Valley Institute, 2013).

69. Nkuba, "Stopping History from Repeating Itself," 1–19.

70. Guilain Mathe, "Investigating Rebel Governance in North Kivu," *Researchers in Exile* 1.1 (April 2016): 110–130.

71. Ntalaja, "The Fragile State and Crisis in Eastern Congo," 15–37.

72. De Vries, *Going Around in Circles*.

73. Kiwuwa, "Accounting for Détente in the Great Lakes Region," 330.

74. Kwibuka, "Rwanda, DR Congo Defence Ministers Hold Talks."

75. Jason Stearns, "The Democratic Republic of the Congo: An Elusive Peace," in *War and Peace in Africa's Great Lakes Region*, ed. G. Khadiagala (Cham: Palgrave Macmillan, 2017), 33–47.

76. Peter Mugabo, "The FDLR Preparing for Mass Surrender."

77. Edmund Kagire, "Congo-Kinshasa: DR Congo Arrests Top Rwandan Rebel Commander," *The EastAfrican*, October 29, 2016, http://allafrica.com/stories/201610311016.html.

78. Paul-Simon Handy, "Rwanda: The Emergence of an African 'Smart Power,'" Institute for Security Studies, September 27, 2021, https://issafrica.org/iss-today/rwanda-the-emergence-of-an-african-smart-power.

79. According to a UN Military Observation member report to the author, Fall 2022.

80. Peter Fabricius, "Tshisekedi Opens a Pandora's Box in Eastern Democratic Republic of the Congo," Institute for Security Studies, June 22, 2022, https://issafrica.org/iss-today/tshisekedi-opens-a-pandoras-box-in-eastern-democratic-republic-of-the-congo.

81. East African Community, "DRC President Presides over Signing of Agreement Giving Green Light to the Deployment of the EAC Joint Regional Force," East African Community Media—International Relations, September 9, 2022, https://www.eac.int/press-releases/151-international-relations/2589-drc-president-presides-over-signing-of-agreement-giving-greenlight-to-the-deployment-of-the-eac-joint-regional-force.

82. Al Jazeera, "DR Congo and Rwanda Agree to Reduce Tensions over M23 Rebels," *Al Jazeera News*, June 7, 2022, https://www.aljazeera.com/news/2022/7/6/dr-congo-and-rwanda-agree-to-reduce-tensions-over-m23-rebels; Laurence Sithole, "DRC Rare Earth Minerals to Accelerate Economic Growth," *The Exchange*, January 10, 2022, https://theexchange.africa/investing/drc-rare-earth-minerals-to-accelerate-economic-growth.

83. International Crisis Group, "Supporting Dialogue and Demobilisation in the DR Congo," *Commentary Africa*, October 10, 2022, https://www.crisisgroup.org/africa/great-lakes/democratic-republic-congo/supporting-dialogue-and-demobilisation-dr-congo.

84. Cristella Ntirenganya, "EAC and AU Sign US$2 Million Grant Agreement to Support Regional Force in DRC," *Region Week*, June 29, 2023, https://regionweek.com/eac-and-au-sign-us2-million-grant-agreement-to-support-regional-force-in-drc.

85. International Crisis Group, *How to Spend It: New EU Funding for African Peace and Security*, Africa Report No. 297 (Brussels: International Crisis Group, 2021), 297, https://www.crisisgroup.org/africa/african-union-regional-bodies/297-how-spend-it-new-eu-funding-african-peace-and-security.

86. International Crisis Group.

87. Feldman and Francis define economic development as "the development of capacities that expand economic actors' capabilities." Maryann Feldman et al., "The Logic of Economic Development: A Definition and Model for Investment," *Environment and Planning C: Government and Policy* 34.1 (2016): 6. Maryann P. Feldman and Johanna I. Francis, "Fortune Favors the Prepared Region: The Case of Entrepreneurship and the Capitol Region Biotechnology Cluster," *European Planning Studies* 11.7 (2003): 765–788; Peace and Security Council Report, "The AU Peace and Security Council Should Discuss the Implications of the European Peace Facility for Africa," Institute for Security Studies, ISS Africa PSC Report, April 5, 2022, https://issafrica.org/pscreport/psc-insights/africa-europe-peace-and-security-partnership-at-a-crossroads.

88. Keohane and Nye, *Power and Interdependence*.

BIBLIOGRAPHY

Adetula, Victor Adebola O., Redie Bereketeab, and Cyril Obi. *Regional Economic Communities and Peacebuilding in Africa: Lessons from ECOWAS and IGAD.* Routledge Studies in African Politics and International Relations. New York: Routledge, 2021.

Al Jazeera. "DR Congo and Rwanda Agree to Reduce Tensions over M23 Rebels." *Al Jazeera News*, June 7, 2022. https://www.aljazeera.com/news/2022/7/6/dr-congo-and-rwanda-agree-to-reduce-tensions-over-m23-rebels.

Anjalo, Roselyn, Pontian Okoth, and Sussy Kimokoti. "Threats to Regional Security and Integration within the Jurisdiction of the East African Community." *International Journal of Education and Research* 6.9 (2018): 83–94.

Arthur, Peter. "Promoting Security in Africa through Regional Economic Communities (RECs) and the African Union's African Peace and Security Architecture (APSA)." *Insight on Africa* 9.1 (2017): 1–21.

Bah, Abu Bakarr. "State Decay and Civil War: A Discourse on Power in Sierra Leone." *Critical Sociology* 37.2 (2011): 199–216.

———. "State Decay: A Conceptual Frame of Failing and Failed States in West Africa." *International Journal of Politics, Culture, and Society* 25.1 (2012): 71–89.

———. "The Contours of New Humanitarianism: War and Peacebuilding in Sierra Leone." *Africa Today* 60.1 (2013): 3–26.

———. "African Agency in New Humanitarianism and Responsible Governance." In *International Security and Peacebuilding: Africa, the Middle East, and Europe*, ed. Abu Bakarr Bah, 148–169. Bloomington: Indiana University Press, 2017.

Bah, Abu Bakarr, and Nikolas Emmanuel. "Migration Cooperation between Africa and Europe: Understanding the Role of Incentives." *Oxford Research Encyclopedia of International Studies*, September 15, 2022. https://doi.org/10.1093/acrefore/9780190846626.013.735.

Buzan, Barry. *From International to World Society? English School Theory and the Social Structure of Globalisation.* Cambridge Studies in International Relations 95. Cambridge: Cambridge University Press, 2004.

Buzan, Barry, and Ole Wæver. *Regions and Powers: The Structure of International Security.* Cambridge: Cambridge University Press, 2003.

Chrétien, Jean-Pierre, and Richard Banégas (eds.), *The Recurring Great Lakes Crisis: Identity, Violence, Power.* London: Hurst, 2008.

Darkwa, Linda, and Philip Attuquayefio. "Analysis of Norm Diffusion in the African Union and the Economic Community of West African States." *African Conflict and Peacebuilding Review* 4. 2 (2014): 11–37.

de Coning, Cedric. "Africa and UN Peace Operations: Implications for the Future Role of Regional Organisations." In *United Nations Peace Operations in a Changing Global Order*, ed. Cedric de Coning and Mateja Peter. Cham: Palgrave Macmillan, 2019.

de Coning, Cedric, Linnéa Gelot, and John Karlsrud (eds.). *The Future of African Peace Operations: From the Janjaweed to Boko Haram.* London: Zed Books, 2016.

de Vries, Hugo. *Going Around in Circles: The Challenges of Peacekeeping and Stabilization in the Democratic Republic of Congo.* Conflict Research Unit (CRU) Report. The Hague: Clingendael Institute, 2015.

Diez, Thomas, Mathias Albert, and Stephan Stetter (eds.). *The European Union and Border Conflicts: The Power of Integration and Association.* Cambridge: Cambridge University Press, 2008.

Diez, Thomas, and Nathalie Tocci (eds.). *The EU, Promoting Regional Integration, and Conflict Resolution.* Berlin: Springer International Publishing, 2017.

Dobbins, James, James Machakaire, Andrew Radin, Stephanie Pezard, Jonathan Blake, Laura Bosco, Nathan Chandler, Wandile Langa, Charles Nyuykonge, and Kitenge Tunda. *Africa's Role in Nation-Building: An Examination of African-Led Peace Operations.* Santa Monica, CA: RAND Corporation, 2019.

Dwyer, Maggie. "The Military in African Politics." In *Oxford Encyclopedia of African Politics*, ed. Nic Cheeseman, Rita Abrahamsen, Gilbert M. Khadiagala, Peace A. Medie, Rachel Beatty Riedl, and Etienne Smith. Oxford: Oxford University Press, 2019. https://doi.org/10.1093/acrefore/9780190228637.013.710.

East African Community. "DRC President Presides over Signing of Agreement Giving Green Light to the Deployment of the EAC Joint Regional Force." East African Community Media—International Relations, September 9, 2022. https://www.eac.int/press-releases/151-international-relations/2589-drc-president-presides-over-signing-of-agreement-giving-greenlight-to-the-deployment-of-the-eac-joint-regional-force.

Fabricius, Peter. "Tshisekedi Opens a Pandora's Box in Eastern Democratic Republic of the Congo." Institute for Security Studies, June 22, 2022. https://issafrica.org/iss-today/tshisekedi-opens-a-pandoras-box-in-eastern-democratic-republic-of-the-congo.

Feldman, Maryann P., and Johanna Francis. "Fortune Favors the Prepared Region: The Case of Entrepreneurship and the Capitol Region Biotechnology Cluster." *European Planning Studies* 11.7 (2003): 765–788.

Feldman, Maryann, Theodora Hadjimichael, Lauren Lanahan, and Tom Kemeny. "The Logic of Economic Development: A Definition and Model for Investment." *Environment and Planning C: Government and Policy* 34.1 (2016): 5–21.

Franke, Benedikt F. "Competing Regionalisms in Africa and the Continent's Emerging Security Architecture." *Africa Studies Quarterly* 9.3 (2007): 34–64. https://asq.africa.ufl.edu/wp-content/uploads/sites/168/Franke-Vol9Issue3.pdf.

———. "Africa's Evolving Security Architecture and the Concept of Multilayered Security Communities." *Cooperation and Conflict* 43.3 (2008): 313–340.

Fukuyama, Francis. *The Origins of Political Order: From Prehuman Times to the French Revolution*. New York: Farrar, Straus & Giroux, 2011.

Gras, Romain. "DRC-Rwanda: Felix Tshisekedi's Headache." *The Africa Report*, July 20, 2022. https://www.theafricareport.com/224594/drc-rwanda-felix-tshisekedis-headache.

Handy, Paul-Simon. "Rwanda: The Emergence of an African 'Smart Power.'" Institute for Security Studies, September 27, 2021. https://issafrica.org/iss-today/rwanda-the-emergence-of-an-african-smart-power.

Herbst, Jeffrey. "States and War in Africa." In *The Nation-State in Question*, ed. Paul V. Thazha, John G. Ikenberry, and John A. Hall, 162–180. Princeton, NJ: Princeton University Press, 2003.

Holmes, Georgina. "Norms and Practices of Peace Operations: Evolution and Contestation." Paper presented at the 4th European Workshop in International Studies, Cardiff, UK, June 7–9, 2017, 16–19.

———. "Situating Agency, Embodied Practices and Norm Implementation in Peacekeeping Training." *International Peacekeeping* 26.1 (2019): 55–84.

Inglehart, Ronald. *Cultural Evolution: People's Motivations Are Changing and Reshaping the World*. Cambridge: Cambridge University Press, 2018.

International Crisis Group. *How to Spend It: New EU Funding for African Peace and Security*. Africa Report No. 297. Brussels: International Crisis Group, 2021.

https://www.crisisgroup.org/africa/african-union-regional-bodies/297-how-spend-it-new-eu-funding-african-peace-and-security.

———. "Supporting Dialogue and Demobilisation in the DR Congo." International Crisis Group, Commentary/Africa, October 10, 2022. https://www.crisisgroup.org/africa/great-lakes/democratic-republic-congo/supporting-dialogue-and-demobilisation-dr-congo.

Iwuoha, Victor C., Ezinwanne N. Ezeibe, and Christian Chukwuebuka Ezeibe. "Glocalization of COVID-19 Responses and Management of the Pandemic in Africa." *Local Environment* 25.8 (2020): 641–647.

Jervis, Robert. *System Effects: Complexity in Political and Social Life.* Princeton, NJ: Princeton University Press, 1997.

Kagire, Edmund. "Congo-Kinshasa: DR Congo Arrests Top Rwandan Rebel Commander." *The EastAfrican,* October 29, 2016. http://allafrica.com/stories/201610311016.html.

Kanengisser, Dubi. "How Ideas Change and How They Change Institutions: A Memetic Theoretical Framework." Paper presented at American Political Science Association Annual Meeting, 2014.

Karlsrud, John. *Norm Change in International Relations: Linked Ecologies in UN Peacekeeping Operations.* Oxford: Routledge, 2015.

Keohane, Robert O., and Joseph S. Nye. *Power and Interdependence.* 4th ed. Glenview, IL: Pearson, 2012.

Kiwuwa, David E. "Accounting for Détente in the Great Lakes Region." In *The Routledge Handbook of Ethnic Conflict,* ed. Karl Cordell and Stefan Wolff, 330–348. London: Routledge, 2016.

Kwibuka, Eugene. "Rwanda, DR Congo Defence Ministers Hold Talks." *The New Times,* September 24, 2015. https://www.newtimes.co.rw/article/122918/News/rwanda-dr-congo-defence-ministers-hold-talks.

Liffan, Oliver, and Joan Tilouine. "East African Community Sets Out Battle Plan for Regional Force in Eastern DRC." *Africa Intelligence,* July 12, 2022. https://www.africaintelligence.com/central-africa/2022/07/12/east-african-community-sets-out-battle-plan-for-regional-force-in-eastern-drc,109798904-art.

Mandelbaum, Michael. *The Ideas That Conquered the World.* New York: Public Affairs, 2004.

Mangula, George. "EAC, EU Sign 10m Euros for Joint Response to Regional and Cross Border Security Threats." *Eagle Online,* December 30, 2019. https://eagle.co.ug/2019/11/30/eac-eu-sign-10m-euros-for-joint-response-to-regional-and-cross-border-security-threats.html.

Mathe, Guilain. "Investigating Rebel Governance in North Kivu." *Researchers in Exile* 1.1 (April 2016): 110–130.

Mugabo, Peter. "The FDLR Preparing for Mass Surrender." *News of Rwanda,* November 4, 2016.

Mulongo, Simon. *Report of Conflict Assessment in the East African Community (EAC) Partner States.* EAC Short Term Consultancy Study. Arusha: EAC, 2010.

Namangale, Clement. "Dynamics of Conflict Management in the Democratic Republic of the Congo." *Prism* 5.2 (2015): 72–83.

Nkuba, Desire. "Stopping History from Repeating Itself: The Case of Forcefully Displaced People from Rwanda and the Need for a Durable Solution through

Political Means." *International Journal of Community Development* 4.1 (2016): 1–19.

Ntalaja, Georges Nzongola. "The Fragile State and Crisis in Eastern Congo." *African Journal of Democracy and Governance* 2.1 (2015): 15–37.

Ntirenganya, Cristella. "EAC and AU Sign US\$2 Million Grant Agreement to Support Regional Force in DRC." *RegionWeek*, June 29, 2023. https://regionweek.com/eac-and-au-sign-us2-million-grant-agreement-to-support-regional-force-in-drc/.

Nyiringabo, Gatete Ruhumuliza. "M23 Rebels Attack Military Positions in Eastern DR Congo." *Al Jazeera*, March 28, 2022. https://www.aljazeera.com/news/2022/3/28/m23-rebels-attack-military-positions-in-eastern-dr-congo.

———. "The M23 Problem, Kigali's Headache and Some Truths Few Want to Hear." *The Africa Report*, July 12, 2022. https://www.theafricareport.com/224594/drc-rwanda-felix-tshisekedis-headache.

———. "Security Crisis and Complex Banyarwanda Equation in DRC." *The EastAfrican*, August 5, 2022. https://www.theeastafrican.co.ke/tea/news/east-africa/security-crisis-and-complex-banyarwanda-equation-in-drc-3904854.

Obasaju, Barnabas Olusegun, Wumi Kolawole Olayiwola, Henry Okodua, Oluwasogo Sunday Adediran, and Adedoyin Isola Lawal. "Regional Economic Integration and Economic Upgrading in Global Value Chains: Selected Cases in Africa." *Heliyon* 7.2 (2021): e06112.

Oyeranmi, Soji. "European Union and African Union: A Study of Regionalism for Global Integration and Development." *Journal for the Advancement of Developing Economies* 3. 1 (2014): 1–16. https://digitalcommons.unl.edu/cgi/viewcontent.cgi?article=1007&context=jade.

Peace and Security Council Report. "The AU Peace and Security Council Should Discuss the Implications of the European Peace Facility for Africa: Africa-Europe Peace and Security Partnership at a Crossroads." Institute for Security Studies, ISS Africa PSC Report, April 5, 2022. https://issafrica.org/pscreport/psc-insights/africa-europe-peace-and-security-partnership-at-a-crossroads.

Prunier, Gérard. *Africa's World War: Congo, the Rwandan Genocide, and the Making of a Continental Catastrophe.* Oxford: Oxford University Press, 2008.

Radziyevska, Svitlana, and Ivan Us. "Regionalization of the World as the Key to Sustainable Future." E3S Web of Conferences, 166 (2020): 13016. https://www.e3s-conferences.org/articles/e3sconf/abs/2020/26/e3sconf_icsf2020_13016/e3sconf_icsf2020_13016.html.

Relief Web. "The African Union and the European Union Join Forces for Ensuring Peace in Africa: The European Union Renews Its Support to the African Peace and Security Architecture with a New Financial Agreement of 40.5 Million Euro." ReliefWeb press release, March 17, 2020. https://reliefweb.int/report/world/african-union-and-european-union-join-forces-ensuring-peace-africa.

Rettig, Michael D. "The Evolution of African Peacekeeping." Africa Center for Strategic Studies, May 26, 2016. https://africacenter.org/spotlight/evolution-african-peacekeeping/.

Richmond, Oliver P. "The Globalization of Responses to Conflict and the Peacebuilding Consensus." *Cooperation and Conflict* 39.2 (2004): 129–150.

Risse, Thomas. "The Diffusion of Regionalism." In *The Oxford Handbook of Comparative Regionalism*, ed. Tanja A. Börzel and Thomas Risse, 87–108. Oxford: Oxford University Press, 2016.

———. *Domestic Politics and Norm Diffusion in International Relations: Ideas Do Not Float Freely*. London: Routledge, 2017.

Robertson, Roland. "Glocalization: Time-Space and Homogeneity-Heterogeneity." In *Global Modernities*, ed. M. Featherstone, S. Lash, and R. Robertson, 25–44. Newbury Park, CA: SAGE, 1995.

Sicurelli, Daniela. *The European Union's Africa Policies: Norms, Interests and Impact*. Farnham, UK: Ashgate Publishing, 2013.

Sithole, Laurence. "DRC Rare Earth Minerals to Accelerate Economic Growth." *The Exchange*, October 1, 2022. https://theexchange.africa/investing/drc-rare-earth -minerals-to-accelerate-economic-growth.

Stearns, Jason. "Laurent Nkunda and the National Congress for the Defence of the People (CNDP)." *L'Afrique des Grands Lacs: Annuaire* (2008): 245–267.

———. *From CNDP to M23: The Evolution of an Armed Movement in Eastern Congo*. London: Rift Valley Institute, 2012.

———. "The Democratic Republic of the Congo: An Elusive Peace." In *War and Peace in Africa's Great Lakes Region*, ed. G. Khadiagala, 33–47. Cham: Palgrave Macmillan, 2017.

———. *The War That Doesn't Say Its Name: The Unending Conflict in the Congo*. Princeton, NJ: Princeton University Press, 2021.

Stearns, Jason, Judith Verweijen, and Maria Eriksson Baaz. *The National Army and Armed Groups in the Eastern Congo: Untangling the Gordian Knot of Insecurity*. London: Rift Valley Institute, 2013.

Swyngedouw, Erik. "Globalisation or 'Glocalisation'? Networks, Territories and Rescaling." *Cambridge Review of International Affairs* 17.1 (2004): 25–48.

Tang, Shiping. *A General Theory of Institutional Change*. London: Routledge, 2011.

———. *The Social Evolution of International Politics*. Oxford: Oxford University Press, 2013.

Telò, Mario (ed.). *European Union and New Regionalism: Competing Regionalism and Global Governance in a Post-hegemonic Era*. Farnham, UK: Ashgate Publishing, 2014.

UN Peacekeeping Open Data Portal. Trop and Police Contributions, 2020. https://peacekeeping.un.org/en/data-troop-and-police-contributions.

Walsh, Barney. "Revisiting Regional Security Complex Theory in Africa: Museveni's Uganda and Regional Security in East Africa." *African Security* 13.4 (2020): 300–324.

Williams, Paul D. *War and Conflict in Africa*. Hoboken, NJ: John Wiley & Sons, 2016.

———. *Fighting for Peace in Somalia: A History and Analysis of the African Union Mission (AMISOM), 2007–2017*. Oxford: Oxford University Press, 2018.

Williams, Paul D., and Alex J. Bellamy. *Understanding Peacekeeping*. 3rd ed. Medford, MA: Polity Press, 2021.

Yusuf, Mohammed. "East African Regional Bloc Begins Deployment of Troops to DRC." *Voice of America*, August 18, 2022. https://www.voanews.com/a/east-african-regional-bloc-begins-deployment-of-troops-to-drc/6706964.html.

Chapter 7

The African Union on the Periphery of Peacebuilding

The Role of External Powers and Regional Bodies in Libya

NORMAN SEMPIJJA, AKRAM ZAOUI, AND NOAMANE CHERKAOUI

Since 2014 the conflict in Libya has increasingly devolved into a battleground of regional and great power competition. Multiple international meetings, conferences, and mediations have largely failed to stabilize the country, reconcile opposing parties, build lasting and functioning institutions, or contribute to efficient and durable peacebuilding, which can be defined as "a process aimed at addressing deep-rooted causes of conflict and establishing a sustainable peace."[1]

The country has experienced multiple armed crises for control of different parts of the territory. It has gone through several phases of conflicts that can be characterized as a contested national order (2011–13), a violent regional division (2013–14), a broken compromise (2014–16), and deeper state fragmentation thereafter.[2] The high risks of conflict relapse, failing democratic transition, and uninterrupted foreign intervention have meant that Libya's underlying conflict dynamics remain unresolved. Indeed, while the third civil war is over, the conflict that reignited in 2014 is not, and hence it will be treated in this chapter as a process that is frozen, a "situation in which war [has] ended yet stable peace did not materialize."[3] Libya's situation can be further delineated in terms of its peace disposition, with the current negative peace lacking the positive "integration of human society."[4] In all of this problem in Libya, external powers have been deeply involved, even more than regional powers and organizations.

The African Union (AU) is a unique pan-African regional organization with wide-ranging peacebuilding skills. Nevertheless, its impacts and influence on the Libyan conflict have been limited, with the interests of more active powers hitherto dominating the conflict and peace process. Arguably, there is a need to include the AU in the Libyan peacebuilding process, which can dovetail with extant efforts to maximize the chances of success. The AU has an intrinsic interest in Libya's stability—more tangible than those of distant countries—and can play a significant role moving forward as the international community gradually withdraws. Therefore, this chapter aims to shed light on how the AU can be a constructive actor in Libya's peacebuilding, given how it embraces a "holistic concept of peace . . . [and] a comprehensive peace architecture that ranges from early warning capacity to post-conflict rebuilding for peace."[5]

The breadth and relevance of the AU's mandate is noteworthy. Its Peace and Security Architecture includes "a Panel of the Wise, which promotes high-level mediation efforts; a rapid-reaction African Standby Force (ASF) built around five subregional brigades; a Continental Early Warning System (CEWS); a Military Staff Committee (MSC); and a Peace Fund."[6] The AU has adopted a holistic approach to peacebuilding that links peace and security to development with an emphasis on national ownership of the peace process. There are eight Regional Economic Communities, namely the Arab Maghreb Union (AMU), the Common Market for Eastern and Southern Africa (COMESA), the Community of Sahel-Saharan States (CEN-SAD), the Economic Community of Central African States (ECCAS), the Economic Community of West African States, the Southern African Development Community, the East African Community, and the Intergovernmental Authority on Development. Some of the Regional Economic Communities (e.g., AMU, COMESA, CEN-SAD, and ECCAS) are directly affected by the Libyan conflict. When coupled with the conflict's distinctive regional history, these dynamics mean that the AU can potentially bring more experience and legitimacy as a mediator in Libya as compared with outside powers.

This chapter will fill a gap in the literature as Libya's complex conflict has rarely been analyzed in a manner that focuses on the actual and the potential contribution of the AU through the frame of marginalization. Existing analysis has overwhelmingly focused on the NATO intervention and the Responsibility to Protect (R2P) doctrine.[7] The marginalization of the AU, despite its profound understanding of both the domestic drivers of the Libyan conflict and the impact of the conflict on the Sahel, poses a critical question for understanding the glocal dimensions of the Libyan conflict. As such, this chapter seeks to examine the Libyan conflict through the lens of the AU's marginalization (despite its unique opportunity to be a critical player). The critical question is, Why has the AU been relegated to a peripheral role in the Libyan peacebuilding process? The central concept in this chapter is glocalization, which is defined as a "twin process whereby, firstly, institutional/regulatory arrangements shift from the national scale both upwards to supra-national or global scales and downwards to the scale of the individual body or to local, urban or regional configurations."[8] The Libyan conflict presents a good case of glocalized security dynamics in which national, regional, and global interests complicate the security situation and peacebuilding efforts.

THE LIBYAN CIVIL WAR: BETWEEN GLOCALIZATION AND INTERNATIONALIZATION

Libya is bordered by the Mediterranean Sea, Egypt, Sudan, Chad, Niger, Algeria, and Tunisia and has a small population of seven million. It is the fourth-largest country in Africa by area, has the continent's largest oil reserves, and is a member of the Organization of the Petroleum Exporting Countries. In 2011, NATO intervened in Libya against Muammar Gaddafi, a brutal dictator who ruled for forty-one years. NATO's intervention was based on the R2P doctrine, a commitment from the 2005 World Summit to prevent mass atrocity. After a NATO military intervention that led to Gaddafi's downfall and death, Libya's first civil war ended. Subsequently, while a burgeoning democratic scene emerged in Libya between 2012 and 2014, it failed to materialize into a peaceful transition to democracy. Instead, it led to conflict and the outbreak of

Libya's second civil war, in 2014. This was followed by a managed peace process facilitated in 2015 by the United Nations (UN) that brought the Government of National Accord to power, though key institutions remained divided between the militants from the western and eastern regions.

In 2019, a year when elections were scheduled after being delayed numerous times, a renegade retired general in the east, Khalifa Haftar, began his offensive against Tripoli, where the UN-recognized Government of National Accord was based. While the latter was supported by Turkey, Haftar's offensive was backed by Russia and other states, resulting in Libya's third civil war that was plagued by an unprecedented level of foreign interference.[9] This round of violent conflict lasted until October 2020, when a permanent ceasefire was signed, thereby freezing the conflict. Since then, foreign powers have remained influential and continue to materially support opposing sides despite the installation of a new UN-recognized government in March 2021. Elections were scheduled for December 2021, but Libyan actors could not hold them for various recycled reasons, including the rigidity of state institutions, the lack of effective mediation, and haphazard peacebuilding and security-sector reform.

Throughout the conflicts, the role of the AU has oscillated between rhetoric and figuration, reduced to symbolic involvement. Indeed, the AU Troika Committee convened a meeting in April 2019, a few days after the offensive led by Khalifa Haftar was launched on Tripoli. Other meetings held by AU mechanisms and institutions on the situation in Libya following the April 2019 offensive on Tripoli included an AU Peace and Security Council meeting in May 2019, a High-Level Committee on Libya meeting in July 2019, an AU-EU-UN meeting on the Situation of Stranded Migrant and Refugees in Libya in September 2019, and a meeting of the AU Contact Group on Libya in May 2020.[10] However, these gatherings appeared to be mostly symbolic and had no significant impacts on resolving the conflict.

Libya's internationalized conflict should be regarded as an inorganically protracted process, with the evolution of intrastate conflicts, which is often a function of the involvement of other third parties.[11] It has been demonstrated that "third-party interventions on the side of both the government and opposition decrease the likelihood of a negotiated settlement."[12] These biased interventions in Libya were based on geostrategic rationale, with international law and moral considerations taking a back seat to national interests.[13] The AU's broader role in African conflicts has, initially, been heavily rooted in mediation and less robust intervention. Though the AU has been part of UN hybrid peacekeeping missions, such as United Nations Hybrid Operations in Darfur (UNAMID), and undertaken independent missions, such as African Union Mission in Somalia (AMISOM), the changing nature of conflicts, especially the fragmentation from within and proliferation of external interventions, has left the AU trying to catch up and struggling to assert itself in the Libyan conflicts. Notably, the AU had to deal with internal players backed by major world powers, including NATO.

It should be noted that, when discussing Libya, scholars have focused mainly on the implications of Gaddafi's demise and the application of R2P, which O'Shea argues has been articulated as a viable solution to a complicated problem.[14] R2P has been associated with the international interventions given Libya's "state of anarchy with human rights abuses being widespread."[15] R2P is also invoked in the peacebuilding effort. Keranen, for example, focused on the "responsibility to rebuild," emphasizing R2P implementation and a state-building plan, which was missing from the initial NATO intervention in Libya.[16] While the R2P approach favored the intervention of major powers, a glocalized approach to the Libya conflict could have created a better space for the AU to contribute to resolving the Libyan conflict. However, because key players in the AU were sympathetic to Gaddafi, NATO and the UN were reluctant to give the AU a meaningful role. Unfortunately, the sidelining of the AU led to further involvement by outside powers, such as the EU, Russia, and Turkey. Each of the outside powers has been imposing its own brand of peacebuilding on Libya. This has led to further fragmentation within the state as external players have coalesced around different local actors who serve their interests. The result has been a continuation of conflict with no strong state in place even as the humanitarian crisis worsened. Thus, it is crucial to go beyond R2P in order to fully understand the AU's role, as the conflict has escalated into dangerous geostrategic competition for influence, with severe domestic and regional implications.

GLOCALIZED SECURITY: INTERNATIONAL INTERVENTIONS AND PEACEBUILDING IN AFRICA

The main discourse on conflict in the immediate aftermath of World War II had been on curbing interstate wars, as shown in the UN Charter of 1945. Mechanisms of collective security were put into place to limit and deal with interstate conflicts. Yet the UN was not consistent in its reactions to acts of aggression. For example, the UN indirectly blamed Vietnam for the intervention in Cambodia in 1978 and was noncommittal on India's intervention in East Pakistan.[17] Later, peacekeeping mechanisms were put in place but were initially intended as a mechanism to prevent superpowers from getting involved in interstate conflicts as their doing so could possibly lead to wider conflicts. However, the emergence of intrastate conflicts such as those in former Yugoslavia, Rwanda, Sierra Leone, and Somalia presented a new dilemma for the international community. Largely referred to as new wars, these conflicts threatened the core of the state.[18] Initially, UN interventions involved lightly armed peacekeepers who could not enforce peace such as in Rwanda and Yugoslavia.[19] Later, UN interventions moved toward robust humanitarian intervention under R2P, which has been applied in places such as Sierra Leone, Somalia, and Kosovo.[20] The discourse of international intervention has now embraced the R2P doctrine, which was applied in Libya. R2P rests on robust international peacebuilding, which entails both military intervention and postwar reconstruction.

Peacebuilding was first articulated by Boutros Boutros-Ghali in the 1992 agenda for peace.[21] Although not in the UN Charter, peacebuilding has become central to the overall peace and security agenda of the UN and the wider international system. The main challenge has been the nature of peacebuilding and the actors therein. The concept of peacebuilding has gone through different definitions as academics, policymakers, and practitioners try to give it a more pertinent role in promoting sustainable peace. For example, Boutros-Ghali perceived peacebuilding as "a series of actions designed to solidify peace and avoid a relapse into conflict."[22] Later, Brahimi defined peacebuilding as "activities undertaken on the far side of the conflict to reassemble the foundations of peace and provide the tools for building on those foundations something more than just the absence of war."[23] The goal of peacebuilding is therefore to establish positive peace, with local ownership central to the process.[24]

Although substantial literature exists on peacebuilding and how integral it is to conflict resolution, there is no clear consensus on who should participate in the process and how those individuals should be selected.[25] For example, having been largely neoliberal in nature, the peacebuilding process has been monopolized by Western-leaning practitioners and nongovernment organizations.[26] This has met many challenges, especially concerning implementation and impact on the viability of the peace process. Thus, there has been a push to include local actors in the process in what Richmond envisaged as a hybrid peacebuilding process.[27] However, even with the role of local actors there is not much attention paid to the agency of the various actors, especially in the selection of key players and the directing of peacebuilding.

Another challenge has revolved around the role of regional actors and the dynamics between the UN and regional actors. Although the UN has the responsibility to maintain international peace and security, it has heavily relied on regional actors like the AU and its subregional bodies under Chapter VIII of its charter in the peacemaking process and, more recently, peacekeeping itself. Yet peacebuilding remains a minefield, especially from a doctrinal perspective. The AU and subregional bodies do not necessarily subscribe to the neoliberal statebuilding perspective. Although Thabo Mbeki of South Africa pushed for the adoption of some neoliberal approaches to governance and development, like the New Partnership for Economic Development and the African Peer Review Mechanism, these are not reflected in the AU's approach to peacebuilding.[28]

Moreover, in many African conflicts, neighboring states are often involved in conflicts. In the DRC, for example, Uganda, Rwanda, Angola, Burundi, Zimbabwe, and Namibia have all been involved by supporting different sides. Similarly, in Somalia, key states like Kenya and Ethiopia have played a role in propping up certain actors. Although neighboring states may be interested in the resolution of conflicts, their involvements sometimes escalate the conflicts. Such involvements affect the relationship between African regional bodies, the UN, and local actors who may not trust the regional bodies or their key actors. Nevertheless, regional bodies act as first responders to conflict, as shown by the Economic

Community of West African States' response to the conflict in Liberia with some success.[29] Although Biswaro contends that regional actors have been generally effective in conflict prevention and management,[30] it can be argued that they have not been very involved in the peacebuilding process. This is because the peacebuilding process has usually taken a neoliberal approach heavily rooted in Western values, which have been critiqued by authors like Abu Bah who have argued for a people-centered liberalism.[31] Nevertheless, there is a need to reposition the regional bodies in peacebuilding. This is because conflicts have become transnational in nature, thereby creating an imperative for a "complementary level of analysis and action for more effective peacebuilding from a regional conflict framework."[32]

The internationalization of conflicts can be viewed though the notion of glocalization, which is an offshoot of globalization. Although globalization was initially defined in economic terms, authors like Robertson contend that globalization has come to entail a homogeneity, especially of culture, as one societal or regional culture dominates the rest.[33] Thus, globalization is inherently homogenizing. On the other hand, the term "glocalization," which is linked to the Japanese word *dochakuka*, refers to an interface between the local and the global.[34] As Swyngedouw notes, glocalization, in the economic sense, "refers to the twin process whereby, firstly, institutional/regulatory arrangements shift from the national scale both upwards to supra-national or global scales and downwards to the scale of the individual body or to local, urban or regional configurations and, secondly, economic activities and inter-firm networks are becoming simultaneously more localized/regionalized and transnational."[35] According to Roudometof, glocalization and globalization are conflated as the former represents the global penetrating the local, or in other cases the global is modified into the local.[36] Hence globalization is not outside of the glocal but within it. Under glocalization, the local is not absorbed by the global but operates in a symbiotic relationship with globalization and shapes the results.

In the context of wars and peacebuilding, glocalization has become more pertinent as no single organization or entity can singlehandedly resolve conflict.[37] In the same vein, it can be argued that no single perspective can be sufficient in approaching or analyzing a conflict. The internationalization of conflict and the increasing acceptance of local and regional actors as part of the solution has resulted in a hybrid approach to peacebuilding, although the discourse on how actors are selected and the dynamics between the different actors remain underexplored. Notably, Sempijja argues for a nondogmatic and more integrated approach to peacebuilding whereby local and regional actors would have agency in applying peacebuilding agendas.[38] Within the peacebuilding framework, exchange of resources between different actors is vital in achieving sustainable peace. For example, the United Nations acts as the legitimizing actor in the international system.[39] However, it often struggles with local issues, such as the proliferation of rebel movements on the ground. In reality the UN has to rely on regional actors to stem the proliferation of such groups. A notable case is the DRC. Following the outbreak of conflict in the DRC in 2008–9, the UN opted for dialogue with Rwanda and Uganda, with the former suspected of funding the National Congress for the Defense of the People (CNDP). This resulted in the arrest of Laurent Nkunda, the leader of the CNDP, and the demise of the CNDP. In many ways, the Libyan conflict and the potential positive role of the AU can be better understood through a glocalization lens.

AU ROLE IN THE LIBYAN CONFLICT: CONTRIBUTIONS AND MARGINALIZATION

Since it erupted in 2011, the Libyan war has been characterized by internal fragmentation and internationalization. The Libyan war started as a revolt against Colonel Muammar Gaddafi's rule, which quickly turned into an armed rebellion as foreign actors armed the rebels. The emergence of various armed groups and the support they receive from foreign powers has led to a fluid international patronage system that is making the Libyan war more complex. The foreign state actors in the Libyan conflict and their conflict-resolution efforts are quite diverse. For example, there are the neighboring Sahelian countries that have suffered from the smuggling of weapons and the incursions of armed groups from Libya. These countries have a stake in peace in Libya. The Maghreb countries have provided Libyan actors with a neutral space for discussion. Notably, the Maghreb countries have provided Libyan actors with a neutral space for them to discuss the issues with the hope of achieving peace. There are also Middle Eastern countries, Turkey, and Russia supporting various armed groups. The other key actors include EU and US/NATO, which are mainly concerned about issues of migration, terrorism, and strategic geopolitical positioning on the Mediterranean. While all of these actors have been very active, the African Union has mainly remained on the periphery, especially after the demise of the Gaddafi regime.

Despite its eventual marginalization, the AU took an early interest in the Libyan conflict, which was largely driven by Gaddafi's prominent role in the transformation of the Organisation of African Unity into the AU. Also, Tripoli had been an important source of funding for several African countries.[40] The AU saw Libya as a place to apply its version of R2P, the principle of non-indifference enshrined in the AU constitution. The Constitutive Act of the AU under Article 4(h) affirms "the right to intervene in a Member State pursuant to a decision of the Assembly in respect to grave circumstances, namely: war crimes, genocide and crimes against humanity," while Article 4(j) enshrines "the right of Member States to request intervention from the Union in order to restore peace and security."[41] The AU was also very interested in the Libyan conflict because of the issue of migration. Human smuggling and massive violations of migrants' rights have been recorded in Libya, which has been a major route for migration from the Sahel to southern Europe.[42]

The AU sought to play a positive role in Libya by offering to mediate the conflict. In August 2011, as the war was raging across Libya, President Jacob Zuma of South Africa visited Tripoli to offer mediation between Libyan rebels and the Gaddafi regime.[43] However, the NATO intervention and the military victory of the rebels thwarted the mediation effort. The AU nevertheless kept offering to mediate as the conflict became more complex, but such mediation efforts were hampered by the perception by Libyan actors that the AU and some of its member states were not neutral in the conflict.[44] In particular, the AU was perceived as sympathetic to the Gaddafi regime and its militias.

One of the first steps taken by the AU to give a common answer to the Libyan conflict was the creation of a high-level ad hoc committee on Libya. The committee was established during the 265th meeting of the Peace and Security Council, held in Addis Ababa on March 10, 2011. Its first members were the heads of state of the DRC, Mali, Mauritania, South Africa, and Uganda, together with the chairperson of the AU Commission.[45] The committee progressively expanded to include eleven members. The AU institutional framework for peace in Libya evolved progressively. A special envoy of the chairperson of the AU Commission was appointed with a mandate that seemed to overlap with that of the high-level committee. In 2020, a contact group on Libya was also established. Coordination between these different bodies and institutions (including the PSC) became an issue that hindered the AU's peace efforts in Libya.[46]

The AU tried to collaborate with other intergovernmental bodies to gain influence in the peace process. For instance, the AU has been part of the Quartet on Libya, which includes the UN, the EU, and the League of Arab States. It was notably involved in the international dimension of the Berlin Conference, which was spearheaded by the United Nations Support Mission in Libya. The aim of the conference was to build consensus among Libyan elites and the international powers involved in the Libyan conflict. The AU managed to participate in the Palermo Conference (November 2018), the first and second Berlin conferences (January 2020 and June 2021), and the November 2021 Paris International Conference for Libya. African states have also advocated for a greater role within the United Nations Support Mission in Libya (UNSMIL) and notably preferred one of their representatives to be considered for the position of head of the mission. The role of mission coordinator and assistant secretary-general was actually assigned to Zimbabwe's Raisedon Zenenga in December 2020, and the role of special representative for Libya and head of the United Nations Support Mission in Libya was given to Senegal's Abdoulaye Bathily in September 2022. There have also been interactions between leaders acting on behalf of the AU and representatives of major powers (including Russia) involved in Libya to further involve the AU in the resolution of the Libyan crisis. However, steps to involve the AU have mostly been tokenism as the AU does not drive the military dynamics of the conflict.[47]

Overall, the AU has largely remained marginalized because the Libyan conflict has morphed into a power competition wherein power politics became central and relied mostly on hard power in the form of combat techniques and provision of hardware. As the multilateral peace process suffered from this competition for power, the EU became more central in the Libyan conflict because of mounting concerns over jihadism and migration into Europe. In addition, other powers are getting more involved, further marginalizing the AU. The marginalization of the AU was exhibited by the AU's inability to implement its own security

PEACEBUILDING EFFORTS AND PROSPECTS FOR PEACE IN LIBYA

The general perception after Gaddafi was ousted was that Libya would move toward peace and democracy. As Yilmaz laid it out, the framework for peacebuilding included transitional justice, national reconciliation, constitutional reform, and popular democracy.[48] These often require improved security and an increased role on the part of the UN, especially in reforming the security organs and overseeing the overall peacebuilding process. However, the role of regional actors like the AU was missing from the peacebuilding process that was pursued in Libya. Alunni and Kappler point to an organic approach to peacebuilding that rests on the cultivation of relationships between international organizations and the multiple stakeholders, rather than a single trusted local partner.[49] To them, this was a culturally intelligent path to reducing the trust deficit in peacebuilding interventions. Moreover, international organizations are usually treated with suspicion when they support social change in a society undergoing social upheaval, especially in cases where there is mistrust between society and state institutions. Unfortunately, the AU's well-known support for Gaddafi placed it at odds with the aspirations of Libyans.

During the start of the conflict, AU peace proposals were inclined more toward seeking negotiation than asking Gaddafi to step down. Also, the AU's failure to recognize the National Transitional Council further undermined the former's influence in the peacebuilding process. According to Apuuli, the AU's mediation efforts, especially the roadmap to end the conflict peacefully, were not compatible with the UN Security Council's authorization of the use of force.[50] The AU was thus discredited in the eyes of the rebels, who were intent on overthrowing Gaddafi. Ani attributes the AU approach to the Libyan conflict to its failure to transition from the old state-centric paradigm of the Organisation of African Unity to the more contemporary human security paradigm imbued in R2P.[51] Even as the AU tried to enforce its "non-indifference to human rights violations" principle of intervention, the AU was unable to act appropriately as it preferred to consent to ruling regimes even when they were somehow discredited because of poor governance and authoritarianism. This problem was most evident in Libya before the fall of Gaddafi. Furthermore, the AU lacked internal cohesion. For example, although it refused to recognize the National Transitional Council, countries like Nigeria and Ethiopia did the exact opposite.[52] In the end, the AU found itself marginal to the peacebuilding process. Even when the AU was involved, its presence was often merely a last-minute symbolic one.[53]

According to Alberts, the AU's initial position against military intervention and opposition to the expansion of NATO action was rooted in the suspicion of Western powers' intentions, rather than deep loyalty to Gaddafi.[54] Colonial history has indeed made African states very suspicious of Western powers, especially when it comes to military intervention. It is important to note that there was no clear postwar reconstruction plan that would follow the NATO regime-change intervention. Also, the UN did not send a stabilization mission as was authorized by the UN Security Council. Regime change actually led to further fragmentation of the state as the coalition that led the rebellion disintegrated. Moreover, other groups such as the Islamic State sought to fill the power vacuum left by the collapse of the Gaddafi regime. Generally, the Arab Spring led to fears that similar uprisings would occur in sub-Saharan Africa.[55] Arguably, African governments' concerns over uprising at the expense of the issues that drove the uprisings point to the AU's failure to take a more human security vision to political and social issues.[56] The AU came to essentially exhibit the attributes of a political class continually out of touch with the needs of the population.[57] This disconnection, along with the failure to produce a post-Gaddafi roadmap, discredited the AU in the eyes of the groups opposed to Gaddafi, rendering its future role in peacebuilding peripheral.

When exploring the role of the AU in resolving the Libyan conflict, Woldemichael and Diatta highlighted the need for a common voice from the organization.[58] For example, as a result of the dire security issues in Libya and their spillover effects, neighboring African states had signed bilateral agreements with different factions in the Libyan conflict, which undermined the possibilities for a unified AU stand and made it difficult for the AU to determine which actions to follow. For example, there were disagreements on whether to set up a collaborative peace support mission with the UN, and which countries would be involved.

A notable fact is that the Libyan peace process has not progressed despite the involvement of so many international actors such as Turkey, Russia, and the EU. Potentially, this lack of progress can provide opportunities for more AU involvement. It is important to note that even the UN has not really made a big impact in the Libyan peace process. The UN Support Mission in Libya (UNSMIL) has kept a light-footed approach, and the consensus is that its mandate has been inadequate. The disarmament, demobilization, and reintegration (DDR) process has not advanced, in part because of the lack of a clear vision and leverage on the part of UNSMIL.[59] A notable problem for UNSMIL is the lack of the manpower needed to oversee DDR, especially as the country is still awash with mercenaries notably from Chad, Sudan, Russia, Turkey, and Arab nations. The prospect of establishing a stronger peacekeeping force is very unlikely because it would not be approved by the UN Security Council given Russian and NATO military presence in Libya. Also, the ongoing war in Ukraine has drained international resources and possibilities for military collaboration. Key international players in the Libyan peace process are pursuing their national interests behind the scenes, as has been the case with Russia and Turkey's meeting in 2022 to discuss their collaboration in Libya.

For the AU, the Libyan conflict remains a major problem, especially given its spillover into Mali through the movement of arms and combatants, which has de-stabilized the Sahel region.[60] The porous nature of the borders makes the Libyan conflict a source of regional instability that is difficult to resolve without the support of regional partners.[61] A key part of this problem is the movement of arms and combatants. As Taraboulsi noted, the cross-border trafficking of arms between Libya and Tunisia has been facilitated by existing ethnic ties and informal networks developed during the arms embargo on Libya during the 1980s.[62] Moreover, Tunisia has received a lot of refugees from both the Gaddafi and opposition camps, which continue to support the war effort.[63] All these regional effects point to the need for regional bodies to be more involved in the peace process. Unfortunately, these regional bodies have been marginalized by major powers, a lack of capacity, and conflicts of interest. Notably, the AU stands out as an example of a regional organization with deep interests in the conflict and an established conflict-resolution mechanism. However, the AU has been largely marginalized in the peace process as a result of excessive external interventions by major powers and by organizational weaknesses.

Roughly ten years after the AU's decision to not fully back the uprising in Libya, the organization is still paying the price by being marginalized despite the regional implications of the Libyan conflict. However, the external powers driving the peace process are struggling to ensure stability. The Libyan situation points to the limits of external interventions and the need for greater involvement by regional actors. The legitimizing power of the UN can be complemented by the regional expertise of the AU. However, for the AU to have a more prominent role, it needs to move away from its Organisation of African Unity state-centric approach to a human security paradigm as enshrined in the AU Constitutive Act.

NOTES

1. Gearoid Millar, *An Ethnographic Approach to Peacebuilding: Understanding Local Experiences in Transitional States* (London: Routledge, 2014), 204.
2. Hamzeh al-Shadeedi, Erwin van Veen, and Jalel Harchaoui, *One Thousand and One Failings: Security Sector Stabilisation and Development in Libya*, CRU Report (The Hague: Clingendael Netherlands Institute of International Relations, 2020).
3. Michal Smetana and Jan Ludvík, "Between War and Peace: A Dynamic Reconceptualization of 'Frozen Conflicts,'" *Asia Europe Journal* 17 (2019): 1.
4. Johan Galtung, "An Editorial: What Is Peace Research?," *Journal of Peace Research* 1.1 (1964): 2.
5. Siphamandla Zondi, "African Union Approaches to Peacebuilding: Efforts at Shifting the Continent towards Decolonial Peace," *African Journal on Conflict Resolution* 17.1 (2017): 127.
6. Mark Paterson, *The AU at Ten: Problems, Progress, and Prospects*, International Colloquium Report (Berlin: Centre for Conflict Resolution and Friedrich Ebert Stiftung, 2012), https://www.africaportal.org/publications/african-union-ten -problems-progress-and-prospects.
7. Eric A. Heinze and Brent J. Steele, "The (D)evolution of a Norm: R2P, the Bosnia Generation and Humanitarian Intervention in Libya," in *Libya, the Responsibility to Protect and the Future of Humanitarian Intervention*, ed. Aidan Hehir and Robert Murray (London: Palgrave Macmillan, 2013); Christopher Hobson, "Responding to Failure: The Responsibility to Protect after Libya," *Millennium* 44.3 (2016): 433–454; Dauda Abubakar, "Responsibility to Protect: The Paradox of International Intervention in Africa," in *International Security and Peacebuilding: Africa, the Middle East, and Europe*, ed. Abu Bakarr Bah (Bloomington: Indiana

University Press, 2017); Abu Bakarr Bah, "Introduction: The Conundrums of Global Liberal Governance," in *International Security and Peacebuilding: Africa, the Middle East, and Europe,* ed. Abu Bakarr Bah (Bloomington: Indiana University Press, 2017).

8. Erik Swyngedouw, "Globalisation or 'Glocalisation'? Networks, Territories and Rescaling," *Cambridge Review of International Affairs* 17.1 (2004): 25.

9. United Nations, "As Foreign Interference in Libya Reaches Unprecedented Levels, Secretary-General Warns Security Council Time Is Not on Our Side, Urges End to Stalemate," United Nations Security Council press release, SC/14243, July 8, 2020, https://www.un.org/press/en/2020/sc14243.doc.htm.

10. African Union, "Final Communiqué of the AU Troika Committee and the AU High-Level Committee on Libya, in Cairo, Arab Republic of Egypt," African Union, April 23, 2019, https://www.peaceau.org/en/article/conclusions-of-the-meeting-of-the-african-anion-au-high-level-committee-on-libya-7-july-2019-niamey-niger; African Union, "The 844th meeting of the African Union Peace and Security Council on the Situation in Libya," African Union Peace and Security Council, last updated May 6, 2019, http://www.peaceau.org/en/article/the-844th-meeting-of-the-african-union-peace-and-security-council-on-the-situation-in-libya; African Union, "Conclusions of the Meeting of the African Union (AU) High Level Committee on Libya," July 7, 2019, Niamey, Niger. https://www.peaceau.org/en/article/conclusions-of-the-meeting-of-the-african-anion-au-high-level-committee-on-libya-7-july-2019-niamey-niger; African Union, "Meeting of the Joint AU-EU-UN Taskforce to Address the Migrant and Refugee Situation in Libya," African Union, September 25, 2019, https://au.int/en/pressreleases/20190925/meeting-joint-au-eu-un-taskforce-address-migrant-and-refugee-situation-libya; African Union, "Communique of the Meeting of the Contact Group on Libya," African Union, May 19, 2020. https://www.peaceau.org/en/article/communique-of-the-meeting-of-the-contact-group-on-libya-19-may-2020.

11. Dylan Balch-Lindsay and Andrew J. Enterline, "Killing Time: The World Politics of Civil War Duration, 1820–1992," *International Studies Quarterly* 44.4 (2000): 615–642.

12. Dylan Balch-Lindsay, Andrew J. Enterline, and Kyle A. Joyce, "Third-Party Intervention and the Civil War Process," *Journal of Peace Research* 45.3 (2008): 360–361.

13. David Carment and Dane Rowlands, "Twisting One Arm: The Effects of Biased Interveners," *International Peacekeeping* 10.3 (2003): 1–24.

14. Elizabeth O'Shea, "Responsibility to Protect (R2P) in Libya: Ghosts of the Past Haunting the Future," *International Human Rights Law Review* 1.1 (2012): 173–190.

15. Christopher Hobson, "Responding to Failure: The Responsibility to Protect after Libya," *Millennium* 44.3 (2016): 454.

16. Outi Keranen, "What Happened to the Responsibility to Rebuild?," *Global Governance* 22.3 (2016): 331–348.

17. Julia Brower et al., "Historical Examples of Unauthorized Humanitarian Intervention" (white paper, Yale School of Law—Center for Global Legal Challenges 5, 2013); A. Rahman, T. Aslam, and S. Shahbaz, "Indian Armed Intervention in East Pakistan and Creation of Bangladesh: A Critical Analysis under International Law," *Global Regional Review* 3 (2020): 344–353.

18. Mary Kaldor, "Old Wars, Cold Wars, New Wars, and the War on Terror," *International Politics* 42 (2005): 491–498; Abu Bakarr Bah, "Introduction: The Conundrums of Global Liberal Governance," in *International Security and Peacebuilding: Africa, the Middle East, and Europe*, ed. Abu Bakarr Bah (Bloomington: Indiana University Press, 2017).

19. Susanne Jacobi, "UNPROFOR—Mission Impossible," *Journal of International Peacekeeping* 2.2–3 (1995): 39–43.

20. Alan Bullion, "India in Sierra Leone: A Case of Muscular Peacekeeping?," *International Peacekeeping* 8.4 (2001): 77–91; Abu Bakarr Bah, "The Contours of New Humanitarianism: War and Peacebuilding in Sierra Leone," *Africa Today* 60.1 (2013): 3–26; Charles T. Hunt, "All Necessary Means to What Ends? The Unintended Consequences of the 'Robust Turn' in UN Peace Operations," *International Peacekeeping* 24.1 (2017): 108–131.

21. Boutros Boutros-Ghali, "An Agenda for Peace: Preventive Diplomacy, Peacemaking and Peacekeeping," *International Relations* 11.3 (1992): 201–218.

22. Boutros Boutros-Ghali, *Agenda for Peace: Preventive Diplomacy, Peacemaking and Peacekeeping* (New York: United Nations, 1992), 11.

23. United Nations General Assembly and Security Council, "Report of the Panel on United Nations Peace Operations," A/55/305 S/2000/809, August 21, 2000 (Brahimi Report), p. 3, https://peacekeeping.un.org/sites/default/files/a_55 _305_e_brahimi_report.pdf.

24. Craig Cohen, *Measuring Progress in Stabilization and Reconstruction*, Stabilization and Reconstruction Series No. 1 (Washington, DC: United States Institute of Peace, 2006); Susanna P. Campbell, *What Is Successful Peacebuilding?* (Baltimore: Catholic Relief Services, 2007); Abu Bakarr Bah and Nikolas Emmanuel, "Positive Peace and the Methodology of Costing Peacebuilding Needs: The Case of Burundi," *Administrative Theory & Praxis* 42.3 (2020): 299–318; Norman Sempijja, "A Critique of the Conceptual Documents That Frame UN and AU Practice of Peacebuilding," in *Researching Peacebuilding in Africa*, ed. Ismail Rashid and Amy Niang (London: Routledge, 2020).

25. Henning Haugerudbraaten, "Peacebuilding: Six Dimensions and Two Concepts," *African Security Review* 7.6 (1998): 17–26; Edward Newman, "A Human Security Peace-Building Agenda," *Third World Quarterly* 32.10 (2011): 1737–1756; Geoff Harris and Neryl Lewis, "Structural Violence, Positive Peace and Peacebuilding," in *Recovery from Armed Conflict in Developing Countries: An Economic and Political Analysis*, ed. Geoff Harris (London: Routledge, 2002).

26. Charles Thiessen, "Emancipatory Peacebuilding," in *Critical Issues in Peace and Conflict Studies: Theory, Practice, and Pedagogy*, ed. Thomas Matyók, Jessica Senehi, and Sean Byrne Lexington Books (Lanham, MD: Lexington Books, 2011), 115–143.

27. Oliver P. Richmond, "Becoming Liberal, Unbecoming Liberalism: Liberal-Local Hybridity via the Everyday as a Response to the Paradoxes of Liberal Peacebuilding," *Journal of Intervention and Statebuilding* 3.3 (2009): 324–344.

28. Victor Adetula, Redie Bereketeab, and Cyril Obi, "Introduction: Regional Economic Communities and Peacebuilding in West Africa and the Horn of Africa," in *Regional Economic Communities and Peacebuilding in Africa*, ed. Victor Adetula, Redie Bereketeab, and Cyril Obi (London: Routledge, 2020).

29. Adetula, Bereketeab, and Obi, "Regional Economic Communities."

30. Joram Mukama Biswaro, *The Role of Regional Integration in Conflict Prevention, Management, and Resolution in Africa: The Case of the African Union* (Brasília: Ministry of External Relations, 2013), http://funag.gov.br/biblioteca/download/1038-Role_of_Regional_Integration_in_Conflict_Prevention_Management_and_Resolution_in_Africa_The.pdf.

31. Abu Bakarr Bah, "People-Centered Liberalism: An Alternative Approach to International State-Building in Sierra Leone and Liberia," *Critical Sociology* 43.7–8 (2017): 989–1007.

32. Necla Tschirgi, "Making the Case for a Regional Approach to Peacebuilding," *Journal of Peacebuilding & Development* 1.1 (2002): 25.

33. Roland Robertson, "Globalisation or Glocalisation?," *Journal of International Communication* 1.1 (1994): 33–52.

34. Adriana Grigorescu and Alexandra Zaif, "The Concept of Glocalization and Its Incorporation in Global Brands' Marketing Strategies," *International Journal of Business and Management Invention* 6.1 (2017): 70–74.

35. Erik Swyngedouw, "Globalisation or 'Glocalisation'? Networks, Territories and Rescaling," *Cambridge Review of International Affairs* 17.1 (2004): 25.

36. Victor Roudometof, "Theorizing Glocalization: Three Interpretations," *European Journal of Social Theory* 19.3 (2016): 391–408.

37. Norman Sempijja, "Does Dependence Lead to Cooperation? The Case of Resource Exchange between the European Union and the United Nations in DR Congo," *African Security* 9.4 (2016): 259–277.

38. Sempijja, "A Critique of the Conceptual Documents."

39. Erik Voeten, "The Political Origins of the UN Security Council's Ability to Legitimize the Use of Force," *International Organization* 59.3 (2005): 527–557.

40. Hussein Solomon and Gerrie Swart, "Libya's Foreign Policy in Flux," *African Affairs* 104.416 (2005): 469–492; Amandine Gnanguênon, *Mapping African Regional Cooperation: How to Navigate Africa's Institutional Landscape* (London: European Council on Foreign Relations, 2020), https://ecfr.eu/publication/mapping-african-regional-cooperation-how-to-navigate-africas-institutional-landscape.

41. African Union, *Constitutive Act of the African Union* (Addis Ababa: African Union, 2000); Tim Murithi, "The African Union and the Libya Crisis: Situating the Responsibility to Protect in Africa: Research Notes/Commentaries," *Journal of African Union Studies* 1.1 (2012): 83–88.

42. Abu Bakarr Bah and Emmanuel Nikolas, "Migration Cooperation between Africa and Europe: Understanding the Role of International Incentives," in *The*

Oxford Research Encyclopedia of International Studies (Oxford: Oxford University Press, 2022).

43. Reuters, "South African President Zuma in Tripoli for Talks," Reuters, May 30, 2011, https://www.reuters.com/article/us-libya-zuma-idUSTRE74T38I20110530.

44. Peace and Security Council Report, *Africa's Place in Resolving Libya's Quagmire: Peace and Security Council Insights* (Pretoria: Institute of Security Studies, 2020).

45. African Union, "The African Union Ad Hoc High-Level Committee on Libya Meets in Nouakchott on 19 March 2011," ReliefWeb press release, March 17, 2011, https://reliefweb.int/report/libya/african-union-ad-hoc-high-level-committee -libya-meets-nouakchott-19-march-2011.

46. Peace and Security Council Report, *Africa's Place in Resolving Libya's Quagmire.*

47. Siba Grovogui, "By Ignoring African Leaders, the West Paved the Way for Chaos in Libya," *Foreign Policy,* November 20, 2020, https://foreignpolicy.com/2020/11 /20/by-ignoring-african-leaders-the-west-paved-the-way-for-chaos-in-libya.

48. Muzaffer Ercan Yilmaz, "Peacebuilding in Libya," *International Journal on World Peace* 29.1 (2012): 45–57.

49. Alice Alunni, Mark Calder, and Stefanie Kappler, *Enduring Social Institutions and Civil Society Peacebuilding in Libya and Syria* (N.p.: British Council, 2017), https:// www.durham.ac.uk/media/durham-university/research-/research-institutes/ durham-global-security-institute/pdfs/h101_enduring_social_institutions_and _civil_society_peacebuilding_in_libya_and_syria_final_web.pdf.

50. Kasaija Phillip Apuuli, "The African Union's Mediation Mandate and the Libyan Conflict (2011)," *African Security* 10.3–4 (2017): 192–204.

51. Ndubuisi Christian Ani, "The African Union Non-indifference Stance: Lessons from Sudan and Libya," *African Conflict and Peacebuilding Review* 6.2 (2016): 1–22.

52. Tim Murithi, "The African Union and the Libya Crisis: Situating the Responsibility to Protect in Africa: Research Notes/Commentaries," *Journal of African Union Studies* 1.1 (2012): 83–88.

53. Farouk Chothia, "How Africa Has Been Frozen Out of Libya Peace Efforts," BBC News, February 4, 2020, https://www.bbc.com/news/world-africa-51293355.

54. Thomas Alberts, *The African Union and Libya: On the Horns of a Dilemma,* African Arguments (London: Hurst, 2011).

55. Ernest Harsch, "'Arab Spring' Stirs African Hopes and Anxieties," *Africa Renewal* 25.2 (2011): 12–14.

56. Ndubuisi Christian Ani, "The African Union Non-indifference Stance: Lessons from Sudan and Libya," *African Conflict and Peacebuilding Review* 6.2 (2016): 1–22.

57. Greg Mills, "Africa's Facelift Generation and the Arab Spring," *Pakistan Horizon* 65.4 (2012): 59–65.

58. Shewit Woldemichael and Mohamed M. Diatta, "Can Africa Help Bring Stability to Libya? To Play a Useful Role, the AU Needs to Present a More Neutral and Unified Front," Institute of Security Studies, March 3, 2020, https:// issafrica.org/iss-today/can-africa-help-bring-stability-to-libya.

59. Stimson Centre, International Peace Institute, and Security Council Report, *The Situation in Libya: Reflections on Challenges and Ways Forward* (New York: Stimson Centre, International Peace Institute, and Security Council Report, 2022), https://www.stimson.org/wp-content/uploads/2022/07/Situation-in-Libya-Meeting-Note-Proofs26.pdf.
60. Scott Shaw, "Fallout in the Sahel: The Geographic Spread of Conflict from Libya to Mali," *Canadian Foreign Policy Journal* 19.2 (2013): 199–210.
61. Lucia Pradella and Sahar Taghdisi Rad, "Libya and Europe: Imperialism, Crisis and Migration," *Third World Quarterly* 38.11 (2017): 2411–2427.
62. Sherine N. El Taraboulsi, *Peacebuilding in Libya: Cross-Border Transactions and the Civil Society Landscape* (Washington, DC: United States Institute of Peace, 2016).
63. Moncef Kartas, *On the Edge? Trafficking and Insecurity at the Tunisian-Libyan Border*, Graduate Institute of International and Development Studies (Geneva: Small Arms Survey, 2013).

BIBLIOGRAPHY

Abubakar, Dauda. "Responsibility to Protect: The Paradox of International Intervention in Africa." In *International Security and Peacebuilding: Africa, the Middle East, and Europe*, ed. Abu Bakarr Bah, 49–76. Bloomington: Indiana University Press, 2017.

Adetula, Victor, Redie Bereketeab, and Cyril Obi. "Introduction: Regional Economic Communities and Peacebuilding in West Africa and the Horn of Africa." In *Regional Economic Communities and Peacebuilding in Africa*, ed. Victor Adetula, Redie Bereketeab, and Cyril Obi, 1–19. London: Routledge, 2020.

African Union. *Constitutive Act of the African Union*. Addis Ababa: African Union, 2000.

———. "The African Union Ad Hoc High-Level Committee on Libya Meets in Nouakchott on 19 March 2011." ReliefWeb press release, March 17, 2011. https://reliefweb.int/report/libya/african-union-ad-hoc-high-level-committee-libya-meets-nouakchott-19-march-2011.

———. "Conclusions of the Meeting of the African Union (AU) High Level Committee on Libya." African Union, July 7, 2019. https://www.peaceau.org/en/article/conclusions-of-the-meeting-of-the-african-anion-au-high-level-committee-on-libya-7-july-2019-niamey-niger.

———. "The 844th Meeting of the African Union Peace and Security Council on the Situation in Libya." African Union Peace and Security Council, last updated May 6, 2019. http://www.peaceau.org/en/article/the-844th-meeting-of-the-african-union-peace-and-security-council-on-the-situation-in-libya.

———. "Final Communiqué of the AU Troika Committee and the AU High-Level Committee on Libya, in Cairo, Arab Republic of Egypt." African Union, April 23, 2019. https://www.peaceau.org/en/article/conclusions-of-the-meeting-of-the-african-anion-au-high-level-committee-on-libya-7-july-2019-niamey-niger.

———. "Meeting of the Joint AU-EU-UN Taskforce to Address the Migrant and Refugee Situation in Libya." African Union, September 25, 2019. https://au.int/en/pressreleases/20190925/meeting-joint-au-eu-un-taskforce-address-migrant-and-refugee-situation-libya.

―――. "Communique of the Meeting of the Contact Group on Libya." African Union, May 19, 2020. https://www.peaceau.org/en/article/communique-of-the-meeting-of-the-contact-group-on-libya-19-may-2020.

Alberts, Thomas. *The African Union and Libya, on the Horns of a Dilemma*. African Arguments. London: Hurst, 2011.

Alunni, Alice, Mark Calder, and Stefanie Kappler. *Enduring Social Institutions and Civil Society Peacebuilding in Libya and Syria*. N.p.: British Council, 2017. https://www.durham.ac.uk/media/durham-university/research-/research-institutes/durham-global-security-institute/pdfs/h101_enduring_social_institutions_and_civil_society_peacebuilding_in_libya_and_syria_final_web.pdf.

Ani, Ndubuisi Christian. "The African Union Non-indifference Stance: Lessons from Sudan and Libya." *African Conflict and Peacebuilding Review* 6.2 (2016): 1–22.

Apuuli, Kasaija Phillip. "The African Union's Mediation Mandate and the Libyan Conflict (2011)." *African Security* 10.3–4 (2017): 192–204.

Bah, Abu Bakarr. "The Contours of New Humanitarianism: War and Peacebuilding in Sierra Leone." *Africa Today* 60.1 (2013): 3–26.

―――. "Introduction: The Conundrums of Global Liberal Governance." In *International Security and Peacebuilding: Africa, the Middle East, and Europe*, ed. Abu Bakarr Bah, 1–24. Bloomington: Indiana University Press, 2017.

―――. "People-Centered Liberalism: An Alternative Approach to International State-Building in Sierra Leone and Liberia." *Critical Sociology* 43.7–8 (2017): 989–1007.

Bah, Abu Bakarr, and Nikolas Emmanuel. "Positive Peace and the Methodology of Costing Peacebuilding Needs: The Case of Burundi." *Administrative Theory & Praxis* 42.3 (2020): 299–318.

―――. "Migration Cooperation between Africa and Europe: Understanding the Role of International Incentives." In *The Oxford Research Encyclopedia of International Studies*. Oxford: Oxford University Press, 2022.

Balch-Lindsay, Dylan, and Andrew J. Enterline. "Killing Time: The World Politics of Civil War Duration, 1820–1992." *International Studies Quarterly* 44.4 (2000): 615–642.

Balch-Lindsay, Dylan, Andrew J. Enterline, and Kyle A. Joyce. "Third-Party Intervention and the Civil War Process." *Journal of Peace Research* 45.3 (2008): 345–363.

Biswaro, Joram Mukama. *The Role of Regional Integration in Conflict Prevention, Management, and Resolution in Africa: The Case of African Union*. Brasília: Ministry of External Relations, 2013. http://funag.gov.br/biblioteca/download/1038-Role_of_Regional_Integration_in_Conflict_Prevention_Management_and_Resolution_in_Africa_The.pdf.

Boutros-Ghali, B. "An Agenda for Peace: Preventive Diplomacy, Peacemaking and Peacekeeping." *International Relations* 11.3 (1992): 201–218.

―――. *Agenda for Peace: Preventive Diplomacy, Peacemaking and Peacekeeping*. New York: United Nations, 1992.

Brower, Julia, Ryan Liss, Tina Thomas, and Jacob Victor. "Historical Examples of Unauthorized Humanitarian Intervention." White Paper, Yale School of Law—Center for Global Legal Challenges 5, 2013.

Bullion, Alan. "India in Sierra Leone: A Case of Muscular Peacekeeping?" *International Peacekeeping* 8.4 (2001): 77–91.

Campbell, Susanna. *What Is Successful Peacebuilding?* Baltimore: Catholic Relief Services, 2007.

Carment, David, and Dane Rowlands. "Twisting One Arm: The Effects of Biased Interveners." *International Peacekeeping* 10.3 (2003): 1–24.

Chothia, Farouk. "How Africa Has Been Frozen Out of Libya Peace Efforts." BBC News, February 4, 2020. https://www.bbc.com/news/world-africa-51293355.

Cohen, Craig. *Measuring Progress in Stabilization and Reconstruction.* Stabilization and Reconstruction Series No. 1. Washington, DC: United States Institute of Peace, 2006.

Ekwealor, Chinedu Thomas, and Ufo Okeke Uzodike. "The African Union Interventions in African Conflicts: Unity and Leadership Conundrum on Libya." *Journal of African Union Studies* 5.1 (2016): 63–82.

El Taraboulsi, Sherine N. *Peacebuilding in Libya: Cross-Border Transactions and the Civil Society Landscape.* Washington, DC: United States Institute of Peace, 2016.

Galtung, Johan. "An Editorial: What Is Peace Research?" *Journal of Peace Research* 1.1 (1964): 1–4.

Gnanguênon, Amandine. *Mapping African Regional Cooperation: How to Navigate Africa's Institutional Landscape.* London: European Council on Foreign Relations, 2020. https://ecfr.eu/publication/mapping-african-regional-cooperation-how-to-navigate-africas-institutional-landscape.

Grigorescu, Adriana, and Alexandra Zaif. "The Concept of Glocalization and Its Incorporation in Global Brands' Marketing Strategies." *International Journal of Business and Management Invention* 6.1 (2017): 70–74.

Grovogui, Siba N. "By Ignoring African Leaders, the West Paved the Way for Chaos in Libya." *Foreign Policy,* November 20, 2020. https://foreignpolicy.com/2020/11/20/by-ignoring-african-leaders-the-west-paved-the-way-for-chaos-in-libya/.

Harris, Geoff, and Neryl Lewis. "Structural Violence, Positive Peace and Peacebuilding." In *Recovery from Armed Conflict in Developing Countries: An Economic and Political Analysis,* ed. Geoff Harris, 49–56. London: Routledge, 2002.

Harsch, Ernest. "Arab Spring Stirs African Hopes and Anxieties." *Africa Renewal* 25.2 (2011): 12–14.

Haugerudbraaten, Henning. "Peacebuilding: Six Dimensions and Two Concepts." *African Security Review* 7.6 (1998): 17–26.

Heinze, Eric A., and Brent J. Steele. "The (D)evolution of a Norm: R2P, the Bosnia Generation and Humanitarian Intervention in Libya." In *Libya, the Responsibility to Protect and the Future of Humanitarian Intervention,* ed. Aidan Hehir and Robert Murray, 130–161. London: Palgrave Macmillan, 2013.

Hobson, C. "Responding to Failure: The Responsibility to Protect after Libya." *Millennium* 44.3 (2016): 433–454.

Hove, Mediel. "Post-Gaddafi Libya and the African Union: Challenges and the Road to Sustainable Peace." *Journal of Asian and African Studies* 52.3 (2017): 271–286.

Hunt, Charles T. "All Necessary Means to What Ends? The Unintended Consequences of the 'Robust Turn' in UN Peace Operations." *International Peacekeeping* 24.1 (2017): 108–131.

Jacobi, Susanne. "UNPROFOR—Mission Impossible." *Journal of International Peace-keeping* 2.2–3 (1995): 39–43.

Kaldor, Mary. "Old Wars, Cold Wars, New Wars, and the War on Terror." *International Politics* 42 (2005): 491–498.

Kartas, Moncef. *On the Edge? Trafficking and Insecurity at the Tunisian-Libyan Border.* Graduate Institute of International and Development Studies. Geneva: Small Arms Survey, 2013.

Keranen, Outi. "What Happened to the Responsibility to Rebuild?" *Global Governance* 22.3 (2016): 331–348.

Millar, Gearoid. *An Ethnographic Approach to Peacebuilding: Understanding LocalExperiences in Transitional States.* London: Routledge, 2014.

Mills, Greg. "Africa's Facelift Generation and the Arab Spring." *Pakistan Horizon* 65.4 (2012): 59–65.

Murithi, Tim. "The African Union and the Libya Crisis: Situating the Responsibility to Protect in Africa: Research Notes/Commentaries." *Journal of African Union Studies* 1.1 (2012): 83–88.

Newman, Edward. "A Human Security Peace-Building Agenda." *Third World Quarterly* 32.10 (2011): 1737–1756.

O'Shea, Elizabeth. "Responsibility to Protect (R2P) in Libya: Ghosts of the Past Haunting the Future." *International Human Rights Law Review* 1.1 (2012): 173–190.

Paterson, Mark. *The AU at Ten: Problems, Progress, and Prospects.* International Colloquium Report. Berlin: Centre for Conflict Resolution and Friedrich Ebert Stiftung, 2012. https://www.africaportal.org/publications/african-union-ten-problems-progress-and-prospects.

Peace and Security Council Report. *Africa's Place in Resolving Libya's Quagmire: Peace and Security Council Insights.* Pretoria: Institute of Security Studies, 2020.

Pradella, Lucia, and Sahar Taghdisi Rad. "Libya and Europe: Imperialism, Crisis and Migration." *Third World Quarterly* 38.11 (2017): 2411–2427.

Rahman, A., T. Aslam, and S. Shahbaz. "Indian Armed Intervention in East Pakistan and Creation of Bangladesh: A Critical Analysis under International Law." *Global Regional Review* 3 (2020): 344–353.

Reuters. "South African President Zuma in Tripoli for Talks." Reuters, May 30, 2011. https://www.reuters.com/article/us-libya-zuma-idUSTRE74T38I20110530.

Richmond, Oliver P. "Becoming Liberal, Unbecoming Liberalism: Liberal-Local Hybridity via the Everyday as a Response to the Paradoxes of Liberal Peacebuilding." *Journal of Intervention and Statebuilding* 3.3 (2009): 324–344.

Robertson, Roland. "Globalisation or Glocalisation?" *Journal of International Communication* 1.1 (1994): 33–52.

Roudometof, Victor. "Theorizing Glocalization: Three Interpretations." *European Journal of Social Theory* 19.3 (2016): 391–408.

Sempijja, Norman. "Does Dependence Lead to Cooperation? The Case of Resource Exchange between the European Union and the United Nations in DR Congo." *African Security* 9.4 (2016): 259–277.

———. "A Critique of the Conceptual Documents That Frame UN and AU Practice of Peacebuilding." In *Researching Peacebuilding in Africa,* ed. Ismail Rashid and Amy Niang, 190–207. London: Routledge, 2020.

Shadeedi, Hamzeh al-, Erwin van Veen, and Jalel Harchaoui. *One Thousand and One Failings: Security Sector Stabilisation and Development in Libya.* CRU Report. The Hague: Clingendael Netherlands Institute of International Relations, 2020.

Shaw, Scott. "Fallout in the Sahel: The Geographic Spread of Conflict from Libya to Mali." *Canadian Foreign Policy Journal* 19.2 (2013): 199–210.

Smetana, Michal, and Jan Ludvík. "Between War and Peace: A Dynamic Reconceptualization of 'Frozen Conflicts.'" *Asia Europe Journal* 17 (2019): 1–14.

Solomon, Hussein, and Gerrie Swart. "Libya's Foreign Policy in Flux." *African Affairs* 104.416 (2005): 469–492.

Stimson Centre, International Peace Institute, and Security Council Report. *The Situation in Libya: Reflections on Challenges and Ways Forward.* New York: Stimson Centre, International Peace Institute, and Security Council Report, 2022. https://www.stimson.org/wp-content/uploads/2022/07/Situation-in-Libya-Meeting-Note-Proofs26.pdf.

Swyngedouw, Erik. "Globalisation or 'Glocalisation'? Networks, Territories and Rescaling." *Cambridge Review of International Affairs* 17.1 (2004): 25–48.

Thiessen, Charles. "Emancipatory Peacebuilding." In *Critical Issues in Peace and Conflict Studies: Theory, Practice, and Pedagogy,* ed. Thomas Matyók, Jessica Senehi, and Sean Byrne Lexington Books, 115–143. Lanham, MD: Lexington Books, 2011.

Tschirgi, Necla. "Making the Case for a Regional Approach to Peacebuilding." *Journal of Peacebuilding & Development* 1.1 (2002): 25–38.

United Nations. "As Foreign Interference in Libya Reaches Unprecedented Levels, Secretary-General Warns Security Council Time Is Not on Our Side, Urges End to Stalemate." United Nations Security Council press release, SC/14243, July 8, 2020. https://www.un.org/press/en/2020/sc14243.doc.htm.

United Nations General Assembly and Security Council. "Report of the Panel on United Nations Peace Operations." A/55/305 S/2000/809, August 21, 2000 (Brahimi Report). https://peacekeeping.un.org/sites/default/files/a_55_305_e_brahimi_report.pdf.

United Nations Peacebuilding Support Office. *UN Peacebuilding: An Orientation.* New York: United Nations, 2010.

Voeten, Erik. "The Political Origins of the UN Security Council's Ability to Legitimize the Use of Force." *International Organization* 59.3 (2005): 527–557.

Woldemichael, Shewit, and Mohamed M. Diatta. "Can Africa Help Bring Stability to Libya? To Play a Useful Role, the AU Needs to Present a More Neutral and Unified Front." Institute of Security Studies, March 3, 2020. https://issafrica.org/iss-today/can-africa-help-bring-stability-to-libya.

Yilmaz, Muzaffer Ercan. "Peacebuilding in Libya." *International Journal on World Peace* 29.1 (2012): 45–57.

Zondi, Siphamandla. "African Union Approaches to Peacebuilding: Efforts at Shifting the Continent towards Decolonial Peace." *African Journal on Conflict Resolution* 17.1 (2017): 105–131.

Contributors

FOLAHANMI AINA is an international security analyst and researcher. He is a lecturer at the Department of Development Studies, School of Oriental and African Studies (SOAS), University of London.

ALFRED BABO is associate professor of anthropology and international studies at Fairfield University and a board member of Scholars-at-Risk (SAR). He is also co-founder of Share the Platform to advocate for refugees' self-representation.

ABU BAKARR BAH is Presidential Research Professor of Sociology at Northern Illinois University (USA) and founding director of the Institute for Research and Policy Integration in Africa (IRPIA). He is also editor-in-chief of *African Conflict & Peacebuilding Review* (*ACPR*) and African Editor for *Critical Sociology*.

NOAMANE CHERKAOUI is a communications professional and analyst whose focuses include Middle Eastern and North African geopolitics. He has an extensive background covering security issues, mainly with the Policy Center for the New South in Morocco.

NIKOLAS EMMANUEL is professor of political science in the Graduate School of International Peace Studies at Soka University of Japan. He also is an external research collaborator with the Centre for Global Criminology (CGC) at the University of Copenhagen. His research emphasizes the use of incentive-based strategies to facilitate international cooperation, as well as to encourage changes in the behavior of various state and non–state actors in Africa and beyond.

CONTRIBUTORS

TENLEY K. ERICKSON is a US Department of Defense Africa analyst and security studies instructor with extensive field experience in the African Great Lakes region. A retired Air Force lieutenant colonel, Erickson served as a foreign affairs officer and squadron commander. She received a PhD in international development from the University of Southern Mississippi.

JOHN MWANGI GITHIGARO is lecturer in peace and conflict studies at St. Paul's University, Kenya. He holds a PhD in international relations from the United States International University (USIU-A), Nairobi, Kenya. He was a Next Generation Social Sciences in Africa Fellow.

MICHAEL NWANKPA is founding director of the Centre for African Conflict and Development in London. He holds a PhD in sociology from the University of Roehampton, London. He teaches and supervises postgraduate students registered on Liverpool John Moore's University and Queen Mary's online MA programs in international relations and supervises PhD students at Unicaf University.

NORMAN SEMPIJJA is associate professor on the faculty of Economics, Governance and Social Sciences at Mohammed VI Polytechnic University in Morocco. He holds a PhD from Kingston University.

AKRAM ZAOUI is an international relations specialist at the Policy Center for the New South in Morocco, where he works on the geopolitics of the Middle East and North Africa. He holds a dual degree in corporate and public management from HEC Paris ("Programme Grande Ecole") and Sciences Po ("Ecole d'Affaires Publiques").

Index

Accord Politique de Ouagadougou, 149
African Peer Review Mechanism, 221
African Standby Force (ASF), 216
African Union (AU), 2, 8, 16, 17, 70, 72, 143, 157, 160, 183, 187–88, 189, 190, 191, 200, 201, 203n12, 216–19, 221, 223, 224
African Union Mission in Somalia (AMISOM), 88–89, 131, 190, 219
African Union Transition Mission in Somalia, 88–89
"Africa's World War," 192
Allied Democratic Forces (ADF), 14, 112, 121, 122, 130, 131, 132, 133, 192
al-Qaeda, 3, 55, 65–66, 71, 92, 112, 121–22, 125, 129, 131, 192
Al-Shabaab, 7–8, 16, 88, 92, 93, 97, 99, 104, 122, 131, 192
Angola, 1, 5, 6, 8, 10, 221
Anti-terrorism Assistance (ATA) program, 123, 124
Arab Maghreb Union (AMU), 216
Arab Spring, 150, 227
armed bandits, 55–56, 58, 64, 69–72, 74
armed groups, 117, 120, 127, 149, 190, 191, 192, 193, 194, 197, 198–99, 200, 223
Arusha Accords, 194
assimilation, 184, 186

Berlin Conference, 36, 225
Berlin Wall, 33, 34–35
Boko Haram (Jamā'at Ahl as-Sunnah lid-Da'wah wa'l-Jihād, JASJ), 7–8, 18, 55–56, 64–66, 68, 70–71, 72, 74, 112, 117, 118–19, 122, 123–25, 128–29, 132
Buhari, Muhammadu, 68, 118, 125–27, 128, 129
Burkina Faso, 3, 7, 64, 147–48, 152, 153, 154, 160, 162
Burundi, 2, 8, 41, 190, 192, 193, 195, 198–99, 221
Bush, George W., 123

Central African Republic (CAR), 6, 130, 145, 159, 162, 163, 190
Chad, 6, 7, 9, 56, 64, 65, 66, 69, 70, 71, 122, 124, 128, 145, 152, 162, 190, 217, 228
China, 7, 60, 73, 123, 162
civil war, 2, 4–5, 8–9, 10, 11, 15, 17, 30, 32, 40–41, 42, 43, 45, 46, 67, 114, 117, 121, 122, 127, 142, 143, 145, 147, 149–50, 154–55, 191, 215–16, 217–18
Cold War, 1, 6, 10, 33, 34–35, 114–15, 144, 181, 184, 187, 188, 189
collective security, 9, 11–12, 13, 16, 17, 115, 187, 220
colonialism, 6, 10, 18–19, 31, 33, 34, 36, 37, 38, 39, 40, 45–46
Common Market for Eastern and Southern Africa (COMESA), 216
Community of Sahel-Saharan States (CEN-SAD), 216
community policing, 17, 18, 88, 89, 90, 93, 94, 95, 96, 97, 98–99, 100–101, 102, 103, 104, 105, 106
conflict drivers, 3, 4, 5, 6, 7, 8, 9, 10–11, 12, 13, 14, 15, 16–17
Congress for the Defense of the People (CNDP), 194, 195, 196, 197, 223
Continental Early Warning System (CEWS), 216
Côte d'Ivoire, 2, 3, 5, 8–9, 15, 18, 41, 42, 43, 45, 142, 143, 144, 145, 147–48, 149, 150, 152, 154, 155, 156, 157, 158–59, 160–62, 190
countering violent extremism (CVE), 12, 88, 89, 90, 91, 96, 98, 100
counterterrorism, 3, 7, 14, 18, 58, 59–60, 61, 62, 65, 72–73, 75, 88, 89, 90, 91, 92, 96–98, 100, 102, 105, 106, 116, 118, 122, 123, 124, 125, 130–31, 132, 188, 201
coup d'état, 142, 144, 145, 151, 153

Dako, David, 145
Dar-es-Salaam, 92

242 INDEX

Democratic Republic of Congo (DRC), 2, 3, 4, 5, 6, 8, 10, 12, 14, 17, 18, 41, 121, 122, 131, 145, 159, 171n93, 184, 187, 190, 191, 192, 193–95, 196, 197, 198–99, 200, 201, 202, 221, 223, 224

democratization, 2, 15, 40, 93, 142

Department of State, US (DoS), 123, 124, 163

Dikko, Umaru, 127

disarmament, demobilization, and reintegration (DDR), 228

Djibouti, 7

domestic factors, 9, 12, 44

East African Community (EAC), 184, 190, 192, 199, 216

Eastern Security Network (ESN), 67, 118, 119–20, 126

Economic Community of Central African States (ECCAS), 216

Economic Community of West African States (ECOWAS), 143, 148, 152, 158–59, 160, 187, 190, 200, 216

elites, 8, 66, 147, 161, 182, 183, 196, 201, 202, 225

environmental factors, 3, 6, 9, 56, 120

Ethiopia, 5, 6, 10, 190, 201, 221, 227

European Union (EU), 18, 70, 72, 74, 123, 151, 156, 159, 185, 186, 188, 189, 200, 201, 218, 219, 223–24, 225–26, 228

external factors, 3–4, 6, 12, 13, 57, 185

external powers, 7, 13, 16, 17, 18, 216, 229

failed states, 143, 144, 145, 146, 147, 159, 163

Failed States Index, 147

Force Integration Brigade (FIB), 197–98

foreign intervention, 143, 144, 145, 146, 148, 151, 153, 163, 215

Françafrique, 143, 161

France, 2, 18, 56, 71, 72, 123, 143, 144, 145, 148, 149, 150, 151–52, 153, 154, 156–57, 158–59, 161, 162–63, 165n7, 186

French Forty-Third Infantry (BIMA), 148, 154

Gaddafi, Muammar, 145, 150, 217, 219, 223, 224, 226, 227, 228

Gbagbo, Laurent, 149, 150, 155, 156–58

genocide, 224

Ghana, 2

globalization, 12–13, 33, 34–35, 59, 115, 116, 181, 182, 183, 222

Global South, 31, 37, 114

Global War on Terror (GWOT), 2, 3, 7, 12, 14, 15, 16, 17, 18, 60, 74, 87, 90, 96, 98, 99, 105, 113, 114, 116, 121, 122, 124, 125, 130, 131–32, 133

glocalization, 9, 12–13, 56, 57, 59, 74, 87, 88, 90, 105, 115, 120, 181, 182, 183, 189, 193, 201–2, 217, 222, 223

glocalized security, 4, 9, 12, 13–14, 15, 16, 18, 57, 59, 61, 63, 75, 90, 105, 106, 125, 130, 144, 146, 147, 148, 159, 161, 163, 164, 182, 184, 217

Government of National Accord, 218

Great Lakes Region, 129, 132, 182, 184, 188, 192, 200

Horn of Africa, 12, 18, 130, 190

humanitarian intervention, 3, 34, 39, 46, 220

Igbo, 66, 67, 72, 117–18, 126, 127, 129

imperialism, 34–35, 38, 39, 115, 120

Indigenous People of Biafra (IPOB), 64–65, 67, 72–73, 74, 117, 118, 119–20, 125, 126, 127, 129, 132, 133

Intergovernmental Authority on Development, 216

internally displaced people (IDP), 131

international community, 11, 40, 41, 42–43, 45, 46, 128, 130, 133, 148, 150–51, 156–57, 157–58, 158–59, 163, 182, 187, 193, 197, 200, 202, 216, 220

International Monetary Fund, 8, 189

international relations (IR), 15–16, 17, 30–33, 34, 35, 36, 37–40, 42, 43, 44, 45, 46, 185, 188, 201

intervention, 2, 3, 7–8, 11–12, 14, 16, 18, 30, 31, 32, 39, 41, 43, 45–46, 56, 57, 59, 88, 89, 90, 91, 92, 93, 95, 96, 98, 101, 105, 143, 144, 145, 146, 147, 148, 149, 150, 151, 152, 153–54, 155, 156, 157, 158, 159, 160, 161, 162, 163–64, 190, 199, 215, 217, 218–19, 220, 224, 226, 227, 228–29

Islamic Movement in Nigeria (IMN), 64–65, 67, 68, 72–73, 125, 126, 127, 129, 133

Islamic Party of Kenya (IPK), 92

Islamic State (ISIS, IS), 3, 55, 66, 67, 71, 99, 121–22, 124, 125, 131, 151, 192, 227

Islamic State in West Africa Province (ISWAP), 55, 64, 65, 66, 70, 74, 112, 117, 118, 124, 125, 132

Israel, 123, 129–30

Jamā'atu Ansāril Muslimīnafī Bilādis-Sūdān (Ansaru), 55, 64, 65–66, 70, 74, 117, 118, 125

jihad, 3, 7, 9, 14, 71, 72, 87, 93, 106, 116, 118–19, 124, 152, 225

Jonathan, Goodluck, 127, 128–29

Index

Kabila, Joseph, 194, 195, 196, 197–98
Kagame, Paul, 194, 195, 196, 198
Kenya, 2, 5, 6, 7, 8, 14, 16, 17, 18, 88–89, 90, 91, 92, 93, 94, 96, 97, 98, 99, 100, 103, 104, 105–6, 121, 122, 126, 129–30, 190, 199, 202, 221
Kenya National Counter-Terrorism Center, 88, 97
Kenya Police Force (KPF), 94–95
knowledge production, 30, 31, 32, 34, 35, 36, 37, 38, 39, 45
Kony, Joseph, 121

League of Arab States, 225
liberal peace, 9, 10–11, 12, 15, 17
liberal peace theory, 15, 17
Liberia, 2, 3, 4, 6, 41, 42, 43, 45, 145, 187, 190, 221–22
Libya, 2, 3, 4, 7, 14, 16, 17, 18, 41, 45, 150, 151, 154, 215, 216–18, 219, 220, 223, 224, 225, 226, 227, 228, 229
Likoni, 89, 95, 98, 99, 101, 102, 103, 105
local: communities and actors, 6, 7, 11, 16, 56, 88, 89, 90, 91, 98, 100, 102, 119, 132, 144, 156, 181, 191, 219, 220–21, 226; conflicts, 16, 114, 120, 122, 132, 143, 154; factors and circumstances, 3, 4, 13, 18, 64, 75, 130, 156, 159, 199, 202–3; relationship of global and, 12, 13, 42, 59, 88, 101, 102, 105, 114, 115, 122, 124, 143–44, 147, 161, 181, 183–84, 202–3, 222–23; security, 93, 95, 132, 143, 147, 151, 152, 153, 182
Lord Resistance Army (LRA), 112, 121, 122, 130, 131, 132, 133

Mali, 2, 3, 7, 14, 15, 16, 18, 41, 42, 43, 45, 64, 69, 72, 73, 142, 143, 144, 145, 147, 148, 150, 151, 152, 153, 155–56, 158–59, 160–62, 163–64, 169n69, 190, 224, 228
March 23 Movement (M23), 193, 194, 197, 199
Marcoussis Accord, 149
military, 2, 3, 4, 5, 7–8, 10, 11, 14, 15, 18, 31, 39, 41, 46, 56, 57, 65, 66, 67, 68, 69, 70, 72, 73–75, 88–89, 90, 93, 115, 117, 122, 123, 124, 125, 126–27, 128, 129, 130, 131, 133, 142, 143, 144, 145, 147, 148, 149, 150, 151, 152, 153, 154–55, 156, 157, 158, 159, 160–61, 162, 163–64, 173n114, 182–83, 190, 191, 193, 195, 197, 198, 200, 217, 220, 224, 225, 227, 228
military cooperation, 162, 191
Military Staff Committee (MSC), 216
mission, 2, 3, 8, 10, 17, 130, 131, 148, 152, 153, 155, 156, 159, 162, 182, 187, 189, 190, 201, 219, 225, 227

Mombasa, 88, 89, 95, 96, 98, 101–2, 104, 105, 129–30
Mombasa Republican Council, 92
Mouvement Patriotique de Côte d'Ivoire (MPCI), 147–48
Movement for the Actualisation of the Sovereign State of Biafra (MASSOB), 67, 117, 127, 129
Mozambique, 1, 3, 187, 190, 191, 192, 202
Multinational Joint Task Force (MNJTF), 56, 70, 71, 74, 124, 128
Museveni, Yoweri, 116, 121, 130–32

Nairobi, 88, 92, 97
Namibia, 2, 8, 221
National Congress for the Defence of the People (CNDP), 193, 194, 195, 196, 197, 223
National Transitional Council, 226, 227
NATO, 3, 7, 16, 18, 150, 151, 154, 169n68, 217, 219, 223–24, 227, 228
natural resources, 1, 4, 5, 6, 8, 10, 14, 70–71
neocolonialism, 9, 10, 12, 13, 38, 46, 153
neoliberal, 3–4, 6, 8, 11, 13, 16, 18–19, 46, 59, 130–31, 221, 222
new humanitarianism, 43, 45–46, 153
New Partnership for Economic Development, 221
Niger Delta, 6, 117, 118, 127, 128
Nigeria, 1, 2, 3, 5, 6, 7, 9, 10, 14, 15, 16–17, 18, 40, 55–56, 57, 58, 63, 64–65, 66–67, 68, 69, 70, 71, 72–74, 75, 112, 113–14, 116, 117, 118–19, 120, 122, 123, 124, 125, 126–29, 130, 132, 133, 144–45, 150, 227
Nigeria-Biafra Civil War, 117, 127
9/11, 12, 60, 87, 88, 90, 96, 102, 112, 114, 117, 121, 122, 123, 124, 129–30, 132, 133
Nkunda, Laurent, 193, 194, 195, 196, 223
non-indifference, 224, 226–27
norms, 16, 17, 57, 147, 181, 182, 183, 184, 186, 187, 191, 193, 195, 200, 201, 202

Obasanjo, Olusegun, 127
O'Odua People's Congress, 117
Operation Amarylis, 145
Operation Barkhane, 3, 152, 155, 162
Operation Barracuda, 145
Operation Bonite, 145
Opération Licorne, 149, 154–55, 157, 158
Operation Sangaris, 145, 159
Operation Serval, 3, 143, 152, 155
Operation Turquoise, 145, 159
Organisation of African Unity (OAU), 203n12, 224, 229

Ouattara, Alassane, 149, 150, 154–55, 156, 157, 160

Panel of the Wise, 216
peace, 16, 17, 32, 41, 42, 56, 57, 58, 59, 62, 74, 114, 115, 122, 127, 128, 144, 146–47, 148, 149, 150, 153, 156–57, 160, 182, 183–84, 186, 188, 189, 190, 191, 192, 193–94, 197–98, 200, 215–16, 218, 220–21, 223, 224, 225, 226, 227, 228–29
Peace and Security Architecture, 187, 216
peacebuilding, 9, 10, 11, 13, 32, 39, 40, 42, 43, 44, 89, 148, 149, 161, 162, 164, 190, 215, 216, 217, 218, 219, 220–21, 222–23, 226, 227
peacekeeping, 10, 11, 41, 130, 182, 183–84, 185, 187, 189, 191, 201, 220, 221, 228
peacekeeping mission, 2, 8, 17, 130, 131, 148, 159, 182, 201, 219
peacekeeping operation, 1, 182, 184, 188, 189, 190, 194
peace talks, 56, 149, 161
people-centered liberalism, 43, 45–46, 222
periphery, 224
piracy, 34, 118, 128
proscription, 15, 16–17, 18, 56, 57, 58, 59–61, 62, 63, 64–65, 67, 68, 70, 72–75, 125–26, 127, 129, 131

Quartet on Libya, 225

Radio Biafra, 117–18
Regional Economic Communities, 2, 17, 187–88, 216
regionalism, 66, 182, 183, 184, 186, 187, 188
Regional Security Complex Theory (RSCT), 182, 183, 184, 185, 186
Responsibility to Protect (R2P), 2, 9, 11, 12–13, 17, 143, 150–51, 153, 157, 217, 219, 220, 224, 226
Russia, 16, 18, 161, 162, 163, 172n104, 188, 218, 219, 223, 225, 228
Rwanda, 1, 5, 8, 121, 145, 159, 192, 193–99, 220, 221, 223; genocide in, 11, 145, 192–93, 193–94
Rwandan Democratic Liberation Forces (FDLR), 192–93, 194, 195, 197–98, 199, 201
Rwandaphone, 192–93, 194, 196

Sahel, 3, 6, 9, 12, 64, 70, 71, 151, 160–61, 162, 163, 217, 224, 228
secession, 5, 55–56, 66–67, 117, 118, 129
securitization, 13, 15, 61, 89, 100, 102, 103, 105, 120, 149, 182, 184, 185, 187–88, 189, 190, 192, 200, 202

Seko, Mobutu Sesse, 145, 195
Senegal, 2, 225
September 11. *See* 9/11
Sierra Leone, 2, 3, 4–5, 6, 9, 41, 42, 43, 45, 145, 163, 187, 190, 220
Social Evolution Theory (SET), 182, 184, 186
Somalia, 2, 3, 7–8, 41, 42, 88–89, 92, 93, 99, 122, 130, 131, 132, 187, 190, 191, 192, 201, 202, 220, 221
South Africa, 1, 150, 221, 224
Southern African Development Community (SADC), 190, 197, 200, 216
South Sudan, 2, 5, 8, 190, 191, 199, 201
sovereignty, 41, 66–67, 68, 73, 117, 142, 144, 155
state building, 2, 38, 41, 184–85, 186, 219, 221
state decay, 4, 11, 15, 42–43, 45–46
Sudan, 4, 5, 6, 7, 8, 121, 122, 130, 190, 191, 217, 228
suicide bombing, 65, 131

terrorism, 2, 3, 6, 7–8, 12, 14, 16, 57, 58, 59, 60, 63, 70–71, 72, 73, 74–75, 88–89, 90, 91–92, 93, 96, 97, 98, 99, 100, 101, 102, 103, 104, 105, 106, 112, 114–15, 121, 122, 123, 124, 126, 130, 131, 143, 146, 153, 156, 161, 162, 163, 191, 192, 223–24
terrorism warfare, 2, 3, 6, 7–8, 12, 16
trafficking, 104, 228
Trans-Sahara Counter-Terrorism Partnership, 123
Tshisekedi, Felix, 193, 194, 198–99
Tuareg, 69, 142–43, 151, 153, 155, 156, 158
Turkey, 16, 18, 218, 219, 223, 228

Uganda, 8, 15, 16, 18, 112, 113, 116, 120, 121, 122, 130, 131–32, 133, 190, 192, 193, 195, 197, 198–99, 201, 202, 221, 223, 224
Ukraine, 9, 188, 228
United Kingdom (UK), 58, 61, 66, 71, 72, 97–98, 103, 123, 126–27
United Nations (UN), 1, 2, 8, 10, 11, 66, 74, 123, 130, 131, 143, 145, 148–49, 150, 152, 155, 156, 157, 159, 160, 163, 182, 187–88, 190, 191, 193, 194, 197, 198, 199, 200, 201, 218, 219, 220, 221, 223, 225, 226, 227, 228, 229
United Nations Development Programme, 55
United Nations Mission in Côte d'Ivoire (UNOCI), 149, 150, 154–55, 157, 158
United States (US), 2, 12, 56, 60, 71, 72, 73, 87, 90, 92, 96, 98, 105, 112, 114, 123, 124, 128, 129, 130, 131–32, 154, 162, 163, 191, 197, 223–24

Index   245

UN Security Council (UNSC), 150, 151–52,
154, 155, 158, 226, 227, 228
UN Stabilization Operation in the Congo
(MONUSCO), 159, 194, 197
UN Support Mission in Libya (UNSMIL),
225, 228
USAID, 98

violent non–state actor (VNSA), 11, 55, 56–
57, 58, 59, 62, 73, 74

warlord, 2, 132
Westphalian state, 38, 40, 148, 183, 185
World Bank, 74, 189
World War II (Second World War), 186, 188, 220

Yoruba, 117, 118, 119

Zaire, 1–2, 6, 8–9, 145
Zimbabwe, 1, 8, 221, 225
Zuma, Jacob, 224

Printed and bound by CPI Group (UK) Ltd, Croydon, CR0 4YY
25/11/2024

14598945-0002